ancient orient
and old testament

ancient orient
and old testament

k. a. kitchen

*Lecturer, School of Archaeology
and Oriental Studies,
University of Liverpool*

*InterVarsity Press
Downers Grove
Illinois 60515*

InterVarsity Press is the book-
publishing division of
Inter-Varsity Christian Fellowship,
a student movement active on campus
at hundreds of universities,
colleges and schools of nursing.
For information about local and regional
activities, write IVCF, 233 Langdon St.,
Madison, WI 53703.

Distributed in Canada through
InterVarsity Press, 1875 Leslie St.,
Unit 10, Don Mills, Ontario
M3B 2M5, Canada.

ISBN 0-87784-907-2

Library of Congress Catalog
Card Number: 66-30697

Printed in the United
States of America

To
V. B. G. *and* T. S. F.

CONTENTS

PART TWO

Illumination and Illustration

PREFACE

The following pages are intended to give some idea of the kind of contribution that Ancient Near Eastern studies can make to the study of the Old Testament, and towards a critical reassessment of problems and methods in the Old Testament field. By way of illustrating these themes, I have deliberately included a wide variety of topics dealing with essentials or salient points rather than attempting to be exhaustive. A full treatment of this width of subjects would call for a dozen or so large tomes, not just one modest book.

Because this book is rooted in primary source-material and is not tied to conventional viewpoints, it has been essential to include running references throughout. Although in no way exhaustive, the notes provide the necessary documentation for facts adduced and views mentioned, and document the paradigmatic examples of principles and points raised in the text. Not every reader may need all the details, but these references will provide the serious student with the indispensable means for verification and for pursuing any special interest.

This book originated in two lectures delivered at the International Student Conferences held under the auspices of the Vereinigte Bibelgruppen von Schweiz at Casa Moscia in September 1962. A German translation of the English original was published at the end of 1965. The present book is a completely revised and up-dated version of the original English text, completed in late summer 1965, only limited revision being possible since then. Expansion of text and notes has been kept down to a minimum; Part Two could very easily have been expanded to match Part One, or even to the size of a separate work.

In some respects, this work has taken on elements of a *Programmschrift*, though not by original intention. It is an invitation to view afresh the Old Testament writings in their

proper Ancient Near Eastern context; only diehards, impri-
soned within the inhibitions of fixed ideas and inflexibly obsolete methods, need fear its contents. Today, more than ever
before, the Ancient Near East offers rich resources for study of
the Old Testament in fresh perspectives.

It is a particular pleasure to express my indebtedness to Mr.
A. R. Millard for various references and, with Mrs. Millard,
for helpful stylistic criticisms; likewise to Mr. T. C. Mitchell
for comments on the original English manuscript; and not least
to the publishers for kindly undertaking to produce the book.
However, any failings noted should not be charged to these
good friends, and the responsibility for views expressed remains
mine.

School of Archaeology & Oriental Studies   K. A. KITCHEN
University of Liverpool

ABBREVIATIONS

AASOR	*Annual of the American Schools of Oriental Research*
AfO	*Archiv für Orientforschung*
ANE	*The Ancient Near East* (J. B. Pritchard), 1958
ANEP	*The Ancient Near East in Pictures Relating to the Old Testament* (J. B. Pritchard), 1954
ANET	*Ancient Near Eastern Texts Relating to the Old Testament* (ed. J. B. Pritchard), ¹1950, ²1955
ARMT	*Archives Royales de Mari, transcrites et traduites* (ed. A. Parrot and G. Dossin), 1950 onwards
ASAE	*Annales du Service des Antiquités de l'Égypte*
AUSS	*Andrews University Seminary Studies*
BA	*The Biblical Archaeologist*
BANE	*The Bible and the Ancient Near East* (*FS* Albright, ed. G. E. Wright), 1961; paperback ed., 1965
BASOR	*Bulletin of the American Schools of Oriental Research*
BIA/UL	*Bulletin of the Institute of Archaeology, University of London*
BIFAO	*Bulletin de l'Institut Français d'Archéologie Orientale*
BZAW	*Beihefte zur ZAW* (*q.v.*)
CAH²	*The Cambridge Ancient History*, revised edition of vols. I and II; cited by vol. and chapter, 1961 onwards
CBQ	*Catholic Biblical Quarterly*
CRAIBL	*Académie des Inscriptions et Belles-Lettres, Comptes Rendus*
DOTT	*Documents from Old Testament Times* (ed. D. W. Thomas), 1958
FS	Denotes anniversary or memorial volume for scholar named
F/T	*Faith and Thought*, continuation of *JTVI*
HdO	*Handbuch der Orientalistik* (ed. B. Spuler),
	I: 1(1) = H. Kees (ed.), *Ägyptologie* (*Äg. Schrift und Sprache*), 1959
	I: 2 = H. Kees *et al.*, *Ägyptologie* (*Literatur*), 1952
	II: 3 = H. Schmökel, *Keilschriftforschung und Alte Geschichte Vorderasiens*, 1957
HTR	*Harvard Theological Review*
IEJ	*Israel Exploration Journal*
JAOS	*Journal of the American Oriental Society*
JBL	*Journal of Biblical Literature*
JCS	*Journal of Cuneiform Studies*
JEA	*Journal of Egyptian Archaeology*

JKF	*Jahrbuch für Kleinasiatische Forschung*
JNES	*Journal of Near Eastern Studies*
JPOS	*Journal of the Palestine Oriental Society*
JRAS	*Journal of the Royal Asiatic Society*
JSS	*Journal of Semitic Studies*
JTS	*Journal of Theological Studies*, new series
JTVI	*Journal of Transactions of the Victoria Institute*
KS	*Kleine Schriften*, I–III (A. Alt), 1953–59
LAAA	*Liverpool Annals of Archaeology and Anthropology*
LXX	Septuagint
MDOG	*Mitteilungen der Deutschen Orient-Gesellschaft zu Berlin*
MIO	*Mitteilungen des Instituts für Orientforschung*
MVÄG	*Mitteilungen der Vorderasiatisch-Ägyptischen Gesellschaft*
NBD	*New Bible Dictionary* (ed. J. D. Douglas, F. F. Bruce, J. I. Packer, R. V. G. Tasker, D. J. Wiseman), 1962
OBL	*Orientalia et Biblica Lovaniensia*
OLZ	*Orientalistische Literaturzeitung*
PEF Annual	*Palestine Exploration Fund Annual*
PEQ	*Palestine Exploration Quarterly*
Proc. APS	*Proceedings of the American Philosophical Society*
RB	*Revue Biblique*
RHA	*Revue Hittite et Asianique*
RSO	*Rivista degli Studi Orientali*
RT	*Recueil de Travaux relatifs à la philologie et à l'archéologie égyptiennes et assyriennes*
SBT	*Studies in Biblical Theology*
THB	*Tyndale House Bulletin*, now *Tyndale Bulletin*
TSF Bulletin	*Theological Students' Fellowship Bulletin*
UM	*Ugaritic Manual*, I–III (C. H. Gordon), 1955
UT	*Ugaritic Textbook*, [I–III] (*idem*), 1965
Urk. IV	*Urkunden IV* (*18. Dynastie*), Hefte 1–16 (K. Sethe), 1927–30; Hefte 17–22 (H. W. Helck), 1955–58
VT	*Vetus Testamentum*
VTS	*Vetus Testamentum, Supplements*, 1953 onwards
WBD	*Westminster Bible Dictionary* (J. D. Davis, ed. H. S. Gehman), 1944 and reprs.
WTJ	*Westminster Theological Journal*
ZA	*Zeitschrift für Assyriologie und verwandte Gebiete*
ZÄS	*Zeitschrift für Ägyptische Sprache und Altertumskunde*
ZAW	*Zeitschrift für die alttestamentliche Wissenschaft*
ZDMG	*Zeitschrift der Deutschen Morgenländischen Gesellschaft*
ZDPV	*Zeitschrift des Deutschen Palästina-Vereins*

PART ONE

PROBLEMS AND SOLUTIONS

1. ANCIENT ORIENT AND OLD TESTAMENT: THE BACKGROUND

1. AN AGE OF CHANGE

We live in times of sweeping change. Through all the millennia of human history, never have the changes effected by man's efforts been so rapid and so revolutionary; and the pace does not slacken.

Taken positively, the advances in human knowledge and discovery are breathtaking. Less than a lifetime separates the pioneer flight of Orville and Wilbur Wright made in 1903 from the orbits of the globe along which rockets have carried astronauts and cosmonauts in our own day. In this time we have also passed decisively from the old theory of an atom as the smallest indivisible unit of matter to the stark fact of the fission and fusion of atomic particles whose possible misuse threatens the very existence of civilization. In medicine, new classes of drugs and surgical techniques, hitherto undreamt-of, have turned former impossibilities into normal practice.

Negatively speaking, the torrents of change have swept away much that was once held to be axiomatic, both in secluded branches of learning and in popular beliefs. In the natural sciences, successive new discoveries and resultant theories chase one another, often far ahead of the standard textbooks. In this world of searching analysis, the things of lasting validity and unchallengeable worth are few indeed.

But these powerful tides of change are not limited in their effect to the natural or medical sciences, or to certain obvious aspects of daily life. Welling up from vast new knowledge in every sphere, their power is visible in every field of human endeavour. This is true even in disciplines which outwardly may seem to be remote from modern metamorphoses – even in such subjects as Ancient Oriental history and literature and study of the Old Testament, the matters with which this book is concerned.

In various spheres,[1] the nineteenth century witnessed a veritable outburst of new activity in human discovery and invention, and in the world of thought. Among other things, the latter realm was marked by reaction against the traditional beliefs and knowledge inherited from earlier epochs and henceforth considered to be 'uncritical' and 'inadequate'. However, the remarkable achievements in discovery and thought which reached a first climax with the end of the nineteenth century have proved not to be definitive. Many of the scientific theories and practical processes of the nineteenth and early twentieth centuries are being pushed into obsolescence by the events and discoveries of the present century, especially in these last few decades. And who now would naïvely subscribe to the evolutionary philosophy of an infallible, ever-upward progress of mankind, unfaltering and inevitable? Much of what was accepted sixty or more years ago as almost definitive seems just as painfully inadequate or mistaken to us now as did the views of earlier ages to the inquiring minds of the nineteenth century.

All his is relevant to our theme. Ancient Near Eastern and Old Testament studies alike can in no way be exempted from these inexorable tides of change any more than the rest of human activity, and for the same reasons. In our time vast new realms of fact, hitherto undisclosed, have come to light, and new methods of study are now becoming necessary and must replace those that are obsolete.

---

[1] In industry, the effects of the 'industrial revolution': steel largely replacing iron; mechanical traction; emerging exploitation of gas and electricity; rise of telecommunications. In medicine, the first major advances since antiquity (*e.g.*, the work of Pasteur, Lister, *etc.*). In zoology, the theories of Darwin; the founding of modern geology. Not unconnected with these, there emerged evolutionary philosophy. The first great advances in astronomy and physics came earlier, of course (Copernicus, Kepler, Galileo; Newton).

II. THE BASIS OF THE MAIN PROBLEMS

Thus, in relation to the Old Testament, the nineteenth century[2] saw the emergence of two major fields of scholarship which both stood in contrast over against earlier ages: Old Testament studies and Ancient Near Eastern studies.

(a) Old Testament Studies

Following on the period of 'Deist' speculation in the eighteenth century, Old Testament studies during the nineteenth century carried the mark of reaction against older beliefs about the Bible and its constituent writings, a mark still perceptible today. In contrast to earlier epochs in which the main concern of biblical study was the exposition of the sacred text and the formulation of doctrine, Old Testament studies of the nineteenth century were more concerned with literary and historical criticism, especially in connection with philosophical treatment of early Hebrew religion. Certain dominant tendencies became apparent. Beside the desire to break with the weight of inherited later tradition (often of dubious value), there was an eagerness to experiment with literary and history-of-religion theories like those then current in Homeric[3] and other

[2] The tentative beginnings long precede the nineteenth century, of course.

For some precursors of nineteenth-century Old Testament scholarship, see the brief summaries (on Introduction and Pentateuchal study) in E. J. Young, *An Introduction to the Old Testament*[3], 1964, pp. 16–21, 107–122, and O. Eissfeldt, *The Old Testament: An Introduction*, 1965, pp. 1–3, 158–163. Since the Reformation, *cf.* also Kraus and Kraeling, works cited in note 7, below.

For Ancient Oriental studies before the nineteenth century, compare E. Iversen, *The Myth of Egypt and its Hieroglyphs*, 1961 (on pre-scientific study of the Egyptian hieroglyphs); S. A. Pallis, *Early Exploration in Mesopotamia*, 1954 (*Kon. Dan. Vidensk. Selskab*, Hist.-fil. Medd., 33, No. 6), or Pallis, *The Antiquity of Iraq*, 1956, pp. 19–70, 94 ff., or A. Parrot, *Archéologie Mésopotamienne*, I, 1946, pp. 13–35 (early travellers in Mesopotamia). For early exploration in Palestine, see W. F. Albright, *The Archaeology of Palestine*[4], 1960, pp. 23–25, and now esp. the Palestine Exploration Fund's Centenary publication, *The World of the Bible*, 1965.

[3] For the instructive parallelism between Homeric and Pentateuchal literary criticism in the nineteenth century see W. J. Martin, *Stylistic Criteria and the Analysis of the Pentateuch*, 1955.

B

studies,[4] and also a wish to view the history of Old Testament religion and literature in terms of the evolutionary philosophies of the age.[5]

One result of all this was the emergence of a marked scepticism not only towards traditions *about* the Bible, but also towards the historical veracity of the Old Testament books and towards the integrity of their present literary form. The existing structure of Old Testament religion and literature could not, as it stood, be fitted into the prevailing philosophical schemes, so it was drastically remodelled until it did. The resultant physiognomy presented by Old Testament studies needs only the briefest summary here; the role of *theory* is preponderant. Thus, the Pentateuch and other books were split up into various supposed source-documents of different authorship of varying epochs (traditionally designated J(ahwist), E(lohist), P(riestly Code), D(euteronomist), *etc.*), and considered to have been assembled into the present books at a relatively late date. Various literary, linguistic and theological criteria were produced in order to justify these divisions and late datings. The prophetical books were also fragmented across the centuries, and the poetry and wisdom-literature assigned to a very late period.[6] Concepts that were held to be theologically 'advanced' (universalism,

[4] For the history-of-religions and anthropological aspects, one need only recall such works as W. Robertson Smith, *Lectures on the Religion of the Semites*, or Sir James G. Frazer, *The Golden Bough. Cf.* chapters II and III of Hahn's work, cited in note 7, below.

[5] For example, the influence of such developmental philosophy upon Wellhausen; *cf.* Eissfeldt, *The OT: An Introduction*, p. 165, and, somewhat differently if more fully, L. Perlitt, *Vatke und Wellhausen*, 1965 (=*BZAW*, 94). Wellhausen's famous *Prolegomena zur Geschichte Israels*, even in its sixth edition of 1905 (repr. 1927), was not marked by any acquisition or use of new, factual data (esp. from the Ancient Orient) so much as by its remoulding of history to accord with his *a priori* philosophical principles. Note the remarks of Kraus (work cited in note 7, below), p. 244 with p. 268, and on a broader basis, S. R. Külling, *Zur Datierung der "Genesis-P-Stücke"*, 1964, pp. 148–165, esp. pp. 153 ff. On unilinear evolution, *cf.* below, pp. 113 f., 148 f., *etc.*

[6] For useful surveys of the more recent phases of Old Testament studies, see H. H. Rowley (ed.), *The Old Testament and Modern Study*, 1951 (paperback, 1961); *cf.* also J. Bright, *BANE*, pp. 13–31.

personification, *etc.*) were also considered to be late developments. With innumerable variations in detail, and some modifications in view of recent developments, Old Testament studies have remained fundamentally the same up to the present day.[7] To this picture, Gunkel and others added *Gattungsforschung* or *Formgeschichte* (form-criticism),[8] and the Scandinavians have laid stress on the supposed role of oral tradition,[9] while Alt and Noth have combined part of these methods with literary criticism and their own theories about aetiological traditions allegedly linked with specific localities.[10]

Contradictions are said to abound in the Old Testament, and its history is still treated with scepticism, especially the earlier periods (*e.g.*, Patriarchs, Exodus and Conquest). It is not merely that (for the historic Christian faith) these results leave a wide gulf between the vision of a dependable and authoritative Word of God, and the spectacle of a tattered miscellany of half-mythical and historically unreliable literary fragments. Rather,

[7] For the last hundred years of Old Testament studies (from a conventional viewpoint), see the excellent, compact and readable work of H. F. Hahn, *The Old Testament in Modern Research*, 1956. For the whole period from the Reformation to the early 1950s, see H.-J. Kraus, *Geschichte der historisch-kritischen Erforschung des Alten Testaments*, 1956, and E. G. Kraeling, *The Old Testament since the Reformation*, 1955 (whose useful work is too often coloured by its author's personal views). Briefer still are chapters VII and VIII by W. Neil and A. Richardson in S. L. Greenslade (ed.), *The Cambridge History of the Bible*, 1963; these essays cover the same period as Kraus and Kraeling, are lively, but in some measure share Kraeling's failings. On OT introduction, *cf.* also G. L. Archer, Jr., *A Survey of Old Testament Introduction*, 1964.

As for the fundamental sameness in the methodology of Old Testament studies, a random example is the use of exactly the same class of criteria (even identical) today (*e.g.*, Eissfeldt, *The OT: An Introduction*, 1965, p. 183) as were used fifty and more years ago (*e.g.*, by S. R. Driver, *Literature of the Old Testament*[9], 1913, p. 119).

[8] See below, pp. 130 ff., and notes 71–74.

[9] See below, pp. 135ff., and notes 92–94.

[10] M. Noth, *Überlieferungsgeschichtliche Studien I*, 1943 (repr. 1957); Noth, *Überlieferungsgeschichte des Pentateuch*, 1948 (repr. 1960); A. Alt, *Kleine Schriften*, I-III, 1953–59, various papers. For a brief summary of Noth's treatment of Hebrew history, and a careful but trenchant critique of Noth's methods, see J. Bright, *Early Israel in Recent History Writing*, 1956 (=*SBT*, No. 19).

on the fundamental level of 'What actually happened in history?', there is above all a very considerable tension between the development of Israelite history, religion and literature as portrayed by the Old Testament and the general reconstructions so far offered by conventional Old Testament studies. An example is afforded by W. Zimmerli who brings out the vast change proposed by Wellhausen in making the 'law of Moses' (especially 'P') later than the prophets instead of preceding them.[11] Nowhere else in the whole of Ancient Near Eastern history has the literary, religious and historical development of a nation been subjected to such drastic and wholesale reconstructions at such variance with the existing documentary evidence. The fact that Old Testament scholars are habituated to these widely known reconstructions, even mentally conditioned by them,[12] does not alter the basic gravity of this situation which should not be taken for granted.

(b) Ancient Near Eastern Studies

During the nineteenth century, Ancient Near Eastern studies first came into their own with the decipherment of Egyptian hieroglyphs and Mesopotamian cuneiform, and the beginnings of scientific excavation and epigraphy.[13] Centuries of human history were recovered, and the life of entire civilizations restored to view. To the resurrection of Egyptian and Mesopotamian civilization, the twentieth century has added that of the Hittites and other Anatolian peoples,[14] the

[11] *The Law and the Prophets*, 1965, pp. 23–25. This developmental pattern has persisted in the thinking of Old Testament scholars ever since (note especially remarks of Bright, *op. cit.*, pp. 23–25 end).

[12] 'The new evidence [*i.e.*, objective Near Eastern data], far from furnishing a corrective to inherited notions of the religion of earliest Israel, tends to be subsumed under the familiar developmental pattern', Bright, *op. cit.*, p. 25 end. And the same applies to other aspects besides history (*e.g.*, literary matters); examples abound – at random, *cf.* McCarthy and covenant-form, pp. 101, n. 53; 127 f., and Eissfeldt's 'Aramaisms' that are early Canaanite, p. 145, below.

[13] For decipherment of Ancient Oriental languages, see the excellent little work of J. Friedrich, *Extinct Languages*, 1962.

[14] The importance of the Hittites was first enunciated by Sayce and Wright, but our modern knowledge of the life and history of early Asia

Canaanites (especially through Ugarit), Hurrians and others.
One factor that influenced many nineteenth-century investi-
gators was the hope of making discoveries that would throw
light on biblical history, a hope that persists today.[15] However,
this factor steadily gave way to the study of the Ancient Oriental
cultures for their own sake, as part of world history. For example, in the years immediately following its foundation in
1882, the English Egypt Exploration Fund (now Society) paid
particular attention to Egyptian sites of biblical interest; this was
reflected in its excavation memoirs on Pithom, 1885 (4th ed.,
1903), Tanis, I/II, 1885–88, Goshen, 1888, Tell el Yahudiyeh,
1890, and Bubastis, 1891. Subsequent activities have always
been devoted to key sites of prime Egyptological importance
(Deir el Bahri, Abydos, Tell el Amarna, Amarah West,
Saqqara, etc.) without any further direct reference to biblical
matters. The same development can be observed in other un-
dertakings. Thus, the Deutsche Orient-Gesellschaft of Berlin included Babylon and Jericho in its vast initial programme, but
since the 1914–18 war has concentrated on Uruk and Boghaz-
köy.
This change was stimulated by two factors: negatively, the
small proportion of discoveries that had an obvious and direct
connection with the Bible;[16] positively, the rapid expansion and

---

Minor was made possible by the excavation of the Hittite state archives at
Boghaz-köy from 1906. The classic synthesis is A. Goetze, *Kleinasien*[2],
1957, supplemented by H. Otten in H. Schmökel (ed.), *Kulturgeschichte des
Alten Orients*, 1961, pp. 311–446, and by G. Walser (ed.), *Neuere Hethiterforschung*, 1964 (=*Historia*, Einzelschriften, Heft 7). In English, a handy outline is O. R. Gurney, *The Hittites*[3], 1961, plus various chapters in *CAH*[2],
I/II. *Cf.* also C. W. Ceram, *Narrow Pass, Black Mountain*, 1956.

[15] For surveys of Ancient Near Eastern discovery in relation to the Old
Testament, see W. F. Albright, *Recent Discoveries in Bible Lands*, 1955; *From
the Stone Age to Christianity*[2], 1957 (also paperback), esp. chapter I; *Archaeology and the Religion of Israel*[3], 1953, esp. chapter II; and *History, Archaeology
and Christian Humanism*, 1964, ch. 5, a revision of *JBL* 59 (1940), pp. 85–112.
Also M. Noth, *Die Welt des Alten Testaments*[4], 1962 = Noth, *The Old Testament World*, 1965; and the essays in *BANE*.

[16] Especially in Palestine itself, where archaeological results were of little
direct use for biblical studies until nearly 1930, and inscriptions were so few.

fast-growing complexity of each section of Ancient Oriental studies (constantly fed by new data), accompanied by trends toward specialization. This change of emphasis in Ancient Oriental studies was partly responsible for two consequences: first, that these studies could develop largely untouched by theological considerations and Old Testament controversies;[17] and secondly, that the impact of Ancient Oriental studies upon Old Testament studies was very small – largely limited to a handful of historical synchronisms and some obvious literary and other comparisons.

Ancient Near Eastern studies have always been fed by a constant supply of new, tangible material. One illustration of this is the steady succession of discoveries of important cuneiform archives: the library of Assurbanipal and related Assyrian finds from 1850; the El Amarna tablets, 1887; the tablet collections from Nippur, 1889–1900, whose Sumerian literary treasures are still being unlocked by S. N. Kramer and others; the Hittite archives from Boghaz-köy since 1906; more Assyrian records from Assur in 1903–14; the Nuzi tablets since the 1920s; the brilliant discoveries at Ugarit since 1929 and 1948; the huge archives from Mari since 1936, *etc.* Other documentary finds (*e.g.*, Egyptian) and other aspects of Near Eastern discovery have been equally fruitful. Thus, in these disciplines, facts have a primary value and theories are mainly subordinated to them. The constant flow of new, objective material has repeatedly enforced the modification or even the wholesale replacement of theories, as in the 'Hatshepsut problem' in Egyptology. Kurt Sethe formulated a brilliant and elaborate theory about the succession of certain monarchs of the Eighteenth Dynasty[18] – a theory which, in its heyday, won the assent of most Egyptologists. But a majority adhesion could not save even this 'scientific' theory from the fatal impact of a series of new facts (and

[17] Apart from the *Babel und Bibel* and Pan-Babylonian episodes; but these had little bearing on Assyriological progress.

[18] In his *Untersuchungen z. Geschichte u. Altertumskunde Ägyptens*, I, 1896, pp. 1–58, 65–129, and *Das Hatschepsut-Problem*, 1932, supported by J. H. Breasted in *Untersuchungen* . . ., II:2, 1900, pp. 27–55; for a thorough critical rebuttal based largely on the American results, see W. F. Edgerton, *The Thutmosid Succession*, 1933.

re-examination of older ones), mainly provided by the American excavations at Deir el Bahri. Scholars in these fields have thus established their studies upon objective, verifiable fact and sound methodology, learnt the hard way, with an emphasis on external, first-hand data; *a priori* philosophical considerations have rarely been allowed to interfere directly.

(c) *Two Disciplines, One World*

A remarkable situation has thus come about. These two neighbouring fields of study have so far developed almost wholly independently of each other, and also along quite different lines: on the one hand, relatively objectively based disciplines of the Orientalists; on the other, idealistic theories of the Old Testament scholars.

This contrast is not unfair. For example, even the most ardent advocate of the documentary theory must admit that we have as yet *no single scrap* of external, objective (*i.e.*, *tangible*) evidence for either the existence or the history of 'J', 'E', or any other alleged source-document. No manuscript of any part of the Old Testament is yet known from earlier than the third century BC.[19] But if, for example, a sufficiently well preserved copy of the supposed pentateuchal document 'J' were to be found in Judaea in an indubitable archaeological context of (for example) the ninth century BC – then we would have *real, verifiable* (genuinely objective) evidence for a documentary theory. Equally, if an archaic copy of one or more of the existing books of the Pentateuch (or even the Pentateuch) were to be discovered in an irreproachable context of the twelfth or eleventh century BC, this would be clear and final evidence against such a theory. It is the lack of *really early* manuscript-attestation which has permitted so much uncontrolled (because unverifiable) theorizing in Old Testament studies.

By contrast, we often have securely dated manuscript evidence extending over centuries for Ancient Oriental literary and other works. Thus, for the Egyptian story of Sinuhe (composed *c.* 1900 BC), we have MSS of *c.* 1800 BC and slightly later, and

---

[19] Dead Sea Scroll fragment of Exodus, *cf.* F. M. Cross, *BANE*, p. 137, fig. 1:3.

a series of ostraca of the thirteenth and twelfth centuries BC.[20] These place the textual and literary history of this work upon a factual basis. This is but one example.

Now geographically, historically and culturally, the Ancient Near East *is* the world of the Old Testament, while humanly speaking the Old Testament is a part of Ancient Near Eastern literature, history and culture. Therefore, what can be known about the history, literatures, linguistics, religion, *etc.*, of the Ancient Orient will have a *direct bearing* upon these same aspects of the Old Testament. The relatively limited Old Testament material must, as appropriate, be set in the *full* context (in both space and time) of *all* the related Ancient Oriental material that is available.

Nevertheless, Old Testament scholarship has made only superficial use of Ancient Near Eastern data. The main reasons, of course, are fairly obvious. Ancient Oriental studies are both complex and highly specialized. To use their original material at first hand, one requires the mastery of Egyptian hieroglyphic and hieratic scripts and language phases, or of the cuneiform syllabaries and several languages of Western Asia, or else of the subtleties of archaeological stratigraphy and typology of pottery and other artefacts – not to mention a control of the essential scholarly literature in these fields. Fresh Near Eastern data, no matter how relevant for the Old Testament, can only be made generally available by those who are suitably trained Orientalists. On the other hand, because they are often more involved in theological work and are largely limited to Hebrew, Aramaic, Greek and languages of early biblical versions (Latin, Syriac, Ethiopic, Coptic, *etc.*), most Old Testament scholars are not in a position to utilize, unaided and at first hand, the raw materials collected by Ancient Oriental research. This is no fault of theirs, and is to be expected; we live in a world of specialization in these realms as much as in the natural sciences or any other. Many Orientalists are not interested or competent in biblical studies, and have enough work of their own to do. Furthermore, not every hieratic ostracon or cuneiform tablet

[20] See G. Posener, *Littérature et Politique dans l'Égypte de la XIIe Dynastie*, 1956, pp. 87 f. and references.

(of the thousands extant) can be fully edited and annotated for non-specialists or for members of other scholarly disciplines. Thus, the Near Eastern material easily accessible to Old Testament scholarship is necessarily limited, and so between the two fields of study there has long been an inevitable gulf. Happily, this situation has begun to change somewhat. More Orientalists are beginning to contribute an increasing flow of new data to Old Testament studies, while Old Testament scholars are making more use of this material than ever before. But this flow is still too small, must be much more increased, and must ultimately achieve a far greater impact.

(d) Two Tensions

One more point must now be briefly considered. Through the impact of the Ancient Orient upon the Old Testament and upon Old Testament studies a new tension is being set up while an older one is being reduced. For the comparative material from the Ancient Near East is tending to agree with the extant structure of Old Testament documents as actually transmitted to us, rather than with the reconstructions of nineteenth-century Old Testament scholarship – or with its twentieth-century prolongation and developments to the present day.

Some examples may illustrate this point. The valid and close parallels to the social customs of the Patriarchs come from documents of the nineteenth to fifteenth centuries BC[21] (agreeing with an early-second-millennium origin for this material in Genesis), and not from Assyro-Babylonian data of the tenth to sixth centuries BC (possible period of the supposed 'J', 'E' sources).[22] Likewise for Genesis 23, the closest parallel comes from the Hittite Laws[23] which passed into oblivion with the fall of the Hittite Empire about 1200 BC. The covenant-forms which appear in Exodus, Deuteronomy and Joshua follow the model of those current in the thirteenth century BC – the period of Moses and Joshua – and *not* those of the first millennium BC.[24]

[21] See below, pp. 51, 153 f.
[22] Compare dates for 'J', *etc.*, given by C. R. North in H. H. Rowley (ed.), *Old Testament and Modern Study*, 1951, p. 81.
[23] See below, pp. 51, n. 88; 154 f.   [24] See below, pp. 90–102, 128.

The background to Syro-Palestinian kingship in 1 Samuel 8 is provided by documents from Alalakh and Ugarit of not later than the thirteenth century BC;[25] this suggests that late in the eleventh century BC is a late enough date for the content of this passage, and would be much more realistic than a date some centuries later still. Personification of abstracts, like Wisdom in Proverbs 8 and 9, finds its real origin not in Greek influences of the fourth century BC but in the wide use of precisely such personified concepts throughout the Ancient Near East in the third and second millennia BC, up to 1,500 years before even Solomon was born.[26] Words once thought to be a mark of post-Exilic date now turn up in Ugaritic texts of the thirteenth century BC, or in even earlier sources.[27]

The proper implications of these and many similar facts are that large parts of the Pentateuch really did originate in the second millennium BC, that Samuel really could (and probably did) issue the warnings recorded in 1 Samuel 8, and that the connection between Solomon's reign and the first few chapters of Proverbs (cf. Pr. 1:1–7) is something more than just the idle fancy of some late scribe; and so on. At least, this is the rational approach that would obtain if this were any part of Ancient Near Eastern literature, history and culture other than the Old Testament.

Such implications have so far found little or no response from Old Testament scholars. Within the framework of their existing theories,[28] they are often willing to admit that this or that detail preserved in a relatively late source (even 'P'!) may indeed go back to a more ancient origin than was hitherto supposed, but nothing more. But what will happen when more and more such details of every kind find their appropriate early analogies, almost always earlier than the inherited theories presuppose? Suppose that every detail and aspect of some given passage or literary unit can be shown by external, objective Ancient Oriental data to be completely consistent with a general date stated or clearly implied by the biblical text – in literary struc-

---

[25] See below, pp. 158 f.   [26] Cf. below, p. 127 and note 57.
[27] See below, pp. 143–146.
[28] Cf. already the citation from Bright on p. 20, note 12, above.

ture, vocabulary and syntax, theological viewpoint and content, or social, political or legal usages, *etc.* – and that not a scrap of residue is left over from this passage or unit to be labelled 'late'. What then will become of time-honoured theory? This has not yet happened, nor does this book make any such attempt; but as time passes, it is increasingly likely that the continuous flow of new material (and fuller utilization of data) may cause this kind of thing to happen, and we must take this prospect very seriously.

There is thus a tension between the basic theories and procedures of much Old Testament scholarship and the frequent and increasing agreement of Ancient Oriental data with the existing Old Testament written traditions. As yet, this tension has barely begun to emerge, but it will inevitably do so increasingly. After all, even the most respected theories are only a means to an end, not an end in themselves. In the light of the vast new knowledge that is becoming available, old problems are amenable to new treatment; they must be dealt with afresh, from the foundations up, taking *no* current theory for granted or as the equivalent of fact, as is too commonly done, for instance, with the methods and general results of conventional literary criticism. Theories must be refashioned or even wholly replaced by new syntheses just as vigorously as in the natural sciences, medicine, or in the rest of Ancient Near Eastern studies, when the accumulating evidence patently requires it. No theory can be sacrosanct, and widespread acceptance of a theory does not guarantee its truth. The geocentric astronomy elaborated by Ptolemy and others was universally accepted until a closer investigation of facts showed that our planetary system revolved round the sun. Likewise, the ingenious system of Descartes commanded general assent (despite Pascal), until Newton – at first in isolation – brought forward contrary facts, and eventually the facts won. Various major theories widely current in Old Testament studies may duly end up in the same fold as those of Ptolemy, Descartes or the 'flat-earthers'.

Then there is an older tension that is being reduced. Not only does the evidence from the Ancient Near East suggest that the existing structure of, and picture given by, the Old Testament writings are nearer to the truth than the commonly accepted reconstructions. Application of Ancient Oriental data and of soundly based principles derived therefrom to Old Testament problems can materially limit and reduce the scope of such problems, especially when their proportions have become rather inflated within Old Testament studies.

III. SOME BASIC PRINCIPLES OF STUDY

As already remarked above (p. 24), the Ancient Orient is the world of the Old Testament, and humanly speaking the Old Testament is an integral part of its Ancient Oriental *milieu*. For example, comparison of biblical and other Ancient Oriental literature reveals very close formal analogies even when there is no linguistic relationship.[29] These basic facts none are likely to deny, but they have certain direct implications which likewise must be conceded, yet which are still not properly appreciated in Old Testament studies. They are that principles found to be valid in dealing with Ancient Oriental history and literature will in all likelihood prove to be directly applicable to Old Testament history and literature – and conversely, that methods or principles which are demonstrably false when applied to first-hand Ancient Near Eastern data should not be imposed upon Old Testament data either.

Within Ancient Near Eastern studies, various basic principles have become so generally established, so tried in the fires of experience, that the scholars concerned hardly ever feel the need even to mention them in print. They include the following.

(a) The Primary Importance of Facts

Priority must always be given to tangible, objective data, and to external evidence, over subjective theory or speculative opinions. Facts must control theory, not vice versa.[30] Source-material

[29] Note, for example, the curious semantic parallel in two wholly unrelated Egyptian and Hebrew texts (below, p. 166); or parallel and independent semantic change in Babylonian, Hebrew and Egyptian (below, pp. 165 f.); or parallelism of Egyptian ʿa and Semitic *yad*, *cf*. Svi Rin, *Biblische Zeitschrift* (*NF*) 7 (1963), p. 32, n. 49.

[30] An example of this was the Hatshepsut problem, in which new facts

must be scrutinized in this light, whether it be biblical or other Oriental.

(b) A Positive Attitude to Source-Material

It is normal practice to assume the general reliability of statements in our sources, unless there is good, explicit evidence to the contrary. Unreliability, secondary origins, dishonesty of a writer, or tendentious traits – all these must be clearly proved by adduction of tangible evidence, and not merely inferred to support a theory.[31]

For example, in modern Egyptology, we accept Shishak's (= Shoshenq I) topographical list at Karnak as an authentic, first-hand document for his having invaded Palestine,[32] an event mentioned in 1 Kings 14:25, 26 and 2 Chronicles 12:1–10. A stela of Shishak from Megiddo, destruction levels in certain Palestinian sites, and a war stela and blocks from Karnak temple in Egypt[33] afford further tangible evidence of Shishak's campaign. Decades ago, in the arrogant manner of Old Testament scholarship of that day, Wellhausen dismissed the list of Shishak as historically worthless, saying, 'He could simply have reproduced an older list of one of his predecessors.'[34] Unlike Old Testament studies, hypercriticism of this kind will not do in Egyptology. In actual fact, Shishak's list uses an orthography different from all earlier lists, because of linguistic changes in

displaced a reigning theory (see p. 22 and note 18, above). In quite another field (study of John's Gospel), H. M. Teeple has also insisted that 'the approach should be objective' and that 'the starting point should be the evidence and not the theory' (*JBL* 81 (1962), p. 279).

[31] As is done by Noth, for example, in dismissing the role of Moses as secondary in the Desert and Exodus traditions of Israel; see J. Bright, *Early Israel in Recent History Writing*, 1956, pp. 106–109, for a cogent and well-deserved criticism of Noth's unrealistic position by analogy from more recent and better-controlled history.

[32] See *NBD*, p. 1181, 'Shishak' and references; Kitchen, *The Third Intermediate Period in Egypt* (forthcoming). The list was published in Chicago Epigraphic Survey, *Reliefs and Inscriptions at Karnak*, III, 1954. Handy part-picture, Pritchard, *The Ancient Near East*, 1958, fig. 94 (=*ANEP*, fig. 349).

[33] See also below, p. 159.

[34] *Israelitische und jüdische Geschichte*[7], 1914, p. 68, n. 4: 'Er kann einfach eine ältere Liste eines seiner Vorgänger reproduziert haben.'

Egyptian before his time and since the known earlier lists.[35] It also contains many names never yet found in earlier lists. The old-style headings of the list (mention of long-defunct Mitanni, *etc.*) were merely intended to put Shishak on the same official plane of achievement as his great Eighteenth and Nineteenth Dynasty predecessors, and have no bearing on the historicity of the list proper or of the campaign, independently attested from other evidence as noted above.

On the other hand, objective evidence suggests that a supposed Libyan campaign of Pepi II (*c.* 2300 BC) *is* an idealistic fiction. For the sculptures of this 'war' in his funerary temple can be seen to have been copied directly in style and subject from corresponding reliefs of the earlier King Sahurēᶜ – even to the proper names of the family of the Libyan chief! Disbelief in Pepi's record is founded not on *a priori* theory but on evidence physically visible to all who care to look.[36]

(c) The Inconclusive Nature of Negative Evidence

Negative evidence is commonly not evidence at all, and is thus usually irrelevant. If some person, event, *etc.* is mentioned only in documents of a later age, the absence of any directly contemporary document referring to such a person or event is *not in itself* a valid or sufficient ground for doubting the historicity of the person, event, *etc.* concerned.

For example, the Egyptian Fourteenth Dynasty consisted of about seventy-six kings (Manetho's figure) mostly listed in the Turin Papyrus of Kings which dates from about 500 years after that period (Nineteenth Dynasty). So far, hardly a single definitely contemporary monument of any of these Delta kings

---

[35] *Cf.* the changes elucidated by Sethe, *ZDMG* 77 (1923), pp. 145–207 and Albright, *RT* 40 (1923), pp. 64–70, and his *Vocalization of the Egyptian Syllabic Orthography*, 1934, pp. 13–16. Some of their results (*e.g.*, on vowel-length, *etc.*) have been modified by J. Vergote, *BIFAO* 58 (1959), pp. 1–19, and G. Fecht, *Wortakzent und Silbenstruktur*, 1960 (= *Münchener Ägyptologische Forschungen*, 21).

[36] See W. Hölscher, *Libyer und Ägypter*, 1937 (*Mün. Äg. Forsch.*, 4), p. 13 and n. 5; the scenes are published in G. Jéquier, *Monument funéraire de Pépi II*, II, 1938, p. 14, plate 9, and L. Borchardt, *Grabdenkmal des Königs Saʾhurēᶜ*, II: 2, 1913, plate 1.

has been recovered (unlike the Memphite/Theban Thirteenth Dynasty), but Egyptologists are not so naïve as to make this a reason for denying the existence of this line of kings.[37] So, although we have no contemporary record of the Abraham of Genesis, this likewise is not a sufficient reason for doubting his real existence. The absolute realism of his social activities as shown by cuneiform documents of the early to middle second millennium BC (see below, pp. 153 ff.) is a warning that any such doubt must be founded on more tangible evidence if it is to be worth any consideration at all. We must have more positive, *tangible* reasons for doubt.[38] Most Egyptologists had too hastily dismissed Manetho's Nephercheres in the Twenty-first Dynasty as fiction – until Montet's excavations at Tanis suddenly revealed the existence of King Neferkarē' Amenemnisu;[39] Manetho's Osochor of the same dynasty has now also been restored to history.[40] However, the King Ramesses of the 'Bentresh Stela' is known never to have existed: three parts of his titulary are those of Tuthmosis IV, and both his cartouches and the story of the stela are based on those of Ramesses II and on events in his reign.[41]

It must always be remembered that such absence of evidence

[37] *Cf.* J. von Beckerath, *Untersuchungen zur politischen Geschichte der zweiten Zwischenzeit in Ägypten*, 1965, pp. 1–11 (on sources and methods), and contrast material for the Thirteenth Dynasty (pp. 226–262) with that for the Fourteenth (pp. 262–269).

[38] *Cf.* my paper, 'Historical Method and Early Hebrew Tradition', *THB* 17 (1966), pp. 63–97; and R. de Vaux, 'Method in the Study of Early Hebrew History' in J. P. Hyatt (ed.), *The Bible in Modern Scholarship*, 1965, pp. 15–29. G. Björkman, 'Egyptology and Historical Method', *Orientalia Suecana* 13 (1964), pp. 9–33, is interesting and salutary, but errs fatally in hypercriticism of sources (pp. 11, 32–33). He is incapable of positively 'faulting' *Merikarē'*, his chosen text, and fails to realize the sheer inadequacy of 'negative evidence'. See also examples of 'negative evidence', p. 44, note 47, below.

[39] See B. Grdseloff, *ASAE* 47 (1947), pp. 207–211; P. Montet, *Psousennès*, 1951, p. 185.

[40] *Cf.* E. Young, *Journal of the American Research Center in Egypt* 2 (1963), pp. 99–101; Kitchen, *Chronique d'Égypte* 40/Fasc. 80 (1965), pp. 320–321, and *Third Intermediate Period in Egypt* (forthcoming).

[41] See W. Spiegelberg, *RT* 28 (1906), p. 181; G. Lefebvre, *Romans et Contes Égyptiens*, 1949, pp. 221–232 (introduction, references, translation).

in these fields of study too often merely reflects the large gaps in *our* present-day knowledge. How great are the gaps in our knowledge even of the relatively well documented culture of Ancient Egypt, and how negative evidence can distort our perspective, has been vividly demonstrated by Professor G. Posener.[42] The relevant evidence still awaits discovery or decipherment,[43] or else it has all too often perished long ago. In the late twelfth century AD, the famous Arab physician 'Abd el-Latif remarked on the huge wilderness of ruins that constituted ancient Memphis; now, only a few temple ruins and remains of mounds among the palms mark the spot, near Mitrahineh village. In 1778 forty or fifty Greek papyri were burned by natives at Giza because they liked the smell of burning papyrus.[44] And countless inscribed limestone monuments have found their way into native lime-kilns. Who can estimate how much priceless historical information has thus been lost? In Palestine, unknown quantities of papyrus documents have perished, their loss often marked by nothing more substantial than the impression of the papyrus-fibres on the back of clay sealings like that of Gedaliah from Lachish.[45]

(d) A Proper Approach to Apparent Discrepancies

The basic harmony that ultimately underlies extant records should be sought out, even despite apparent discrepancy.

[42] Cf. Posener, Collège de France (Chaire de Philologie et Archéologie Égyptiennes), Leçon Inaugurale, 6. Déc. 1961, Paris, 1962, especially pp. 7–12 (written documents) and 13–16 (types of site); this also appeared (abridged) in Annales (Économies, Sociétés, Civilisations) 17: No. 4 (1962), pp. 631–646. For Mesopotamia, note the remarks by A. L. Oppenheim, Ancient Mesopotamia, 1964, pp. 11, 24–25, 334 and passim.

[43] Although cuneiform tablets and fragments in the world's museums are numbered in the hundred-thousands (cf. D. J. Wiseman, The Expansion of Assyrian Studies, 1962, p. 8 and n. 16), they are but a fraction of all that were written – perhaps 99 per cent are still in the ground (E. Chiera, They Wrote on Clay, 1938 (repr. 1956, paperback), p. 233), while in the words of C. H. Gordon (Adventures in the Nearest East, 1957, p. 13) 'for every mound excavated in the Near East, a hundred remain untouched'.

[44] See J. Černý, Paper and Books in Ancient Egypt, 1952, p. 31.

[45] See G. E. Wright, Biblical Archaeology, 1957, p. 178 and fig. 128. For Byblos, see below, p. 137 and note 103.

Throughout ancient history, our existing sources are incomplete and elliptical. Apparent discrepancies even in first-hand sources *can* be caused by (and thus indicate) the presence of *error* in one or more sources. Thus, errors in the Assyrian King Lists concerning the family relationships between successive kings can be detected by comparison with independent original documents.[46] Note also the differing order of early Sumerian kings in two versions of the Tummal building chronicle, one agreeing with the Sumerian King List and one not,[47] and the difficulties in using this chronicle, the Sumerian King List and other data to establish the chronological relationships of these kings.[48] Yet not infrequently, such 'discrepancies' imply nothing of the kind. Thus the succession of kings at the end of the Egyptian Nineteenth Dynasty has long been complicated by first-hand data that seemed mutually contradictory. Ramesses-Siptah and Merenptah-Siptah are certainly only variant names of one king. Yet Ostracon Cairo 25515 clearly announces the death of Sethos II and accession of Ramesses-Siptah, while the titles of Sethos II have equally clearly been subsequently carved in palimpsest over those of Merenptah-Siptah on a slab from Memphis and in the tomb of Queen Tewosret at Thebes. Total contradiction! The solution is in principle simple: later rulers recognized Sethos II as having been a legitimate king, but not Siptah; thus, the latter's titles were replaced *post mortem* with those of his 'legitimate' predecessor, Sethos II.[49] Again, it is difficult to bring together agreeably the evidence of thirty-three year-dates for King Zimri-lim of Mari and the synchronism of Hammurapi of Babylon with Shamshi-Adad I of Assyria (all in first-hand sources) into a clear chronological and historical relationship.[50]

[46] Examples in A. Parrot, *Archéologie Mésopotamienne*, II, 1953, p. 361, after A. Poebel, *JNES* 1 (1942), p. 481.

[47] E. Sollberger, *JCS* 16 (1962), pp. 40–41; M. E. L. Mallowan, *Iraq* 26 (1964), pp. 67–68, nn. 16, 19.

[48] *Cf.* S. N. Kramer, *The Sumerians*, 1963, pp. 46–50; M. B. Rowton, *CAH²*, I:6 (*Chronology*), 1962, pp. 30–32, 53–56, 65–67.

[49] See Sir A. H. Gardiner, *JEA* 44 (1958), pp. 12–22.

[50] *Cf.* references given by Rowton, *op. cit.*, pp. 40–41, and H. B. Huffmon, *Amorite Personal Names in the Mari Texts*, 1965, pp. 8–9.

C

Instead, such 'discrepancies' can serve to warn us that, in order to obtain a full picture, we must weigh and take into account *all* relevant sources, and make allowance for missing or ill-interpreted factors. At first sight, various inscriptions of Sargon II of Assyria appear to give irreconcilable accounts of events (and especially their dates) in his reign; but a full study of all the relevant texts by H. Tadmor[51] has suggested principles of composition and reckoning which would underlie and explain the apparent differences.

Or, again, the apparent anomaly of a vizier Nesipeqashuty (serving under Shoshenq III) whose father was a contemporary of Shoshenq I (biblical Shishak) eighty to a hundred years earlier caused Kees to doubt the validity of a genealogy attested by half a dozen monuments.[52] Here, a reconsideration of the family history would eliminate Kees' doubts completely, and would allow as alternative a simple scribal slip in just one badly written stela (Liverpool City Museum M.13916).[53]

Finally, in speaking of error, one must distinguish clearly between primary errors (mistakes committed by the original author of a work) and secondary errors (not in the original, but resulting from faulty textual transmission or the like).

Such principles are implicit throughout Ancient Near Eastern studies. It should be emphasized that a positive approach does not exclude searching, critical scrutiny of material, but it does seek to avoid the grave distortions produced by hypercriticism. If positive principles of this kind had been properly applied in Old Testament studies (in line with other Ancient Oriental studies), such studies would have followed a pattern quite different from their present one, and many problems would be reduced to more natural proportions. We now turn to a brief, positive treatment of a necessarily limited but varied handful of problems.

[51] *JCS* 12 (1958), pp. 22–40, 77–100.
[52] *Das Priestertum im Ägyptischen Staat*, 1953, pp. 237–238.
[53] *Cf.* Kitchen, *The Third Intermediate Period in Egypt* (forthcoming), Part III, on Neser-Amun/Nebneteru families.

2. EARLY HEBREW CHRONOLOGY

I. BEFORE ABRAHAM

For the period before Abraham, the Old Testament data are very limited and concise.[1] From the chronological point of view, they raise questions which cannot be fully answered from our present knowledge. But comparative Ancient Near Eastern data can perhaps throw a little light on the Old Testament material.

(a) The Old Testament Data

The genealogies of Genesis 5 and 11 are the principal sources. These serve as formal connecting links between earliest Man and the Flood (the first great crisis), and between the Flood and Abraham as ancestor of the Hebrews and of the line of promise. Such genealogies were not intended to serve just a narrowly chronological purpose in the modern sense; like those in Matthew 1 or Luke 3, their main purpose was theological, but this does not necessarily mean that they are without any factual basis at all. One may compare the primarily religious purpose of some Egyptian King Lists. The Table of Kings at Abydos was related to the cult of the royal ancestors,[2] but this does not affect the chronological order or historicity of the kings that it lists; and certain groups of kings are omitted deliber-

[1] On possible historical relationships of Genesis 1–11 with early antiquity, cf. T. C. Mitchell, *F/T* 91 (1959), pp. 28–49, and Kitchen, *ibid.*, pp. 195–197. On historical status of Genesis 1–11, theologically viewed, cf. K. Cramer, *Genesis 1–11: Urgeschichte? Zur Problem der Geschichte im Alten Testament*, 1959; also J. B. Bauer, *Die biblische Urgeschichte, Vorgeschichte des Heils, Genesis 1–11²*, 1964. On genealogies, cf. Mitchell and Bruce, *NBD*, pp. 456–459 and references.

[2] On which, see H. W. Fairman in S. H. Hooke (ed.), *Myth, Ritual and Kingship*, 1958, pp. 77, 98–104.

ately but without stating the fact.[3] The royal offering-lists of the Hittite monarchy are also cultic documents, but their historical and chronological value is beyond all real doubt.[4] The Sumerian King List expresses a certain concept of kingship in early Mesopotamia, but contains data of great value.[5]

(b) Problems and External Evidence

1. *Degree of Continuity.* From earliest Man (Adam) to Abraham, the time covered by the genealogies (if taken to be continuous throughout) is far too short when compared with external data. Thus, if the birth of Abraham were to be set at about 2000 BC,[6] then on the Hebrew figures[7] the Flood would occur some 290 years earlier, about 2300 BC. This date is excluded by the Mesopotamian evidence, because it would fall some 300 or 400 years *after* the period of Gilgamesh of Uruk[8] for whom (in both Epic and Sumerian King List) the Flood was already an event of the distant past.[9] Likewise, the appearing of earliest Man (Adam) some 1,947 years or so before Abraham on the Hebrew figures, in about 4000 BC, would seem to clash rather

---

[3] On the lists, *cf.* Sir A. H. Gardiner, *Egypt of the Pharaohs*, 1961, pp. 429–453, and W. Helck, *Untersuchungen zu Manetho und den Ägyptischen Königslisten*, 1956.

[4] See H. Otten, *MDOG* 83 (1951), pp. 47–71; A. Goetze, *JCS* 11 (1957), pp. 53–55, 58; Kitchen, *Suppiluliuma and the Amarna Pharaohs*, 1962, pp. 1, 52–55 (Excursus II).

[5] *Cf.* T. Jacobsen, *The Sumerian King List*, 1939 (repr. 1964), esp. pp. 138–140, 165 ff.

[6] It would hardly be much earlier on any calculation, *cf.* Section II, pp. 41–56, below.

[7] Some variant figures in the LXX and Samaritan versions do not affect the main point at issue here; *cf. WBD*, p. 103.

[8] So also M. E. L. Mallowan, *Iraq* 26 (1964), pp. 67–68, with whose paper, *cf.* R. L. Raikes, *Iraq* 28 (1966), pp. 52–63. Rowton, *CAH²*, I:6 (*Chronology*), 1962, pp. 64–67, *cf.* 54–56, offers a date of roughly 2700 BC for Gilgamesh; Kramer, *The Sumerians*, 1963, pp. 49–50, suggests about 2600 BC; somewhere in the twenty-seventh century BC seems safe enough.

[9] Gilgamesh Epic, Tablet XI; translations by A. Heidel, *The Gilgamesh Epic and Old Testament Parallels²*, 1949 (paperback, 1963), and E. A. Speiser in *ANET²*, 1955, pp. 72–99, 514–515,=*ANE*, pp. 40–75. Studies on Gilgamesh and his Epic with rich bibliography are to be found in P. Garelli (ed.), *Gilgameš et sa Légende*, 1960.

badly with not just centuries but whole millennia of pre-
literate civilization throughout the Ancient Near East[10] prior
to the occurrence of the first written documents just before the
First Dynasty in Egypt, c. 3000 BC, and rather earlier in Mesopotamia.[11] One may well question therefore whether these
genealogies are really to be understood as being continuous
throughout. There are several indications which may suggest
that this is not the case.

First, there is the symmetry of ten generations before the
Flood and ten generations after the Flood. With this, one may
compare the three series of fourteen generations in Matthew's
genealogy of Christ (Mt. 1:1–17, esp. 17), which is *known* to be
selective, and not wholly continuous, from the evidence of the
Old Testament. Thus Matthew 1:8 says 'Joram begat Uzziah',
but from the Old Testament (2 Ki. 8:25; 11:2; 14:1, 21) it is
clear that in fact Joram fathered Ahaziah, father of Joash, father

[10] Examples: For Palestine, we have Jericho as a walled town with
towers by c. 7000 BC (K. M. Kenyon, *PEQ* 92 (1960), pp. 97–98; Kenyon,
Archaeology in the Holy Land[2], 1965 (also paperback), p. 44). For Syria, *cf.*
traces of a similar fortified settlement in level V at Ugarit (C. F. A. Schaeffer
et al., *Ugaritica IV*, 1962, pp. 153–160, 317–322 (esp. 319–321)). For Mesopotamia, *cf.* Jarmo with settlements from roughly 9000 to 4500 BC (G. E.
Wright in *BANE*, pp. 76, 77 and n. 13). For Asia Minor, note the remarkable
settlements at Çatal Hüyük (shrines with paintings and plasterwork, c.
6200–5800 BC), Can Hasan and Hacilar. For Çatal Hüyük and Hacilar,
see J. Mellaart's reports in *Anatolian Studies* 12–14 (1962–4) and 8–11
(1958–61) respectively; for Can Hasan, *cf.* D. H. French, *ibid.*, 12–15
(1962–5); in general, see Mellaart, *CAH*[2], I:7 (§§ xi–xiv), *Anatolia Before
c. 4000 BC*, 1964. The amazingly early evidence for metalworking c.
6500–5800 BC at Çatal Hüyük (levels IX–VI, *cf.* Mellaart, *Anatolian Studies*
14 (1964), pp. 111, 114) reminds one of Tubal-cain in Gn. 4:22 (but *cf.*
Mitchell, *F/T* 91 (1959), p. 42).
    The above dates are based on Carbon-14, but find some measure of sup-
port in the long stratigraphic sequences in these sites and regions. For Near
Eastern C-14 dates, see: Wright, *BANE*, 76–77: E. L. Kohler and E. K.
Ralph, *American Journal of Archaeology* 65 (1961), pp. 357–367; H. S. Smith,
Antiquity 38 (1964), pp. 32–37 (Egypt); J. G. D. Clark, *Antiquity* 39 (1965),
pp. 45–48; R. W. Ehrich (ed.), *Chronologies in Old World Archaeology*, 1965.
    [11] *Cf.* S. Schott, *Hieroglyphen*, Abh. Akad. Mainz, 1950, and in *HdO*, I: I
(1), *Ägyptologie*, 1959, pp. 18–36, for Egypt. For Mesopotamia, *cf.* references
in C. J. Gadd, *CAH*[2], I: 13 (*Cities of Babylonia*), 1962, pp. 3–6, and Rowton
in *CAH*[2], I: 6 (*Chronology*), 1962, pp. 56–57.

of Amaziah, father of Uzziah; *i.e.*, we must understand 'Joram begat (the line culminating in) Uzziah' as far as chronology is concerned. A much earlier parallel is provided by the eight, nine or ten rulers[12] who reigned from the beginning of kingship until the Flood according to an old Mesopotamian tradition prefixed to the Sumerian King List about 1800 BC.[13] And after the Flood at least, the Sumerian King List itself is known to have sometimes omitted both individual kings and whole dynasties.[14]

Secondly, the terminology of the genealogies does not prove that they are continuous throughout. Sometimes the adjoining narrative would suggest that certain parts of the genealogies are continuous (so: Adam to Enosh; Lamech to Shem; Nahor(?) to Terah; Terah to Abraham). Everywhere else, a continuous sequence cannot be automatically assumed without proof. Such a mixture of continuous and selective genealogy is in no way abnormal. Besides the obvious example of Matthew 1:1–17, the Abydos King List in Egypt silently omits three entire groups of kings (Ninth to early Eleventh, Thirteenth to Seventeenth Dynasties and the Amarna pharaohs) at three separate points in an otherwise continuous series; other sources enable us to know this. Or compare Jacobsen,[15] who derived from other sources the procedure of arrangement probably followed by the ancient author of the Sumerian King List and not obvious from its structure, as well as from certain King List statements.

The phrase 'A begat B' does not always imply direct parenthood. This is shown by its use in Matthew 1 in cases where

[12] *Cf.* W. G. Lambert, *JSS* 5 (1960), p. 115.

[13] On date and composition of this King List, see T. Jacobsen, *The Sumerian King List*, 1939, pp. 55–68, 128 ff.; F. R. Kraus, *ZA* 50 (1952), pp. 49 ff.; Rowton, *JNES* 19 (1960), pp. 156–162 and in *CAH²*, I: 6 (*Chronology*), 1962, pp. 30–31; Gadd, *CAH²*, I: 13 (*Cities of Babylonia*), 1962, pp. 15–17. Translations of the King List, Jacobsen, *op. cit.*, pp. 71–127; A. L. Oppenheim, *ANET*, pp. 265–266 (partial), and Kramer, *The Sumerians*, 1963, pp. 328–331.

[14] Gadd, *op. cit.*, p. 16; *cf.* Jacobsen, *op. cit.*, pp. 180–183 (dynasties of Lagash, Umma and elsewhere; reasons for this).

[15] *The Sumerian King List*, 1939, p. 160.

links are known (from the Old Testament) to have been omitted (*cf.* pp. 37–38, above). Likewise, in Genesis 46:18, the
children that 'Zilpah bare to Jacob' are known to include
great-grandsons. Terms like 'son' and 'father' can mean not only
'(grand)son' and '(grand)father' but also 'descendant' and
'ancestor' respectively. The noted charioteer Jehu 'son' of
Nimshi (1 Ki. 19:15; 2 Ki. 9:20) was strictly son of a Jehoshaphat, and so *grandson* of Nimshi (2 Ki. 9:2). Likewise in
Amarna Letter No. 9, Burnaburiash III, King of Babylon,
calls Kurigalzu I his 'father'; but '(grand)father' is to be understood, because he is more precisely entitled 'eldest son' of an
intervening king.[16] Ramesses II is called 'father' of Sethos II
in Pap. Gurob 2:7, although he could not be closer than
grandfather;[17] *cf.* the address to Belshazzar in Daniel 5:11
where 'father'='predecessor' in both cases. An extreme example
from Egypt is that of King Tirhakah (Twenty-fifth Dynasty,
c. 680 BC) who honours[18] *'it.f*, 'his father', Sesostris III
(Twelfth Dynasty, *c.* 1880 BC) – who lived 1,200 years earlier!
One thinks also of Christ called 'Son of David' (*e.g.*, Mt. 9:27).

So in Genesis 5 and 11, 'A begat B' may often mean simply
that 'A begat (the line culminating in) B';[19] in this case, one
cannot use these genealogies to fix the date of the Flood or of
earliest Man.

2. *High Numbers and Historicity.* The figures for the life-spans in
the genealogies seem much too high, and suggest to the superficial observer that the individuals concerned may be purely
legendary.

These high figures may be puzzling but they are not unique,

[16] Knudtzon, *Die El Amarna Tafeln*, I, No. 9. *Cf.* K. Jaritz, *MIO* 6 (1958),
pp. 212 n. 89, 241 No. 81; Kitchen, *Suppiluliuma and the Amarna Pharaohs*,
1962, p. 10 n. 5.

[17] Gardiner, *JNES* 12 (1953), p. 146.

[18] Altar-inscription in a temple of Tirhakah at Semna West; Sir E. A. W.
Budge, *The Egyptian Sudan*, I, 1907, p. 483 and figure.

[19] Precisely the same approach (Sumerian DUMU, 'son', as 'descendant')
is adopted for Gilgamesh and Ur-lugal in the Sumerian King List by
Rowton, *CAH²*, I: 6 (*Chronology*), 1962, p. 55.

and probably have no direct bearing on the possible historicity of the characters concerned.

First, the figures in Genesis 5 and 11 cannot in both cases be scaled down to 'natural' proportions by some arbitrary mathematical formula. In Genesis 5, all the figures are large; but in Genesis 11, each individual begets the next generation at a 'reasonable' age (at twenty-nine to thirty-five years of age; only Terah begets late in life at seventy),[20] even if his total lifespan is very long.

Secondly, however bizarre they seem in themselves, the Hebrew figures are much more modest and precise than the tens of thousands of years' reign attributed to the antediluvian kings of Mesopotamian tradition, varying from 43,200 years (En-men-lu-anna) to 18,600 years (Ubara-tutu).[21] After the Flood and before Gilgamesh, the longest reign is that of Etana of Kish (1,560 or 1,500 years), and the shortest that of Dumuzi of Uruk (100 years).[22]

Thirdly, incredibly large figures for lives or reigns (especially after the Flood) have, in fact, no necessary bearing on historicity. Thus, we may reject in its present form the 900 years' reign attributed to Enmebaragisi, king of Kish, as pure myth, but the stubborn fact remains that this king was real enough to leave behind him early Sumerian inscriptions, so he himself must be counted as historical, regardless of how one accounts for the Sumerian King List figure.[23] Scholars are now beginning to recognize as originally historical various early figures who were once considered to be purely mythical heroes because of later legends that became attached to them; these include such famous names as Dumuzi (deified to become later Tammuz) and

[20] As probably did the father of the Egyptian vizier Nesipeqashuty, referred to p. 34, above.

[21] See *ANET*, pp. 265–266, or Jacobsen, *Sumerian King List*, pp. 71/73, 75/77, or Kramer, *The Sumerians*, p. 328.

[22] *Cf. ANET*, pp. 265–266, Jacobsen, *op. cit.*, pp. 81, 89, or Kramer, *op. cit.*, pp. 328, 329. *Cf.* also J. J. Finkelstein, *JCS* 17 (1963), pp. 39–51.

[23] Gadd, *CAH²*, I: 13 (*Cities of Babylonia*), 1962, p. 17, and Rowton, *CAH²*, I: 6 (*Chronology*), 1962, pp. 54–55, after D. O. Edzard, *ZA* 53 (1959), pp. 9–26.

Gilgamesh of Uruk.[24] Thus, whatever one may make of the large figures in Genesis 5 and 11, the names themselves – on the closest Ancient Oriental analogy – are not necessarily to be considered as unhistorical merely because these figures are attached to them.

(c) The Literary Structure of Early Genesis (1–9)

This now finds early parallels. New evidence bearing on the Atrakhasis Epic shows that in Mesopotamia there also existed the literary schema: creation, development and degeneration of man, list of names before the Flood, then the Flood itself.[25] As various fragments indicate that the Atrakhasis Epic certainly goes back as far as the Old Babylonian period,[26] this literary pattern had its *floruit* at least as early as Abraham, an interesting point in regard to the antiquity of this form of the tradition. This is also true of the Sumerian King List, composed not later than the Third Dynasty of Ur, *c.* 2000 BC, and embodying the antediluvian tradition in its final form, *c.* 1800 BC.[27]

II. THE DATE OF THE PATRIARCHAL AGE[28]

As Noth has recently pointed out,[29] scholars are not all agreed upon the date of the Patriarchal Age. Does Abraham belong

[24] *Cf.* Gadd, *op. cit.*, pp. 19–22; Rowton, *loc. cit.;* and W. G. Lambert in P. Garelli (ed.), *Gilgameš et sa Légende*, 1960, pp. 39–56, esp. 46–52. Note that in the Tummal building-chronicle, Gilgamesh is included on the same level as, and in the midst of, such historically attested kings as Enmebaragisi, Mesannepadda, *etc.*; translation, *cf.* Kramer, *The Sumerians*, 1963, pp. 48–49, 47. Kingship in Gn. 6:1–4, *cf.* Kline, *WTJ* 24 (1962), 187–204.

[25] See W. G. Lambert, *JSS* 5 (1960), pp. 113–123, esp. 115–116; for the reconstructed cuneiform text of Atrakhasis, *cf.* W. G. Lambert and A. R. Millard, *Cuneiform Texts . . . (British Museum)*, XLVI, 1965. See also references in A. L. Oppenheim, *Ancient Mesopotamia*, 1964, p. 372, n. 45.

[26] Lambert, *JSS* 5 (1960), p. 114 and references.

[27] See p. 38, above, and references in note 13.

[28] The literature on the Patriarchs grows constantly; only a selection can be cited here. Best over-all survey is (in French) R. de Vaux, *RB* 53 (1946), pp. 321–348; *RB* 55 (1948), pp. 321–347; *RB* 56 (1949), pp. 5–36 (in book-form collected in German as R. de Vaux, *Die hebräischen Patriarchen und die modernen Entdeckungen*, 1961), supplemented by de Vaux in *RB* 72

to *c.* 2000–1700 BC (so Albright,[30] Glueck,[31] de Vaux,[32] Wright,[33] *etc.*)? Or to the seventeenth century BC (so Rowley[34] and Cornelius[35])? Or to the fourteenth century BC (so C. H. Gordon[36] and Eissfeldt[37])? Which date, if any, is correct? Is the evidence really so ambiguous? In point of fact, the divergences are more apparent than real, and a positive approach yields a reasonable solution when all the main data are taken into proper consideration. There are three independent 'main lines' of approach:

(1965), pp. 5–28 (as German booklet, *Die Patriarchenerzählungen und die Geschichte,* 1965). Elementary books include C. F. Pfeiffer, *The Patriarchal Age,* 1961 (good outline, but bibliography is too generalized) and J. M. Holt, *The Patriarchs of Israel,* 1964 (readable, but diffuse, too often neglects primary data in favour of secondary sources, and is partly obsolete, *e.g.* ignores Vergote, *Joseph en Égypte,* 1959). For Abraham, see D. J. Wiseman, *The Word of God for Abraham and Today,* 1959, and A. Parrot, *Abraham et son temps,* 1962. Recent studies of varying value include H. Cazelles, 'Patriarches' in H. Cazelles and A. Feuillet (eds.), *Supplément au Dictionnaire de la Bible,* VII/ Fasc. 36, 1961, cols. 81–156 (valuable survey, good bibliography to 1959); W. F. Albright, *BASOR* 163 (1961), pp. 36–54 (valuable material); and three papers by J. C. L. Gibson, *JSS* 7 (1962), pp. 44–62, S. Yeivin, *RSO* 38 (1963), pp. 277–302, and F. Vattioni, *Augustinianum* 4 (1964), pp. 331–357, all with useful points but unsatisfactory in various details. Very inadequate is O. Eissfeldt, *CAH²,* II: 26a (*Palestine in the Nineteenth Dynasty: Exodus and Wanderings*), 1965, pp. 5–16; *cf.* my review-article, *THB* 17 (1966), pp. 63–97, on the nature and possible historicity of the Patriarchs.

[29] *VTS,* VII, 1960, pp. 265–271.

[30] Most recently in *BASOR* 163 (1961), pp. 49–52.

[31] *BA* 18 (1955), pp. 4, 6–9; *BASOR* 152 (1958), p. 20; *Rivers in the Desert,* 1959, pp. 68–76.

[32] *RB* 55 (1948), pp. 326–337 (= *Die hebräischen Patriarchen . . .,* 1961, pp. 33–44) and *RB* 72 (1965), pp. 26–27.

[33] *Biblical Archaeology,* 1957, p. 50 (and 42–43, 44–45); *BA* 22 (1959), p. 99.

[34] *Cf. BJRL* 32 (1949), p. 63; *From Joseph to Joshua,* 1950, pp. 113–114, *cf.* p. 164 (Appendix).

[35] *ZAW* 72 (1960), pp. 1–7, by setting Gn. 14 in the seventeenth century BC.

[36] *Journal of Bible and Religion* 21 (1953), pp. 238–243; *JNES* 13 (1954), pp. 56–59; *JNES* 17 (1958), pp. 28–31 (implicit on parallels); *The World of the Old Testament,* 1960, ch. 8, esp. pp. 115–117; in A. Altmann (ed.), *Biblical and Other Studies,* 1963, pp. 4–5. *Cf.* L. R. Fisher, *JBL* 81 (1962), pp. 264–270.

[37] *CAH²,* II: 26a (*Palestine in the Nineteenth Dynasty . . .*), 1965, p. 8.

First, we must look to see if any major events in the Patriarchal narratives can be linked with external history.

Secondly, we must note evidences of date preserved in details of the narratives (personal names, legal usages, *etc.*) in Near Eastern context.

Thirdly, we must consider possible chronological links between the Patriarchal and later epochs.

(a) Major Events and External History

The main event of this kind is the raid of the four Eastern kings recorded in Genesis 14. Three lines of evidence are available.

First, during his archaeological surveys in Transjordan, Glueck found evidence of a sharp decrease in the density of occupation there for the period between the nineteenth and thirteenth centuries BC,[38] and he would link this with the destructive campaign mentioned in Genesis 14.[39] Harding's discovery of remains of the intervening period near Ammān[40] does not affect the general picture for the rest of Transjordan. This suggests a date for Abraham before *c.* 1800 BC.

Secondly, the names of the four Eastern kings fit the period *c.* 2000–1700 BC (and some also later periods). Arioch is an Arriyuk or Arriwuk (*cf.* Mari archives, eighteenth century BC)[41] or Ariukki (*cf.* Nuzi archives, fifteenth century BC);[42]

[38] Full reports of the surveys in N. Glueck, *Explorations in Eastern Palestine*, I–IV (=*AASOR*, Vols. 14, 15, 18/19, 25/28), 1934–51.

[39] See Glueck, *The Other Side of the Jordan*, 1940, pp. 114–125 (esp. 114, 121, 124–5), and his *Rivers in the Desert*, 1959, pp. 71–74. *Cf.* Albright, *BASOR* 163 (1961), p. 50 n. 68 (to eighteenth century BC).

[40] G. L. Harding, *PEF Annual*, VI, 1953, pp. 14–15; *PEQ* 90 (1958), pp. 10–12; plus Albright, *BASOR* 90 (1943), pp. 17–18 n. 77a (but referring to the main Jordan valley). *Cf.* Albright, *BASOR* 68 (1937), p. 21 n. 21; Glueck, *BASOR* 75 (1939), p. 28; *ibid.*, 142 (1956), p. 35 n. 40; *ibid.*, 159 (1960), p. 3. On Dibon, *cf.* F. V. Winnett, *BASOR* 125 (1952), pp. 18, 20; W. H. Morton, *ibid.*, 140 (1955), p. 6; also G. E. Wright, *BA* 22 (1959), pp. 99, 100, and F. V. Winnett and W. L. Reed, *AASOR* 36/37 (1964), p. 66.

[41] C. F. Jean, *ARMT*, II, Letters 63 and 64 (see *ARMT*, XV, p. 142); J.-R. Kupper, *Les Nomades en Mésopotamie au temps des Rois de Mari*, 1957, p. 232 n. 1.

[42] I. J. Gelb, P. M. Purves, A. A. MacRae, *Nuzi Personal Names*, 1943, p. 30a. Over a millennium later, perhaps *cf.* an Arioch in Dn. 2:14, 15.

Tid'al is a Tudkhalia, a Hittite name known from the nineteenth century BC onwards,[43] and borne by four or five Hittite
kings in the eighteenth to thirteenth centuries BC.[44] Chedor-la'-
omer is typically Elamite (Kutir $+ x$)[45] of the Old Babylonian
period (2000–1700 BC) and later. Amraphel is uncertain, but is
most unlikely to be Hammurapi.[46] The individuals themselves
have not yet been identified in extra-biblical documents, but
this is not surprising when one considers the gaps in our knowledge of the period.[47]

[43] Albright, *BASOR* 163 (1961), p. 49, n. 66a (no references); see J.
Lewy, *ZA* 35 (1924), p. 148 n. 2; F. J. Stephens, *Personal Names from Cuneiform Inscriptions of Cappadocia*, 1928, p. 33; I. J. Gelb, *Inscriptions from Alishar
and Vicinity*, 1935, p. 34. Tudkhalia is a name derived from topography (*cf.*
E. Laroche, *Les Hiéroglyphes Hittites*, I, 1960, No. 4, and P. Garelli, *Les
Assyriens en Cappadoce*, 1963, p. 160, both with references), and is perhaps
(proto-) Hattian rather than strictly Hittite (*cf.* E. Bilgiç, *AfO* 15 (1945–51),
p. 16, No. 4); also Laroche, *Les Noms des Hittites*, 1966, pp. 191, 276, 283.

[44] It may occur at Ugarit as *Tdǧl(m)*, *cf.* C. Virolleaud, *Palais Royal
d'Ugarit*, II, 1957, p. 65, No. 39: 21; *ibid.*, V, 1965, pp. 18, 20, No. 11: 21;
cf. Gordon, *UM*, III, 1955, No. 1923a. Dietrich and Loretz, *Welt des
Orients* 3:3 (1966), 201, take this as a word denoting an occupation.

[45] *Cf.* the Elamite royal names Kudur or Kutir-Naḫḫunte, Kutir-
Shilḫaḫa (W. Hinz, *CAH²*, II: 7 (*Persia, c. 1800–1550 BC*), 1964, p. 19);
Kudur-mabug of Larsa (Schmökel, *HdO*, II: 3, pp. 75, 77, 79; Gadd, *CAH²*,
I: 22 (*Babylonia, c. 2120–1800 BC*), 1965, pp. 46–48). For -*la'omer*/Lagamar/l,
cf. de Vaux, *RB* 55 (1948), p. 334 n. 2 (= *Die hebr. Patr.*, p. 41, n. 2).
For the goddess Lagamal or Lakamar at Mari, *cf.* Kupper, *ARMT*, XIII,
1964, Letter 111: 5; in third millennium and later, *cf.* W. Hinz, *CAH²*,
I: 23 (*Persia, c. 2400–1800 BC*), 1963, p. 25, and esp. I. J. Gelb, *A Glossary
of Old Akkadian*, 1957, p. 118 (seal in Legrain, *Publications of Babyl. Section,
Univ. Mus., Univ. of Pennsylvania*, XIV, No. 138); Scheil, *Revue d'Assyriologie*
25 (1928), 46. In general, *cf.* W. Hinz, *Das Reich Elam*, 1964, Index, *s.v.*

[46] *Cf.* Albright, *op. cit.*, p. 49 n. 67, and earlier studies (n. 66); K. Jaritz,
ZAW 70 (1958), pp. 255–256; favouring Hammurapi, F. Cornelius, *ZAW*
72 (1960), p. 2 n. 4. Against the equation, note (i) the initial '*aleph*-sound
in 'Amraphel as opposed to the underlying initial '*ayin* in Hammurapi
shown by '*mrpi* (='Ammurapi) at Ugarit (Virolleaud, *Palais Royal d'Ugarit*,
V, 1965, pp. 84, 85, No. 60: 2); *cf.* also Speiser, *Genesis (Anchor Bible)*,
1964, pp. 106–107; and (ii) element -*l* in Amraphel and not in Hammurapi.
Some would compare Amraphel with names like Amud-pi- (or pa-) ila
(reading Heb. *r* as *d*); on latter name, *cf.* H. B. Huffmon, *Amorite Personal
Names in the Mari Texts*, 1965, pp. 128–129.

[47] On the irrelevance of such negative evidence, *cf.* above, pp. 30 f. and

Thirdly, the system of power-alliances (four kings against five) is typical in Mesopotamian politics within the period c. 2000–1750 BC, but *not* before or after this general period when different political patterns prevailed.[48] In the eighteenth century BC, for example, a famous Mari letter mentions alliances of ten, fifteen and twenty kings.[49] At least five other Mesopotamian coalitions are known from the nineteenth/eighteenth centuries BC.[50] One may also note the role of Elam in the

notes 37–38, with the example of the Egyptian Fourteenth Dynasty. For gaps elsewhere, compare the four empty centuries in the known history of Ugarit between the 'dynastic founders' Niqmad I and Yaqarum (eighteenth century BC) and the line of Ammistamru I in the fourteenth century BC. Only two doubtful names, Ibira (J. Nougayrol, *Palais Royal d'Ugarit*, III, 1955, pp. xxxvi-xxxvii, xli) and Puruqqu (H. Klengel, *OLZ* 57 (1962), col. 454) could be attributed to this whole period, until the recent discovery of a list of former kings of Ugarit (some fourteen names preserved out of about thirty), *cf.* Virolleaud, *CRAIBL: 1962*, 1963, p. 95; Schaeffer/ Weidner, *AfO* 20 (1963), p. 215, and in Schaeffer (ed.), *Ugaritica V: 1*, 1966, alphabetic text No. 5. Even now, nothing is known of most of these kings. Gordon's remarks about 'dark ages' (in Altmann (ed.), *Biblical and Other Studies*, 1963, p. 5) are wide of the mark. And from Mesopotamia, we know of hardly any names of kings of the Second Dynasty of Ur – a major Sumerian city-state – from either king lists or monuments (*cf.* Gadd, *CAH²*, I: 13 (*Cities of Babylonia*), 1962, p. 23).

[48] The upper limit is the hegemony of the Third Dynasty of Ur; the lower limit, the ephemeral supremacy of Hammurapi of Babylon; *cf.* D. O. Edzard, *Die 'Zweite Zwischenzeit' Babyloniens*, 1957, pp. 1–2, 9–10, 44–49, 180–184. After his day, Mesopotamia was temporarily divided between the 'Sea-land', Babylon, the Kassites, Assyria and a brief Khana-dynasty (*cf.* Gadd, *CAH²*, II: 5 (*Hammurabi and the End of his Dynasty*), 1965, pp. 47–54), but these in due time were reduced to Assyria and Kassite rule in Babylonia (*cf.* Schmökel, *HdO*, II: 3, pp. 172–174). Likewise, in Asia Minor the Old Hittite state became the main power from the seventeenth century onwards (*cf.* Schmökel, *op. cit.*, pp. 123–124; O. R. Gurney, *The Hittites*, 1961, pp. 22–24; H. Otten, *Saeculum* 15 (1964), 115–124). In Upper Mesopotamia, in the great west bend of the Euphrates, there arose the Mitanni-kingdom from c. 1600 BC (*cf.* R. T. O'Callaghan, *Aram Naharaim*, 1948, p. 81, Table; I. J. Gelb, *Hurrians and Subarians*, 1944, pp. 70 ff.; Schmökel, *op. cit.*, pp. 159–160; A. Goetze, *JCS* 11 (1957), pp. 67, 72).

[49] G. Dossin, *Syria* 19 (1938), pp. 117–118; S. Smith, *Alalakh and Chronology*, 1940, p. 11.

[50] First, an alliance of Belakum of Eshnunna with Akkad and three tribal peoples (Edzard, *op. cit.*, pp. 105, 106, 108, 121). Second, Rimanum

eighteenth century BC (even exchanging envoys with Qatna in Syria),[51] and perhaps earlier. 'Tid'al, king of nations' resembles the federal great chiefs in Asia Minor of the nineteenth to eighteenth centuries BC (*e.g.*, Anittas). At this period, Assyrian merchant archives in Cappadocia mention almost a dozen different cities each under its own *rubā'um* or ruler.[52] From time to time, one of these rulers would, by subduing his neighbours, become a paramount chief (*rubā'um rabium*) or Great King; so Anittas of Kussara supplanted the ruler of Burushkhatum as chief ruler.[53] Tid'al could well have been just such an overlord, or else a commander of warrior-groups like those known as Umman-manda from at least *c.* 1700 BC onwards.[54]

(of Malgium?) defeated a four-power alliance (*ibid.*, pp. 157, 160). Third, Rim-Sin of Larsa defeated a coalition of five powers (*ibid.*, pp. 108, 155, 157). Fourth, Hammurapi did so in his twenty-ninth year (*ibid.*, p. 181); and fifth, defeated an alliance of four groups in his thirty-first year (*ibid.*, p. 182).

[51] For Elam and Qatna, *cf.* J. R. Kupper, *ARMT*, VI, Letters 19, 22; Hinz, *CAH²*, II: 7 (*Persia, c. 1800–1550 BC*), 1964, p. 10. Power of Elam more generally at this time: J. Bottéro and A. Finet, *ARMT*, XV, 1954, p. 124 sub *Elamtum;* Kupper, *ARMT*, VI, 1954, Letters 27, 51, 66; Hinz, *op. cit.*, pp. 10–13; Dossin, *Syria* 20 (1939), p. 109: 1–3, and *Orientalia* 19 (1950), p. 509.

[52] A. Goetze, *Kleinasien²*, 1957, p. 75 and references; P. Garelli, *Les Assyriens en Cappadoce*, 1963, p. 206 and n. 4, and pp. 205–215 on these rulers.

[53] Cappadocian tablets, Goetze, *loc. cit.*; Deeds of Anittas, Otten, *MDOG* 83 (1951), pp. 42, 43; Garelli, *op. cit.*, pp. 63–65.

[54] Note Zaluti, 'Chief of the Umman-manda', *c.* 1700 BC (before or after Labarnas I of Hatti), Otten, *MDOG* 86 (1953), pp. 61, 63, and Albright, *BASOR* 146 (1957), p. 31 and n. 15. In fifteenth century BC, *cf.* S. Smith, *Statue of Idrimi*, 1949, p. 58, and Albright, *BASOR* 118 (1950), p. 18 and n. 28; in the Hittite Laws §54, *cf.* F. Sommer, *Hethiter und Hethitisch*, 1947, pp. 5–6, Goetze, *op. cit.*, p. 109, and *ANET*, p. 192, and J. Friedrich, *Die hethitischen Gesetze*, 1959, p. 35. In thirteenth century BC, *cf.* Nougayrol, *Palais Royal d'Ugarit*, IV, 1956, p. 180. Literary reference in Legend of Naram-Sin, *cf.* O. R. Gurney, *Anatolian Studies* 5 (1955), pp. 97, 101; military character of Umman-manda (with dubious 'Indo-germanisch' speculations), F. Cornelius, *Iraq* 25 (1963), pp. 167–170. Later, *cf.* D. J. Wiseman, *Chronicles of Chaldaean Kings*, 1956, pp. 15, 16, 18, 81, and S. Smith, *Isaiah XL–LV*, 1944, pp. 127–128. For the word *goyim*, 'nations', *cf.* E. A. Speiser, *JBL* 79 (1960), pp. 157–163, and *Genesis (Anchor Bible)*, 1964, pp. 107–108; *JAOS* 72 (1952), pp. 100–101 and n. 36.

For early Mesopotamian expeditions into the Westland like that of Genesis 14, one may in some measure compare the texts about Sargon of Akkad and Naram-Sin (*c.* twenty-fourth to twenty-third centuries BC) invading to Amanus in Syria and possibly further north-west,[55] mention of relations with Didanum (between Euphrates and Syria?)[56] during the Third Dynasty of Ur (*c.* twenty-second to twenty-first centuries BC),[57] and the expedition of Shamshi-Adad I of Assyria to Lebanon (nineteenth or eighteenth century BC).[58]

The overthrow of the cities of the plain (including particularly Sodom and Gomorrah) by seismic movement and conflagration (Gn. 19)[59] cannot be independently dated at present; their ruins are apparently under the Dead Sea, and the neighbouring site of Bab-edh-Dhra may have come to an end in the twenty-first century BC before they did.[60]

(*b*) *Indications of Date in the Narratives*

1. Power-alliances between Mesopotamian states (Gn. 14) are typical for *c.* 2000–1750 BC (see above, pp. 45 f.).

[55] See Gadd, *CAH*², I: 19 (*Dynasty of Agade and Gutian Invasion*), 1963, pp. 10–16, 27–29. From a still earlier period, note the discovery of archaic Sumerian tablets in a Neolithic site in S. Rumania(!), although probably not brought by Sumerians *so* far (N. Vlassa, *Dacia*, (NF), 7 (1963), pp. 485–494, esp. 490); my thanks go to Frau I. Fuhr for this reference.

[56] So I. J. Gelb, *JCS* 15 (1960), p. 30. For Sargon of Akkad and Iahdun-Lim of Mari in the West, *cf.* Malamat in *Studies in Honor of Benno Landsberger*, 1965 (*Assyriological Studies*, 16), pp. 365–373.

[57] Gelb, *loc. cit.;* Albright, in *Geschichte und Altes Testament* (*FS Alt*), 1953, pp. 11–12. For links between Byblos and the Third Dynasty of Ur, *cf.* E. Sollberger, *AfO* 19 (1960), pp. 120 ff.

[58] *ANET*, p. 274b; Kupper, *CAH*², II: 1 (*N. Mesopotamia and Syria*), 1963, p. 5. On the realism of the expedition in Gn. 14, *cf.* de Vaux, *RB* 55 (1948), pp. 328, 330–331 (=*Die hebr. Patr.*, 1961, pp. 35, 37–38). The opinion of some Old Testament scholars that Gn. 14 is merely a late midrash (*e.g.*, *ZAW* 74 (1962), p. 116) wholly fails to account for the authentic early detail of power-alliances pointed out above.

[59] See J. P. Harland, *BA* 5 (1942), pp. 17–32, and esp. *BA* 6 (1943), pp. 41–54. Popular presentation in W. Keller, *The Bible as History*, 1956, pp. 93–97.

[60] *Cf.* earlier Albright, *BASOR* 14 (1924), pp. 5–9, *AASOR*, vol. 6, 1926, pp. 58–62, 66; and now, *BASOR* 163 (1961), p. 51 n. 73 with *BASOR* 95 (1944), p. 9 n. 18.

2. The personal names of the Patriarchs and their families can be directly compared with identical or similarly formed names in Mesopotamian and Egyptian[61] documents of the twentieth to eighteenth centuries BC and occasionally later. Thus, one may compare Abram with Aba(m)rama in tablets from Dilbat,[62] Abraham with Aburahana (execration-texts),[63] Jacob with Ya'qub-il (Chagar-Bazar, etc.),[64] Zebulon with Zabilanu (Egyptian[65] and Old Babylonian[66] sources), Asher with Ashra, etc.[67] The (Marē-) Yamina of the Mari texts may be

[61] The so-called Execration Texts. Earlier series in K. Sethe, *Die Ächtung feindlicher Fürsten, Völker und Dinge auf altägyptischen Tongefässscherben des mittleren Reichs*, 1926; cf. Albright, *JPOS* 8 (1928), pp. 223–256 and references. Later series in G. Posener, *Princes et Pays d'Asie et de Nubie*, 1940, cf. Albright, *BASOR* 81 (1941), pp. 16–21, and *BASOR* 83 (1941), pp. 30–36 and references. Cf. also W. Helck, *Die Beziehungen Ägyptens zu Vorderasien im 3. und 2. Jahrtausend v. Chr.*, 1962, pp. 49–68, and further references in H. B. Huffmon, *Amorite Personal Names in the Mari Texts*, 1965, p. 12 n. 68. New such texts have just been found in Nubia, cf. J. Vercoutter, *CRAIBL: 1963*, 1964, pp. 97–102.

[62] A. Ungnad, 'Urkunden aus Dilbat', *Beiträge zur Assyriologie*, VI: 5, 1909, p. 82; cf. de Vaux, *RB* 53 (1946), p. 323 (=*Die hebr. Patr.*, p. 3). Disputed by Speiser, *Genesis (Anchor Bible)*, 1964, p. 124: 5, overlooking the possibility that an Akkadian name may have been assimilated to a similar-sounding W. Semitic name in Palestine. De Vaux, *RB* 72 (1965), p. 8, also compares from Ugarit (fourteenth–thirteenth centuries BC) the name Abiramu (Nougayrol, *Palais Royal d'Ugarit*, III, 1955, p. 20) or Abrm (Virolleaud, *ibid.*, V, 1965, pp. 117–118, No. 95: 2, 4), an equation tacitly accepted by Speiser, *loc. cit.*, but rejected by Albright, *BASOR* 163 (1962), p. 50 n. 69, perhaps overlooking the possibility of i being a connecting-vowel, not always 1st pers. sing. suffix.

[63] Posener, *Princes et Pays* . . . , E.55; see Albright, *BASOR* 83 (1941), p. 34; n alternating with m.

[64] References, Albright, *JAOS* 74 (1954), p. 231: 37, and de Vaux, *RB* 72 (1965), p. 9; S. Yeivin, *JEA* 45 (1959), pp. 16–18; Huffmon, *op. cit.*, 203–204. Cf. A. R. Millard, *Archaeology and the Life of Jacob* (forthcoming).

[65] Sethe, *Ächtung feindlicher Fürsten* . . . , p. 47, and Albright, *JPOS* 8 (1928), p. 239; Posener, *Princes et Pays* . . . , p. 73 (E. 16) and Albright, *BASOR* 83 (1941), p. 34.

[66] A. Goetze, *BASOR* 95 (1944), pp. 23–24; W. L. Moran, *Orientalia* 26 (1957), p. 342.

[67] Albright, *JAOS* 74 (1954), pp. 229, 231 (for Asher) and 227–228 (for Issachar); comparisons for Gad and Dan (Mari), cf. M. Noth, *Geschichte und Altes Testament (FS Alt)*, 1953, pp. 145–146, and for Dan, cf. Dani-AN,

semantically parallel in name with Hebrew Benjamin.[68] All these parallels fit well into the nineteenth to seventeenth centuries BC.

3. Seasonal occupation[69] of the Negeb region on the south-west borders of Palestine is archaeologically attested[70] for the twenty-first to nineteenth centuries BC (Middle Bronze Age I) – but *not* for a thousand years earlier or for eight hundred years afterwards. Abraham and Isaac spent time in this area (Gn. 20:1; 24:62); as they were keepers of flocks and herds[71] and occasionally grew crops of grain (Gn. 26:12; 37:7), their activities there would best fit the Middle Bronze Age I period, *c.* 2100–1800 BC,[72] considering their need of assured water sup-

---

Huffmon, *Amorite Personal Names in the Mari Texts*, 1965, pp. 88, 183. For Levi, *cf.* Moran, *op. cit.*, pp. 342–343, but note Goetze, *BASOR* 151 (1958), pp. 31–32, and now Huffmon, *op. cit.*, pp. 225–226.

[68] On the reading of DUMU.MES-Yamina in the Mari texts (formerly read as 'Binu-Yamina'), see Dossin, *Revue d'Assyriologie* 52 (1958), pp. 60–62, but *cf.* also Gelb, *JCS* 15 (1961), pp. 37–38, and H. Tadmor, *JNES* 17 (1958), p. 130 n. 12. Contrast Albright, *The Biblical Period*[4], 1963, p. 101, n. 70.

[69] For the probably mainly seasonal nature of this occupation, *cf.* Albright, *BASOR* 142 (1956), p. 31 n. 35, and *BASOR* 163 (1961), p. 50 n. 68.

[70] Further work by Glueck; see *BA* 18 (1955), pp. 1–9; *BA* 22 (1959), pp. 81–97; *Rivers in the Desert*, 1959; reports in *BASOR* 131 (1953), pp. 6–15; *ibid.*, 137 (1955), pp. 10–22; *ibid.*, 138 (1955), pp. 7–29; *ibid.*, 142 (1956), pp. 17–35; *ibid.*, 145 (1957), pp. 11–25; *ibid.*, 149 (1958), pp. 8–17; *ibid.*, 152 (1958), pp. 18–38; *ibid.*, 159 (1960), pp. 3–14.

[71] It is going far beyond the biblical evidence to turn Abraham into a full-time donkey caravaneer or a professional merchant (-prince) as suggested by Albright (*BASOR* 163 (1961), pp. 26–54 *passim*) on the one hand and by Gordon (*JNES* 17 (1958), pp. 28–31) and Fisher (*JBL* 81 (1962), pp. 264–270) on the other. The verb *shr* in Hebrew can as easily be 'to move around' as 'to trade' (*cf.* Speiser, *BASOR* 164 (1961), pp. 23–28, plus note by Albright); in any case, opportunity to trade (simply, buy and sell) does not necessarily make one a professional merchant. We await with interest Albright's promised evidence for 'Apiru = donkeyman, caravaneer, but share the misgivings of de Vaux (*RB* 72 (1965), p. 20), in view of the many contexts of Ḫ/'apiru that would not fit this interpretation.

[72] On the date, see Albright, *BASOR* 163 (1961), pp. 38–40 (in agreement with Glueck, *e.g.* in *BASOR* 152 (1958), p. 20, or *Rivers in the Desert*, 1959, p. 68). Noth's date of the twenty-first–twentieth centuries BC (*VTS*, VII, p.

D

plies and pasture or fodder for their livestock (especially as so-
journers and not just passing straight through the area).

4. Freedom and wide scope of travel is particularly evident
in the Old Babylonian period.[73] In the Mari archives, envoys
and others criss-cross the whole Near East from Hazor in Palestine to Elam in the far south-east,[74] while earlier still we have
record not only of innumerable merchant caravans but also
of detailed 'itineraries' all the way from Babylon or Assur into
the heart of Asia Minor.[75] And as Abraham in Palestine was
prepared to send all the way for his son's wife to North Mesopotamian Harran, so similarly we find Shamshi-Adad I of
Assyria sending to the King of Qatna in Syria for the same purpose.[76] Semi-nomadic tribes ranged far and wide[77], and sometimes took to crop-cultivation and more settled life.[78]

5. The religion of the Patriarchs included prominently the
concept of the 'God of the fathers', first stressed by Alt.[79] However, the best parallels for this come not from his Nabataean
examples (about 2,000 years later) but, as Albright and Cross
have pointed out,[80] from the Old Assyrian tablets of the nine-

---

266) thus ends a century too early, and hence he exaggerates unwittingly
the supposed divergence between this and other data, *e.g.* Nuzi.

[73] *Cf.* latterly the remark by A. L. Oppenheim, *Ancient Mesopotamia*, 1964,
p. 120, top.

[74] *ARMT*, I–VI, *passim*; *e.g.*, *ARMT*, VI, Letters 14, 15, 23, 78, *ARMT*,
XIII, Letter 46, On Elam and the West, *cf.* pp. 45 f. and note 51, above,
plus *ARMT*, XIII, Letters 31, 32.

[75] For the itineraries, see A. Goetze, *JCS* 7 (1953), pp. 51–72; M. Falkner,
AfO 18 (1957-8), pp. 1–37; W. W. Hallo and Goetze, *JCS* 18 (1964), pp.
57–88, 114–119; P. Garelli, *Les Assyriens en Cappadoce*, 1963, pp. 81–125.
Cf. also E. Weidner, *AfO* 21 (1966), 42–46, for later such data.

[76] See Albright, *BASOR* 78 (1940), p. 25, being Letter 77 in G. Dossin,
ARMT, I, 1950. For other inter-dynastic marriages of Shamshi-Adad's
social level, *cf.* J. M. Munn-Rankin, *Iraq* 18 (1956), pp. 94–95.

[77] *Cf.* Kupper, *Les Nomades en Mésopotamie au temps des Rois de Mari*, 1957,
passim, *e.g.* pp. 47 ff., 71, 74 f., 78–81, 90 f., 96 ff.

[78] *E.g.*, Kupper, *op. cit.*, p. 31; *cf.* G. Posener in *CAH²*, I: 21 (*Syria and
Palestine*), 1965, pp. 24–29.

[79] A. Alt, *Der Gott der Väter*, 1929; now in *KS*, I, 1953, pp. 1–78.

[80] Albright, *BASOR* 163 (1961), pp. 48–49, and F. M. Cross, *HTR*
55 (1962), pp. 225–259. *Cf.* H. Hirsch, *AfO* 21 (1966), 56–58.

teenth century BC from Cappadocia as noted by Lewy.[81] There is no evidence that the different designations, 'the God of Abraham', 'the Fear[82] of Isaac', 'the Mighty One of Jacob', were applied to separate minor deities as Alt suggested; as so often in the Ancient Near East, they are but multiple epithets of a single God.[83]

6. Patriarchal customs of inheritance find close parallels in the Nuzi archives from Mesopotamia, c. 1500 BC.[84] These parallels do not necessarily imply a date for the Patriarchs as late as 1500 BC,[85] because Old Babylonian tablets from Ur (nineteenth to eighteenth centuries BC) would afford equally good parallels,[86] a point unknown to most Old Testament scholars. Also the parallel with the Hittite laws[87] in Genesis 23 may likewise go back long before the date of the extant copies of these laws (fourteenth to thirteenth centuries BC).[88]

[81] J. Lewy, *Revue de l'Histoire des Religions* 110 (1934), pp. 50–55, 64–65. A similar reference occurs in *ARMT*, V, Letter 20, line 16, in the eighteenth century BC, as noted by J. P. Hyatt, *VT* 5 (1955), p. 131 and n. 4 (note that the eighth-century Hittite Hieroglyphic example from Topada (after Del Medico) is illusory; *cf.* my *Hittite Hieroglyphs, Aramaeans and Hebrew Traditions*, forthcoming).

[82] Or possibly 'Kinsman'? So Albright, *From the Stone Age to Christianity*, 1957 ed., p. 248 and n. 71.

[83] Interchangeability of names and epithets in the Old-Assyrian data was long ago demonstrated by Lewy, *op. cit.*; *cf.* also Cross, *op. cit.*, pp. 228 ff. Alt's plurality of deities is also rejected by Parrot, *Abraham et son temps*, 1962, p. 101, n. 7 end. Last full survey of El Shaddai is by M. Weippert, *ZDMG* 111 (1961), pp. 42–62. On patriarchal religion, *cf.* also M. Segal, *Jewish Quarterly Review* 53 (1962–3), pp. 226–256. An Egyptian example of multiple names, p. 121, below.

[84] See references, p. 154, note 2, below.

[85] As is assumed by Gordon, *JNES* 13 (1954), pp. 56–57; *cf.* discussion by Noth, *VTS*, VII, pp. 266–267, 270.

[86] *Cf.* briefly D. J. Wiseman, *JTVI* 88 (1956), p. 124, with reference to H. H. Figulla and W. J. Martin, *Ur Excavations Texts*, V, 1953.

[87] See below, pp. 154–156, and note 7.

[88] *Cf.* J. Friedrich and H. Zimmern, *Hethitische Gesetze*, 1922 (=*Der Alte Orient* 23:2), p. 4; and for older fragments, H. G. Güterbock, *JCS* 15 (1961), pp. 64–65 (Old Hittite ductus). Early date, *cf.* Goetze in Walser, *op. cit.* (p. 21, n. 14, above), p. 27 and n. 23; Gurney, *CAH²*, II: 15a (*Anatolia, c. 1600–1380 BC*), 1966, p. 12, and H. Otten and V. Soucek, *AfO* 21 (1966), 1–12 *passim*; O. Carruba, *Kratylos* 7 (1962), p. 159.

There is no positive reason why there should not be some Hittites in Palestine in the nineteenth to eighteenth centuries BC. They intervened politically in Syria in the eighteenth to seventeenth centuries BC.[89] As early as *c.* 1800 BC, a Lycian from West Asia Minor – 'Kukun's son Luqq(a)' (= 'the Lycian') – is attested at Byblos in Phoenicia;[90] limited Anatolian penetration of Phoenicia and Palestine can be found quite early.[91]

The parallels in social themes between the Patriarchal narratives and the Ugaritic epics on tablets of the fourteenth to thirteenth centuries BC do not prove a late date either,[92] for it is known on clear linguistic evidence that those epics originated in the twentieth to sixteenth centuries BC.[93]

Finally, the price of twenty shekels of silver paid for Joseph in Genesis 37:28 is the correct average price for a slave in about the

[89] Note Albright, *BASOR* 146 (1957), pp. 30–31 (Zukrasi, *etc.*) and H. Otten, *MDOG* 86 (1953), pp. 61, 63; *cf.* Kupper, *CAH²*, II: 1 (*N. Mesopotamia and Syria*), 1963, pp. 32–35; Wiseman, *NBD*, p. 66b. For non-documentary data, *cf.* note 91 below.

[90] See Albright, *BASOR* 155 (1959), pp. 33–34, along with *BASOR* 176 (1964), p. 42 n. 17 (on order of names); on date of Luqqa's obelisk, *cf.* Helck, *Die Beziehungen Ägyptens zu Vorderasien . . .*, 1962, p. 646 to p. 64; S. H. Horn, *AUSS* 1 (1963), pp. 58–59, and Kitchen, 'Byblos, Egypt and Mari in Early 2nd Millennium BC', *Orientalia* 36 (1967), in press. Helck's doubts on the Asianic linguistic affiliation of the names are not justified.

[91] As a parallel for Hittites being mainly in Anatolia and just a few in Palestine (the sons of Heth in Genesis), one may note not only the similar penetration by Horites or Hurrians (*cf.* I. J. Gelb, *Hurrians and Subarians*, 1944, pp. 52–62, 69–70; Wiseman, *Alalakh Tablets*, 1953, p. 9, for Syria), but also the earlier examples of northern newcomers to Syria-Palestine (not all Amorites) with distinctive metalwork (*cf.* K. M. Kenyon, in *CAH²*, I: 21 (*Syria and Palestine, c. 2160–1780 BC*), 1965, pp. 52–53 and refs.), and of penetration of Syria-Palestine by the bearers of Khirbet Kerak pottery and material culture in the twenty-fourth century BC (*cf.* C. A. Burney, *Anatolian Studies* 8 (1958), pp. 173–174, and references p. 165 n. 21, plus K. Bittel, *Prähistorische Zeitschrift* 34/35: 2 (1953), pp. 142–143. For early Hittites and Horites, see my *Hittite Hieroglyphs, Aramaeans and Hebrew Traditions* (forthcoming), chapter II: 1.

[92] So, *contra* Gordon, *JNES* 13 (1954), pp. 56–57.

[93] *Cf.* Albright, in Rowley (ed.), *Old Testament and Modern Study*, 1951, pp. 31–32, *BASOR* 150 (1958), pp. 36, 38, and especially M. Held, *JAOS* 79 (1959), pp. 171 n. 49 (phases of Ugaritic), 174–175 and nn. 93–107 (linguistic differences).

eighteenth century BC:[94] earlier than this, slaves were cheaper (average, ten to fifteen shekels), and later they became steadily dearer.[95] This is one more little detail true to its period in cultural history.

(c) Links with Later Periods

Genesis 15, Exodus 12:40 and certain genealogies link the Patriarchs to the period of the Exodus.

First, Abraham was warned that his descendants should dwell in an alien land for 400 years (Gn. 15:13). (There is no reason why the figure '400 years' should not refer to the whole of verse 13: i.e., to the sojourn as a whole, *culminating* in enslavement and oppression, rather than be forced unnecessarily to mean that the Hebrews were to be slaves for four centuries against the evidence of Genesis 41 to 50.) In due course, it is recorded that the Israelites left Egypt on the 430th anniversary of their ancestor's entry into Egypt.[96] The 400 years is a round figure in prospect, while the 430 years is more precise in retrospect;[97] there is no contradiction in this.

[94] So in the 'Laws' of Hammurapi, §§116, 214, 252 ($\frac{1}{3}$ mina = 20 shekels), *ANET*, pp. 170, 175, 176; and in Mari legal documents, *cf.* G. Boyer, *ARMT*, VIII, 1958, p. 23, No. 10, lines 1–4.

[95] *E.g.*, in fifteenth century BC and later, 30 or even 40 shekels; in the first millennium BC, the general price rose to 50 shekels and even to 90 or 120 shekels by Persian times. See I. Mendelsohn, *Slavery in the Ancient Near East*, 1949, pp. 117–155, and in *IEJ* 5 (1955), p. 68; Kitchen in *NBD*, pp. 1195–1196.

[96] The LXX interpretation of 430 years in Egypt *and Canaan, i.e.* 215 years in each land, is excluded because of (i) Ex. 12: 41 (the 430 years are counted from entering *Egypt*), and (ii) Abraham and Isaac were not 'children of Israel' but ancestors of Israel, and so their time in Canaan could not be included in the sojourn of Israel and his descendants.

[97] Paul in Gal. 3:17 is concerned to establish one single point: that the Law came long after God's covenant with Abraham. He therefore makes his point, not by laboriously calculating the actual interval between these events, but simply and incisively by citing the one well-known figure – the 430 years – included within that interval. That Paul made use of the LXX interpretation of the 430 years is a gratuitous and unnecessary assumption, where the wish of the modern commentator is perhaps too often father to the thought.

Secondly, Abraham is told that his descendants will re-enter Canaan in 'the fourth generation' (Gn. 15:16, Hebrew *dôr*). The simplest explanation is that the four *dôr* correspond to the 400 years, not to 'generations' in the modern sense. This is suggested not by a mere wish for harmonization but by perfectly clear evidence from Ugaritic[98] and early Assyrian sources that *dôr* or *dāru* can mean a 'span' or 'cycle of time' of eighty years or more.[99]

Thirdly, we have the genealogies. Some scholars[100] dismiss the figure of four centuries between the Patriarchs and the Exodus by appealing to Exodus 6:16–20, a 'genealogy' of Moses and Aaron, which they interpret as four literal generations lasting only a century or more.[101] In doing so, they overlook the following facts.

1. Exodus 6:16–20 is not a full genealogy, but only gives the tribe (Levi), clan (Kohath) and family-group (Amram by Jochebed) to which Moses and Aaron belonged, and *not* their actual parents (also not named in Exodus 2). The Amramites are shown as being already numerous at the Exodus (*cf.* Nu. 3:27, 28), so Amram must be considered as having lived much earlier.[102]

[98] See Albright, *BASOR* 163 (1961), pp. 50–51; C. H. Gordon, *UM*, III, 1955, p. 256, No. 506 (=*UT*, p. 386 f., No. 697); F. J. Neuberg, *JNES* 9 (1950), pp. 215–217; *cf.* Rowley, *From Joseph to Joshua*, 1950, pp. 69 (with n. 2), 70.

[99] Albright, *loc. cit.*, also noting eighty years in Syriac; R. C. Thompson, *LAAA* 19 (1932), pp. 105–106: in the eighteenth century BC, Shamshi-Adad I of Assyria spoke of 7 *dāru* having elapsed between the end of the kingdom of Akkad and his own reign, which would work out at *c.* 70 years in practice (*cf. Chicago Assyrian Dictionary*, 3/D, 1959, p. 115b), allowing five centuries to have elapsed (*cf.* Albright, *The Biblical Period from Abraham to Ezra*⁴, 1963, p. 9, for dates; or *CAH*² dates sixty years earlier). But, like later Assyrian kings, Shamshi-Adad may have considered the period longer than it really was, and so his *dāru* may be longer. The Hebrew *dôr* certainly was (*cf. WBD*, p. 153a, 2).

[100] Latterly, Gordon, *JNES* 13 (1954), p. 58; *The World of the Old Testament*, 1960, pp. 116–117; in A. Altmann (ed.), *Biblical and Other Studies*, 1963, p. 4.

[101] So Rowley, *From Joseph to Joshua*, pp. 70–73; Gordon, *loc. cit.*

[102] *Cf.* already, *WBD*, p. 153b, top; the classification tribe – clan – family group is also partly seen by D. N. Freedman, *BANE*, pp. 206–207

2. The statement that 'Jochebed bore to (Amram) Aaron and Moses' in Exodus 6:20 does not prove immediate descent: in Genesis 46:16–18, the children that Zilpah 'bore' to Jacob include great-grandsons.[103]

3. As we have already noted, Ancient Near Eastern genealogies were often selective, not continuous. From Egypt, in the eighth century BC, we have a statue (Cairo 42,212) which would appear to give its owner the priest Tjaenhesret a continuous ancestry of six generations. But the fuller genealogy of Cairo statue 42,211 shows that six generations are omitted at one point and three more at another on the first statue. Likewise, several generations are missing between Ramesses II and the Twenty-first Dynasty in the Berlin genealogy published by Borchardt.[104] In other genealogies for our period, Bezalel is in the seventh generation from Jacob (cf. 1 Ch. 2:1, 4, 5, 9, 18–21); Elishama (Nu. 1:10) is in the ninth generation from Jacob with Joshua (younger contemporary of Moses) in the eleventh (cf. series Jacob–Joseph–Ephraim, plus 1 Chronicles 7:22–27). And there is no guarantee that these and others are wholly continuous. Compare, for example, that of Nahshon, head of the tribe of Judah (Nu. 1:7), who in 1 Chronicles 2:1, 4, 5, 9, 10, is in the sixth generation after Jacob.

The genealogies cannot, therefore, be used to contradict the 430-year period of the other references. In cases like this, continuity of genealogies has to be proved, not assumed. Four centuries from Jacob in about the late eighteenth century BC would bring us to the thirteenth century BC for the date of the Exodus, a date known to be suitable on independent grounds now to be considered.

(mixed with some unnecessary speculation). This classification also applies to Jos. 7:1 and entries in Nu. 26, cited by Gordon, in Altmann (ed.), *Biblical and Other Studies*, 1963, p. 4 and n. 4.

[103] See also the material on genealogies and lists noted above, pp. 38 f. with notes 15–19. Nu. 26:59 and 1 Ch. 6:3 merely follow Ex. 6.20 and have no separate evidential value.

[104] For these, cf. Kitchen, *The Third Intermediate Period in Egypt* (forthcoming) and recent parallels quoted by Albright, *Biblical Period from Abraham to Ezra*, 1963, p. 9 and n. 26.

The total evidence, therefore, accords very well with a date for the Patriarchs in the twentieth to eighteenth centuries BC, and shows a reasonable degree of consistency when properly interpreted.[105]

[105] Contrast O. Eissfeldt, *CAH*², II: 26a (*Palestine in the Nineteenth Dynasty, Exodus and Wanderings*), 1965, pp. 8, 10, whose treatment of this topic is superficial and misleading; *cf.* my review article in *THB* 17 (1966), pp. 63–97.

3. LATER HEBREW CHRONOLOGY

I. THE DATE OF THE EXODUS AND ISRAELITE INVASION OF CANAAN[1]

Here also the biblical and other evidence is very complex, and is often considered to contain a variety of serious contradictions.[2] But the difficulties and supposed contradictions are less serious than they are often made to appear, if the available data is treated positively and in proper accord with known Ancient Near Eastern usage. The material is here dealt with under five heads.

(a) Egyptian Evidence

First, Exodus 1:11 links the oppression of the Israelites with the building of the store-cities of Pithom and Ra'amses, giving thereby an indication of date for the *end* of the oppression and for the Exodus.[3] Ra'amses is most probably[4] the Pi-Ramessē of

---

[1] On the date of the Exodus, *cf.* earlier C. de Wit, *The Date and Route of the Exodus*, 1960 (good conspectus of previous studies), and Kitchen and Mitchell, *NBD*, pp. 214–216 (brief outline of treatment used here).

[2] *Cf.* the detailed and painstaking study by H. H. Rowley, *From Joseph to Joshua*, 1950, who offers a rather too complicated reconstruction of the course of events.

[3] Giving no hint as to how long the oppression lasted, Ex. 1:7–14 describes the oppression very briefly in general terms, esp. verse 14, a general summary of building and other field-work. The failure of this oppression to reduce the Hebrews led to the edict of Ex. 1:16 and the Hebrew evasion of it that sets the stage for the birth of Moses in Ex. 2. The narrator gives just *one* concrete example of the work done by the Hebrews, 'and they built for Pharaoh store-cities, Pithom and Ra'amses', 1:11b. We have *no* warrant to assume either that the Hebrews were employed exclusively on Pithom and Ra'amses (note 1:14, 'and in all manner of service . . .'), or that the oppression began only with this project. In fact, it is much more likely that Pithom and Ra'amses were their *last* major taskwork before the Exodus itself, because (i) they actually set off from the vicinity of Ra'amses (*cf.*

Egyptian texts,[5] founded by Sethos I and mainly built (and named) by Ramesses II. The Exodus, therefore, is best dated after the accession of Ramesses II (1304 or 1290 BC).[6] There is no reason to doubt the Hebrew text at this point, and the possible sites of Pi-Ramessē – Tanis[7] or Qantir,[8] or both[9] –

Ex. 12:37; Nu. 33:3, 5), and (ii) they would retain most vividly in memory and record the names and scenes of their last labours before leaving Egypt, not those of a generation earlier. In other words, it should not be lightly assumed that Moses' birth was later than the start of Hebrew labours on Pithom and Ra'amses (as did Rowley, *Expository Times* 73 (1962), pp. 366–367, thereby imposing artificial problems on Ex. 1, and *NBD*, pp. 214–216). For the literary usage in Ex. 1 of general terms and a specific isolated point, *cf.* the generalities and specific reference to the Shardana in Tanis stela II of Ramesses II, J. Yoyotte, *Kêmi* 10 (1949), pp. 62, 63.

⁴ Recently, J. Yoyotte suggested that the biblical Ra'amses should perhaps be identified not with the great metropolis Pi-Ramessē, but with a smaller place Ramessē-pa-demi (Ramessē-the-town), *cf.* J. Sainte Fare Garnot, *Revue Historique*, fasc. 459 (1961), p. 118, n. 2; but this does not affect the chronological argument.

⁵ References first collected by Gardiner, *JEA* 5 (1918), pp. 127–138, 179–200, 242–271; subsequent references and discussion in Gardiner, *Ancient Egyptian Onomastica*, II, 1947, A.410, pp. 171*–175*, 278*–279*. The treatment of Ex. 1:11, Pithom and Ra'amses by D. B. Redford, *VT* 13 (1963), pp. 401–418, is misleading and almost worthless; *cf.* the able refutation and corrections given by W. Helck, *VT* 15 (1965), pp. 35–48.

⁶ A combination of astronomical (lunar) and historical data makes it certain that the accession of Ramesses II occurred either in 1290 BC or fourteen years earlier in 1304 BC (*cf.* R. A. Parker, *JNES* 16 (1957), pp. 42–43). The 'high date' 1304 BC is advocated by Rowton (*JCS* 13 (1959), pp. 1–11; *JNES* 19 (1960), pp. 15–22), while the more commonly accepted 'low date' 1290 BC is methodically defended by E. Hornung, *Untersuchungen zur Chronologie und Geschichte des Neuen Reiches*, 1964. In point of fact, the available evidence is still indecisive; see my review of Hornung's valuable monograph in *Chronique d'Égypte* 40/Fasc. 80 (1965), pp. 310–322. Hence I retain dates based on 1290 for the accession of Ramesses II merely provisionally; 1304 dates must also be reckoned with at present.

⁷ P. Montet, *RB* 39 (1930), pp. 5–28; *Géographie de l'Égypte ancienne*, I, 1957, pp. 194–197; *Revue Archéologique*, 1958–I, pp. 1–20; *L'Égypte et la Bible*, 1959, pp. 54–55; H. Kees, *Tanis*, 1942, pp. 150–155.

⁸ M. Hamza, *ASAE* 30 (1930), pp. 31–68 (esp. 64–68); L. Habachi, *ASAE* 52 (1954), pp. 443–447, 500, 510–514, 545–559. Also W. C. Hayes, *Glazed Tiles from a Palace of Ramesses II at Kantir*, 1937, pp. 5–8; and *Scepter of*

were original foundations by Sethos I and Ramesses II,[10] so that the Exodus can hardly be dated in the preceding Eighteenth Dynasty as was once thought by some scholars,[11] who argued that the name Ra'amses was original neither in the Hebrew text nor in the name of the city on Egyptian monuments.

Secondly, the so-called 'Israel Stela' commemorates a victory of Merenptah over the Libyans in his fifth year (c. 1220 BC), and mentions places and peoples in Syria-Palestine claimed as subdued by Merenptah – including Israel. This clearly suggests that Israel was already in Western Palestine by 1220 BC.[12] Some scholars, however, have doubted whether Meren-

---

Egypt, II, 1959, pp. 332–333, 334–339. Good discussion of pros and cons (without final verdict) is B. Couroyer, *RB* 53 (1946), pp. 75–98.

[9] Taking Pi-Ramessē in the broad (and administratively-correct) sense of 'Estate (*not* "House") of Ramesses', including Tanis and Qantir in one domain of scattered settlements and institutions. See Gardiner, *Anc. Eg. Onomastica*, II, p. 175*; C. F. Nims, *JNES* 9 (1950), p. 261; A. Alt, *FS Zucker*, 1954, pp. 7–8 (=*KS*, III, 1959, pp. 181–182); H. Kees, *Ancient Egypt, A Cultural Topography*, 1961, p. 201; W. Helck, *VT* 15 (1965), p. 41. This view is probably the most realistic at present.

[10] *Cf.* Montet (note 7 above) and Habachi (note 8 above).

[11] As the official building-works of the Ramesside kings in the E. Delta are usually found to be the first original works there since the Hyksos period four centuries earlier, they are not mere usurpations of Eighteenth Dynasty structures as is sometimes suggested by advocates of a fifteenth-century date for the Exodus (*e.g.*, J. W. Jack, *The Date of the Exodus*, 1925, pp. 22–32). This can be seen from (*e.g.*) the frequency of genuine Ramesside (and absence of Eighteenth Dynasty) monuments in Lower Egypt in B. Porter and R. L. B. Moss, *Topographical Bibliography of Ancient Egyptian Hieroglyphic Texts (etc.)*, IV, 1934, pp. 1–68 (esp. 1, 6–44, 52–58); so far, only Bubastis has both (*cf.* L. Habachi, *Tell Basta*, 1957), and this city is no candidate for identification with Ra'amses/Pi-Ramessē.

[12] The equation of the name *Ysr'r* (Egyptian for *Ysr'l*) on the Merenptah stela with Hebrew Israel is universally recognized by all competent philologists in Egyptian and Semitic, and likewise with the Israelites who left Egypt explicitly and uniformly commemorated in the Pentateuch and other OT writings. Yet Eissfeldt, without evidence, would claim that *Ysr'l* is ambiguous because it could well be for Jezreel (*CAH*[2], II: 26a (*Palestine in the Nineteenth Dynasty* . . .), 1965, p. 14). This is an incredible 'howler'; Heb. *z* appears as *d* or *t* in Egyptian, not *s* (*cf.* Helck, *Beziehungen*, pp. 589, 554: 18), and *Ysr'l* wholly lacks the '*ayin* of Jezre' 'el! Noth's idea that *Ysr'l* could be some earlier entity than OT Israel bearing the same name

ptah ever warred in Palestine, and so they suggest that the stela indicates merely that Israel left Egypt in Merenptah's first years.[13] But independent proof that Merenptah *did* conduct at least one small campaign in Palestine is given by an inscription at the temple of Amada in Nubia – overlooked completely by most scholars – in which the title 'Binder of Gezer' (in Palestine) is given equal prominence with the strictly parallel title 'Seizer of Libya' that refers to his well-known Libyan war.[14] Some Israelites must, therefore, have had a minor clash with Merenptah's troops in West Palestine before 1220 BC, and so the Exodus and first phase of the Israelite conquest must be earlier than 1220 BC as well as later than 1290 (or 1304) BC (earliest date for Ra'amses).

(b) Duration of the Wilderness Journeyings

Originally, Israel were to go from Egypt through Sinai directly to Canaan; the forty years in the wilderness was a punishment for disobedience, and its explicit purpose was to replace the rebellious generation by a new generation (Nu. 14:21–23; 32:9–13; Dt. 2:14). The forty years should not be dismissed as a meaningless round figure, because it is explicitly made up of

---

(*History of Israel*[2], 1960, p. 3) is equally baseless. No evidence exists for such a 'double'; and why not also claim that Egyptian 'Moab', 'Edom' and 'Se'ir' are different from their OT homonyms? Why these evasions? Simply that the tribal Israel as an entity in W. Palestine in 1220 BC, pictured by the Old Testament and tacitly by the Merenptah-stela (by determinative of 'people'), does not suit their particular theories about Israelite origins, and they prefer these theories to the first-hand evidence of the stela. No wonder that, in another context, Albright found himself writing that 'German [OT] scholars are inclined . . . to close their eyes' to archaeological and linguistic data (*History, Archaeology and Christian Humanism*, 1964, p. 267) – a situation distressingly close to obscurantism. *Cf. THB* 17 (1966), pp. 90–92 (where read $\underline{d}$, $\underline{t}$, in **ydr'*, **ytr'*, p. 91).

[13] See E. Drioton, 'La Date de l'Exode' in *La Bible et l'Orient*, 1955, p. 45, and C. de Wit, *The Date and Route of the Exodus*, 1960, p. 10.

[14] Published by U. Bouriant, *RT* 18 (1896), p. 159; H. Gauthier, *Le Temple d'Amada*, 1913, pp. 187–189 and pl. 41: B, and *Livre des Rois d'Égypte*, III, p. 118. New copy by J. Černý, *Amada: Stela of Amenophis II and Inscription of Meneptah*, Cairo, Centre of Documentation, n.d.; *cf.* A. Youssef, *ASAE* 58 (1964), pp. 273–280 and plate.

thirty-eight years[15] (Dt. 2:14) plus other short periods of time, totalling forty years altogether (Nu., *passim*; Dt. 1:3). Therefore, this particular forty-year period must be taken seriously in dealing with this epoch. This means that if the Exodus is after 1290 BC, the start of the conquest under Joshua cannot then precede *c*. 1250 BC; similarly, if the conquest began before 1220 BC, the Exodus would not be later than *c*. 1260 BC. The limits for the date of the Exodus are then roughly 1290/1260 BC, and for the start of the conquest about 1250/1220 BC. A rough average date would be *c*. 1280 and *c*. 1240 BC respectively, or perhaps up to a decade later (*cf*. p. 67, below). (If Ramesses II's accession were in 1304 rather than in 1290, all these dates would then average some fourteen years earlier.)

(c) Palestinian Evidence

First, in Transjordan, Glueck's surveys show a renewed density of occupation from about 1300 BC, after a lapse of five centuries since the Patriarchal age,[16] a situation reflected in Egyptian sources, where in the Nineteenth Dynasty we suddenly find references to the Transjordan lands and peoples lacking in the Eighteenth Dynasty – to Moab, Seʻir, Edom – and evidence for forces of Ramesses II having campaigned in Moab and Seʻir, presumably before the Israelites under Moses reached the 'plains of Moab'.[17] As Israel were opposed by strong kingdoms in Edom and Moab and had to go round these (Nu. 20:14–21; Jdg. 11:17), the Exodus and wanderings of

---

[15] This thirty-eight years, a real and not 'round' or schematic figure, was occupied by wanderings as is clearly stated in Dt. 2:14, and was not simply spent at Kadesh as Rowley states (*From Joseph to Joshua*, p. 133), perhaps by a slip of the pen. His conclusion as to its artificiality is wishful thinking unsupported by any tangible evidence and therefore invalid; the same is true of Alt, *KS*, I, 1953, p. 163 n. 3.

[16] *Cf*. notes 38, 40 to p. 43, above; also Glueck, *The Other Side of the Jordan*, 1940, pp. 125 ff., 128 ff., 134 ff., 140 ff. For a note of caution (but applying more to the Jordan valley), see also Albright, *BASOR* 90 (1943), note 77a to pp. 17–18.

[17] For details and the new data on Moab and Dibon, *cf*. Kitchen, *JEA* 50 (1964), pp. 50, 53–55, 63–67, 69–70.

Israel are unlikely to have been earlier than *c.* 1300 BC, the approximate date of foundation of these kingdoms.

Secondly, let us look at the situation in Western Palestine. After the crossing of Jordan,[18] the capture of Jericho and Ai, and the submission of the Gibeonites, Joshua had to conduct one campaign in Southern Palestine and then another in Galilee; then he and his contemporaries and successors had to try to occupy a Canaan defeated but not fully or finally conquered. Joshua continued the work of Moses in apportioning the land (Jos. 13). At Gilgal, he assigned land to Caleb, his tribe Judah, and to the Joseph-tribes (Jos. 14–18); and at Shiloh allotted land for the other tribes to occupy (Jos. 18–22). Before his death, Joshua exhorted the leaders and people privately (Jos. 23) and publicly (Jos. 24). Caleb was some forty years old when Moses sent him and others to spy out Canaan; he claimed his inheritance forty-five years later, after the campaigns of Joshua 6 to 11, aged eighty-five years (Jos. 14:6–11). As nearly forty of those forty-five years were spent in the wilderness journeyings, this suggests that the events of Joshua 1 to 12 occurred within five or six years of Moses' death. During what remained of the lifetimes of Joshua and the elders, the tribes had the task of beginning to occupy the territories assigned them at Gilgal and Shiloh.

Excavations at several sites in Palestine suggest that the Israelite conquest began during the second half of the thirteenth century BC, thus agreeing with the Egyptian evidence, although two sites have produced results which appear divergent at first sight.

At Jericho (Tell es-Sultan), the Late Bronze Age levels appear to have been almost completely washed away[19] during the four centuries that the mound lay desolate from Joshua until Ahab's time;[20] in barely half that length of time (during *c.*

18 *Cf.* J. Garstang, *Joshua, Judges,* 1931, pp. 136–138 and plate 25.

19 For what follows, *cf.* Kitchen, *NBD,* pp. 215–216, and esp. 612–613. For re-dating of Garstang's 'Late Bronze' wall as Early Bronze, see K. M. Kenyon, *Digging Up Jericho,* 1957, pp. 170–171, 176–177, and esp. 181.

20 It is possible, also, that the Late Bronze Age inhabitants continued to use the Middle Bronze Age ramparts (oral suggestion by Prof. Y. Yadin);

1600–1400 BC), most of the Middle Bronze Age city had been eroded away,[21] so that this is a real factor to be reckoned with and not just a harmonistic excuse.[22] Excavations at Et-Tell have failed to produce any proper evidence of occupation there after the Early Bronze Age (c. 2400 BC),[23] apart from a small Israelite settlement (Iron I) of c. 1200–1050 BC. Despite assertions sometimes made to the contrary, this situation suggests that Et-Tell is *not* Ai but another ancient site (Beth-Aven?),[24] and that Ai must be looked for somewhere else in the area and not on Et-Tell. When mounds and literary records fail to agree in other cases, topographers and archaeologists do not panic but simply use their common sense, recognize that they were probably mistaken in their identification,[25] and proceed to search elsewhere

---

cf. also Albright, *The Biblical Period*[4], 1963, p. 28, citing Tell Beit Mirsim where this is attested.

[21] Kenyon, *op. cit.*, pp. 170–171; *cf.* pp. 45, 93, 259–260, 262–263; *PEQ* 92 (1960), p. 108. *Cf.* Albright, *op. cit.*, pp. 28–29.

[22] Positive evidence that a settlement existed at Jericho in the thirteenth century BC comes from the tombs, these yielding Mycenaean pottery and imitations of such. The pottery is of thirteenth-century type (*cf.* Albright, *op. cit.*, p. 100 n. 59, and in *Bibliotheca Orientalis* 21 (1964), p. 69). Its rarity merely reflects the inland location of Jericho, like Hama(th) which yielded only two such sherds from its thirteenth-century occupation (Kitchen, *NBD*, p. 216 top, after Hanfmann, *JNES* 12 (1953), pp. 206–207).

[23] G. E. Wright, *Biblical Archaeology*, 1957, p. 80; Albright, *op. cit.*, 1963, p. 29 and n. 60.

[24] See J. M. Grintz, *Biblica* 42 (1961), pp. 201–216; note how well the occupational history of Et-Tell corresponds to the literary evidence for Beth-Aven, and is utterly different from that for Ai (Grintz, *op. cit.*, pp. 213–215, with p. 207)! Ai may not be a full-sized tell, but only separate (if neighbouring) Middle Bronze, Late Bronze and Iron II settlements in this area, and not easily found. One thinks of the searches for Teiman or pre-Hellenistic Gerasa in Transjordan (*cf.* N. Glueck, *The Other Side of the Jordan*, 1940, pp. 21–26, 121–123).

[25] It is only the approximate geographical suitability and the presumed play on the name that has recommended Et-Tell as the site of Ai, and no scrap of positive *proof* (such as inscriptions *in situ* as at Gezer) exists to justify Noth's uncritical belief (*VTS*, VII, p. 273) that the equation of Et-Tell with Ai is 'beyond all doubt'. There are very serious doubts on both grounds cited, *cf.* Grintz, *op. cit.*, pp. 208–211 (name), 207 end (locus). New excavations at Et-Tell have as yet added little, but at least the neighbouring

in the region.[26] The problem of Ai should be regarded in exactly the same way. Jericho and Ai are lessons in negative evidence: the absence of the expected body of remains of Late Bronze Age date does not automatically imply that the biblical narratives are inventions or aetiological tales.[27] The circumstantial realism of the topographical allusions and of Joshua's leadership suggest otherwise, as does the analogy of archaeological failure to produce remains tallying with other – and indisputably original – Ancient Oriental written documents.[28]

Khirbet Haiyan can apparently be ruled out as purely Islamic (cf. E. F. Campbell after J. A. Callaway, BA 28 (1965), p. 28).

[26] Thus, 'Aqir was once thought to be Ekron, but no pottery-evidence could be found to support this, despite similarity of name; Ekron may rather be located at Khirbet el Muqanna which shows a suitable history of occupation and is topographically acceptable (see J. Naveh, IEJ 8 (1958), pp. 166 ff.; cf. B. Mazar, IEJ 10 (1960), pp. 106 ff.). Similarly, Khirbet Tarrama with nothing earlier than Hellenistic pottery could not be Debir as Noth suggested; hence Albright and Wright suggested the more fitting Tell Beit Mirsim (cf. Wright, JNES 5 (1946), p. 110, n. 12). Specially instructive is the case of Arad in S. Palestine, where the ancient town was apparently located at Tel Arad and Tell el-Milh in different epochs; both mounds together (and neither alone) would fit the whole history; see Y. Aharoni and R. Amiran, IEJ 14 (1964), pp. 144–147; cf. also B. Mazar, JNES 24 (1965), pp. 297–303; Yadin, IEJ 15 (1965), p. 180. There is no inherent reason for treating Ai as any more of a special problem than Ekron, Debir or Arad.

[27] As has been the tendency with Alt and Noth, for example (references, cf. Grintz, op. cit., p. 205 and nn. 2–5); on their over-use of aetiology, cf. J. Bright, Early Israel in Recent History Writing, 1956, pp. 91 ff. The supposed standing still of the sun, or 'long day', of Jos. 10:12–13 sometimes causes difficulty, but it may rest on nothing more than mistranslation. Possibly cease shining rather than cease moving should be understood, and for 'about a whole day' one may definitely render 'as when day is done'; cf. provisionally R. D. Wilson, Princeton Theological Review 16 (1918), pp. 46–54.

[28] Thus in Egypt, for example, many stone temples are mentioned in documents (e.g., the great Papyrus Harris I) or on monuments of their officials, but have never been found by archaeologists. Cf. lists in W. Helck, Materialen zur Wirtschaftsgeschichte des Neuen Reiches, I, 1961, pp. 137–139 (eight royal funerary temples never yet found); ibid., II, 1961, pp. 157–190 (temples of provincial capitals, etc.). No trace of Ninth-Dynasty Heracleopolis has yet been found although that dynasty originated there, and so on.

The excavations at Gibeon[29] afford a further sharp lesson on the unreliability of negative evidence: the first three seasons of excavation found no trace of the Late Bronze Age city presupposed in Joshua 10:2.[30] But in the fourth campaign, the discovery of a few very fine tombs of that particular period has shown that there must in fact have been a Late Bronze Age settlement somewhere on the general site as required by Joshua 10:2.[31]

With the beginning of the conquest have been associated archaeological destruction-levels at Lachish (Tell ed-Duweir), Debir (if Tell Beit Mirsim), Bethel (Beitin), Tell el-Hesi (Eglon?), and Hazor (Tell el-Qedah or Waqqas).[32] All of these show traces of catastrophic destruction in the later part of the thirteenth century BC, although the fall of Bethel has been thought to be earlier than the others. If one identifies these destructions at Lachish and Debir as resulting from Joshua's Southern campaign (Jos. 10), the earlier fall of Bethel (before Israel crossed the Jordan?) might seem a difficulty. To 'solve' it by postulating a separate history of the Joseph-tribes (as some do), or similar counsels of despair, would seem quite unnecessary, however.

First, the notion that Bethel perhaps fell earlier than Lachish and Debir is based on the superior quality of its pottery compared with that from the destruction-levels at the other two sites.[33] But this overlooks the fact that *all* the material culture at Bethel is of a high standard: well-built houses, paved or plastered floors, excellent drainage-system, exotic art ('Astarte

---

[29] On the identification of El-Jib as the site of Gibeon on the basis of inscribed jar-handles found there, *cf.* J. B. Pritchard, *VTS*, VII, 1960, pp. 1–2, and *Gibeon where the Sun stood still*, 1962, pp. 45–52 (topographical indications, *ibid.*, pp. 24–45 *passim*).

[30] Except for a single sherd of Cypriote ware (*VTS*, VII, p. 8 n. 2), but reported as two sherds of a bowl in *BA* 24 (1961), pp. 22–23.

[31] *BA, loc. cit.; Gibeon* . . . , 1962, pp. 135–138, 156–158: *The Bronze Age Cemetery at Gibeon*, 1963.

[32] Wright, *Biblical Archaeology*, 1957, pp. 80–83; with references, *JNES* 5 (1946), pp. 110–111.

[33] *Cf.* Albright, *BASOR* 58 (1935), p. 13.

E

cylinder-seal), and so on.[34] Thus, the Bethelites may simply have maintained a higher over-all cultural standard than did less important Debir, or Lachish subject to greater foreign (Egyptian) exploitation, and the chronological time-lag may be illusory.[35] The fall of Bethel to the Joseph-tribes is mentioned in Judges 1:22–26, but is given no explicit date; this incident could have been associated with the fall of Ai, or with the end of Joshua's Southern campaign, or with some other occasion.[36]

Secondly, the final destruction of Canaanite Debir and Lachish probably represents the work of the Judah-tribe led by Caleb (Jos. 14:13–15; 15:13–19; Jdg. 1:10–15, 20) subsequent to the Southern campaign of Joshua (Jos. 10, esp. verses 31–33, 38–39). It is clear from these references that Debir was smitten twice by the Hebrews; once during Joshua's flying campaign, and a second time by Caleb and the Judahites beginning a permanent settlement. The major destruction of Debir (if Tell Beit Mirsim, end of stratum C) should be associated with the second occasion (Caleb) – the first would leave little separate trace – as it was followed by an entirely different kind of occupation (stratum B_1) which is best identified as that of the newly settling Hebrews.[37] It is therefore possible that the major destruction of Canaanite Lachish also belongs to the follow-up campaigns of Caleb and Judah. Unlike Debir, however, the city was not immediately settled by Israel after its destruction; instead, the Philistines had a garrison there for a time.[38] The fall of Lachish may even perhaps be dated to the fourth or

---

[34] Wright, *op. cit.*, p. 81: more detail, J. L. Kelso, *BA* 19 (1956), pp. 38–40; Albright, *Archaeology of Palestine and the Bible*[2], 1933, p. 101.

[35] Thus, metropolitan Ugarit in the thirteenth century BC enjoyed higher living standards than anything attested in Palestine then – but it was destroyed (by the 'Sea Peoples') later than any of the sites dealt with here, at *c.* 1200 BC (plus or minus a few years).

[36] Note that Jdg. 1:1, 'After the death of Joshua', does *not* refer to everything in Jdg. 1, only to verses 1–9 and 16–19. Jos. 14:13–15 and 15:13–19 show that Jdg. 1:10–15, 20 belongs in the lifetime of Joshua; the rest of Jdg. 1 (verses 21, 22–26, 27 ff.) is undated.

[37] Albright, *Archaeology of Palestine and the Bible*[2], 1933, pp. 101 ff.; *cf.* references in note 45 below.

[38] Possibly under Ramesses III of Egypt; *cf.* T. Dothan, *IEJ* 10 (1960), pp. 62–63.

fifth year of the Egyptian king Merenptah (*i.e.*, *c.* 1220/1219 BC), for among the Late Bronze Age ruins was found an Egyptian hieratic ostracon dated 'Year 4' in the script of this period, relating to taxes (tribute for Egypt?) on the grain-harvest.[39] In other words, Caleb's campaign was perhaps not later than *c.* 1220/1219 BC, and may have begun a little earlier at Debir, while Joshua's Southern and Northern (and perhaps other, unmentioned) campaigns were earlier still, within about five years (see p. 62 above). This might put Israel's crossing of the Jordan at *c.* 1230/1225 BC, and the Exodus forty years earlier at about 1270/1265 BC, roughly. The fall of Bethel (if linked with Ai or the Southern campaign) might also be about 1230/1225 BC.[40] These dates are realistic, but of course must not be pressed; the 'Year 4' on which they are based is most probably that of Merenptah, but not certainly so.

The main destruction of Canaanite Hazor (enclosure level Ia) would fall into the same period.[41] Rowton's attempt[42] to equate this fall of Canaanite Hazor (stratum XIII of the Tell; enclosure level Ia) with the campaign of Deborah and Barak in Judges 4 to 5 instead of that by Joshua in Joshua 11 (so pushing the Exodus and initial conquest back into the fourteenth or early thirteenth century BC) flies in the face of *all* other collateral evidence, and glosses over certain hints in Joshua 11 and Judges 4. It should be noted that in Joshua 11 all the emphasis is on Jabin I as king of *Hazor*, and on *Hazor* as 'formerly head of all those kingdoms', and it alone was burnt (Jos. 11: 10, 13). It is therefore natural to associate this with the main end of Canaanite Hazor and its burnt remains. But in Judges 4, Jabin II is more often called king of *Canaan* (Jdg. 4:2, 23, 24 twice) than king of Hazor (Jdg. 4:2, 17), and

---

[39] See Albright, *BASOR* 68 (1937), pp. 23–24, and *ibid.*, 74 (1939), pp. 20–22; and now, J. Černý in O. Tufnell, *Lachish IV: The Bronze Age*, 1958, pp. 132–133, *cf.* p. 36.

[40] If 1304 BC be preferred for the accession of Ramesses II, then all dates in this section must be raised by about fourteen years (*cf.* above, p. 58, note 6).

[41] Y. Yadin, *BA* 22 (1959), pp. 1–20, esp. 4–6, 13–15.

[42] M. B. Rowton, *CAH²*, I:6 (*Chronology*), 1962, pp. 67–69; *cf.* F. H. Stubbings, *ibid.*, pp. 75–76, on difficulties of dating Mycenaean III pottery.

his main strength is curiously not in Hazor but with Sisera in Harosheth. No emphasis whatever is placed on the *city* Hazor. This could simply mean that the later Jabin had a small fortified residence somewhere on (or near) Tell el-Qedah that has not yet been touched by the excavators, or else merely that he still ruled the *state* of Hazor but from a different town in the area.[43] (Only a small proportion of the Tell has been dug down to Canaanite levels; the examples of Gibeon and Arad should be a warning against too hasty an assumption that a further (but secondary) Canaanite occupation by Jabin II (or a residence nearby) is to be excluded.[44]) The occurrence of two kings Jabin is, of course, no more of a doublet than two Niqmads (II and III) and two Ammistamrus (I and II) in Ugarit, two Suppiluliumas (I and II) and two Mursils (II and III) of the Hittites, and two Amenophis (III and IV), two Sethos (I and II) and two Ramesses (I and II) in Egypt – all in the fourteenth/thirteenth centuries BC.

Furthermore, the type of occupation found on several of these destroyed Canaanite sites is of a quite different and simpler kind, best explained as that of the occupying Israelites.[45] The biblical account cannot, therefore, be reduced to a peaceful, marginal infiltration by the Hebrews as required by Noth's

[43] *E.g.*, in Gn. 20:1, Abraham dwells between Kadesh and Shur, and sojourns 'in Gerar' – obviously, in the territory so named, not the walled city itself (probably Tell Abu Hureirah, Albright, *BASOR* 163 (1961), pp. 47–48 n. 59). City and state often have the same name in the Ancient Orient, although distinct entities. This applied to Carchemish in Hittite politics, for example, where city and land (same name) had distinct roles (*cf.* H. Klengel, *Geschichte Syriens im 2. Jahrtausend v.u.Z.*, I, 1965, pp. 41, 48 n. 54). Assur-uballit II, last king of 'Assyria', reigned in the West at Harran (outside his home territory) when Babylonians and Medes had destroyed the ancient capitals of Assyria proper, occupying the land (*cf.* D. J. Wiseman, *Chronicles of Chaldaean Kings*, 1956, pp. 17–19, 45, 61–63).

[44] J. Gray, *VT* 16 (1966), 26–52, compactly surveys the history and archaeology of Hazor (not using *Hazor III–IV*), but his treatment of the conquest marks no advance, while his sceptical view of Joshua's role rests on no tangible, objective basis.

[45] On this matter see G. E. Wright, *JBL* 60 (1941), pp. 27–42, esp. 30–33; *Biblical Archaeology*, 1957, pp. 81, and esp. 88–89; Albright, *op. cit.* in note 37, p. 66, above.

arbitrary theories,[46] while the contrast commonly drawn between Judges 1 and Joshua 10 (usually to the grave disadvant-
age of the latter) is tenable only if one is content with a superficial view of the matter.[47]

(d) Some False Trails

Some factors that have been supposed to have some bearing on
the date or nature of the Exodus and conquest are actually
irrelevant, and so can be eliminated.

1. *The Habiru or 'Apiru.* People so designated were a source of
unrest in Canaan in the fourteenth century BC, as is shown by
the Amarna tablets.[48] Their name is probably etymologically
connected with that of the 'Hebrews', but it includes people
scattered in place and time as far apart as Egypt, Anatolia and
Mesopotamia from the eighteenth to twelfth centuries BC.
There are too many differences in the data provided by Joshua–
Judges and the Amarna tablets to identify the biblical and
Amarna-period Hebrews. Thus, the Israelites were invaders
from without and opposed the Canaanites, but the Habiru were
native to Canaan and served under rival Canaanite princes
who sometimes called *each other* 'Habiru' pejoratively.[49] In any

[46] *Cf.* M. Noth, *History of Israel*[2], 1960, pp. 68 top, 68–70.

[47] As is, for example, O. Eissfeldt, *CAH*[2], II:34 (*The Hebrew Kingdom*),
1965, pp. 4 (on Jos. 10 and Jdg. 1), 7, 9, 10–11, 12–13 (denial of Joshua
commanding 'all Israel'), who seems to have learnt little or nothing from
Wright, *JNES* 5 (1946), pp. 105–114. It must be remembered that Joshua's
swift campaigns temporarily disabled a series of Canaanite city-states and
were *not* (and not considered) an exhaustive conquest (despite Eissfeldt,
op. cit., pp. 10–11); when (Jos. 10) 'he left none remaining', common sense
suggests that (like pedestrians on our roads) it is a question of 'the quick and
the dead'; whoever had not got away perished. Eissfeldt has not allowed for
Jos. 13 ff., where it is obvious that Joshua left very much land to be actually
possessed, and not merely swept through or assigned by lot.

[48] Most of the data on the Ḫabiru/'Apiru will be found in J. Bottéro
(ed.), *Le Problème des Ḫabiru*, 1954, and in M. Greenberg, *The Ḫap/biru*,
1955; for some later studies, see J.-R. Kupper, *Revue d'Assyriologie* 55 (1961),
pp. 197–200, esp. 197 n. 2, and next note.

[49] So E. F. Campbell, *BA* 23 (1960), pp. 13–15 (esp. 15), and Wright,
Biblical Archaeology, 1957, p. 75 (after Mendenhall); *cf.* earlier, E. Dhorme,
JPOS 4 (1924), pp. 162–168 and Greenberg, *op., cit.*, pp. 70–76, 86–87. G. E.

case, the larger number of South Palestinian city-states in Joshua as opposed to the Amarna tablets would indicate a later situation under Joshua than in the tablets.[50] The Amarna Habiru, therefore, have no direct bearing on the date of the Exodus or conquest (except indirectly to precede them) and so cannot support a date for these events in the fifteenth and fourteenth centuries BC as was once held. As has been said long ago, the Hebrews may have been Habiru – but not all Habiru are biblical Hebrews, nor can any particular group in the external data be yet identified as corresponding to the Hebrews.

2. *Asher in Palestine before the Exodus.* In Egyptian documents of *c*. 1300–1250 BC,[51] a place-name *i-s-r* in Palestine was identified by some with the biblical tribe of Asher, and it was then argued that this tribe was already in Palestine before the main Exodus took place: either they had a separate Exodus, or were never in Egypt.[52] But recently, the proper Egyptian transcription of the name Asher has been recovered: it is *i-sh-r* (*i-š-r*) not *i-s-r* – so the references to *i-s-r* have nothing to do with the biblical Asher, and the theories based on this false equation must be abandoned.[53] The supposed references to Asher,

---

Mendenhall, *BA* 25 (1962), pp. 65–87, is interesting but in large measure dubious.

[50] Wright, *Biblical Archaeology*, 1957, pp. 75–76; note also the differences between the situation in Joshua and in the Amarna tablets mentioned by Wiseman, *NBD*, pp. 67–68 (Lachish and Gezer supporting Habiru, not destroyed by them; differing names of city-kings). The Jashuia whom Meek compares with 'Joshua', without identifying him outright, in *Hebrew Origins*[2], 1960, pp. 21–22, is a lesser member of the Egyptian administration of Palestine (Amarna letter 256:18), not an invader. These differences invalidate Meek's general comparisons, *loc. cit.*

[51] In topographical lists: J. Simons, *Handbook . . . of Egyptian Topographical Lists*, 1937, pp. 147 (XVII:4), 162 (XXV:8). In Papyrus Anastasi I: Gardiner, *Egyptian Hieratic Texts*, I, 1911, p. 25* note 12, and *Ancient Egyptian Onomastica*, I, 1947, pp. 191*–193* (No. 265); M. Burchardt, *Altkanaanäische Fremdworte und Eigennamen . . .* , 1911, No. 139.

[52] For example, Rowley, *From Joseph to Joshua*, pp. 3, 33–35, *etc.*

[53] See Albright, *JAOS* 74 (1954), pp. 229–231 and n. 51, 232 and n. 58a (on Papyrus Brooklyn 35.1446 of eighteenth century BC). S. Yeivin, *Mélanges Bibliques André Robert*, 1957, pp. 98–9, preferring the old combination, dismissed Albright's view as hasty. But Yeivin has himself been too hasty. (i)

Zebulon, *etc.*, in the Ugaritic epics were proved to be non-existent long ago.[54]

3. *More than one Exodus and Some Tribes Never in Egypt.* The *uniform* biblical tradition at all levels records that *all* of Jacob's sons entered Egypt (*e.g.*, Gn. 46:8–27; Ex. 1:1–5), and knows of only *one* Exodus by their descendants (*cf.* Ex. 24:4; Nu. 1, 2, 10:14 ff.). They were accompanied by a variety of heterogeneous elements (*cf.* Ex. 12:38; Nu. 11:4), and yet more were joined with Israel subsequently (*e.g.*, the Kenites, Nu. 10:29; Jdg. 1:16; 1 Sa. 27:10). There is not a scrap of clear, explicit evidence for more than one Exodus or for some tribes never going into Egypt. The supposed Egyptian and Ugaritic evidence is illusory (see previous paragraph). The events of Genesis 34 belong explicitly to the time of Jacob, and have nothing to do with any later period (the Amarna age, for example; Labayu and his sons, not Hamor, ruled Shechem then).[55] The fact that Joshua and Judges do not record an Israelite conquest of the Shechem area of Palestine may show nothing more than the fact that our biblical records are not exhaustive sources for the period, and were never intended to be so read. One cannot (and should not) build theories on a void.[56] It should be evident from

---

Heb. Asher and Eg. '*i-sh-r* do not go with '*i-s-r* and the goddess Ashirat, because the latter has nothing to do with the root 'good fortune' but in Ugaritic is '*Athirat-yammi*, 'She who walks the Sea' or the like (cf. Albright, *Archaeology and the Religion of Israel*[3], 1953, pp. 77–8). (ii) Albright's *JAOS*-equation *is* in line with the table *BASOR* 110 (1948), p. 15 n. 42, see remarks on Eg. equivalents before the table, and *cf.* table of F. M. Cross, *HTR* 55 (1962), p. 245 n. 95. Hence Albright's view must be retained.

[54] On this, see Albright, *BASOR* 63 (1936), pp. 27–32, and *ibid.* 71 (1938), pp. 35–40; R. de Langhe, *Les Textes de Ras Shamra-Ugarit . . .* , II, 1945, pp. 469–519.

[55] Both Rowley, *From Joseph to Joshua*, pp. 113–114, 124, *etc.*, and Eissfeldt, *CAH*[2], II: 26a (*Palestine in the Nineteenth Dynasty . . .*), 1965, pp. 13, 24 with p. 8 (date of patriarchs) and *CAH*[2], II:34 (*The Hebrew Kingdom*), 1965, pp. 7–8, put the patriarchs and the events of Gn. 34 in the Amarna age; as noted, Labayu, not Hamor, was at Shechem then, and as shown in §II of chapter 2, the patriarchs must be dated much earlier than the Amarna age.

[56] This is not to deny that some Hebrews could have left Egypt long before *the* Exodus; but if so, we have no explicit biblical record of such –

this whole chapter that assumptions of more than one Exodus, or of tribes not entering Egypt, or that the order of Moses and Joshua should be reversed[57] are wholly superfluous.

(e) Links with Other Periods

1. *With the Patriarchs.* As shown above (pp. 53–56), a four centuries' interval agrees very well with a date for the descent of the Patriarchs into Egypt about 1700 BC (round figure) and for the exodus of their descendants (and associates) in the early thirteenth century BC, each established on independent grounds. 2. *From the Exodus to Solomon.* Here, the evidence is rather more complicated. The primary evidence and biblical data used so far would indicate an interval of roughly 300 years from the Exodus to the early years of Solomon (*c.* 971/970 BC).[58] For the same interval, 1 Kings 6:1 gives 480 years, while addition of all the individual figures in the books from Exodus to 1 Kings gives a total of some 553 years plus three unknown amounts which will here be called '*x*'.[59] Furthermore, David's genealogy of five generations in Ruth 4:18–22 can hardly easily extend over the 260 years or so between him and the Exodus, and so it is probably a selective one; but that of the priest Zadok (1 Ch. 6:3–8) of ten generations would about cover the 300 years. The

---

the Patriarchs are people, not tribal personifications. The silence on central Palestine *could* reflect a rapid link-up with Hebrews already there, but of itself does not constitute direct evidence and so proves absolutely nothing except the incompleteness of the data. The assumption is possible but lacks proper evidence.

[57] As assumed by A. T. Olmstead, *History of Palestine and Syria*, 1931, pp. 197, 248; T. J. Meek, *Hebrew Origins*[2], 1950 (repr. 1960), pp. 43–46.

[58] The date 971/0–931/0 BC for Solomon's reign rests initially on Thiele's date for the beginning of the Divided Monarchy (E. R. Thiele, *Mysterious Numbers of the Hebrew Kings*, 1951, pp. 42–54); 961–922 BC is preferred by Albright and his associates (*e.g.*, *BANE*, pp. 209–210). I prefer 971/0–931/0 BC for detailed Near Eastern and Egyptian reasons to be published in my *Hittite Hieroglyphs, Aramaeans and Hebrew Traditions* and *The Third Intermediate Period in Egypt* respectively (both forthcoming).

[59] *Cf.* the convenient table in Rowley, *From Joseph to Joshua*, pp. 87–88; he gives 554 + (*etc.*) years, where I have taken only three complete years of Solomon up to his fourth year.

genealogies need be no problem; but what shall we make of the 480 and 553-plus-x years, as compared with the roughly 300 years' interval required by our primary evidence?

In principle, this problem is not quite so contradictory as it may appear, if we remember that the Old Testament is also a part of the Ancient Near East, and therefore that Ancient Oriental principles must be applied. Thus, in ordinary king lists and historical narratives, ancient scribes and writers did not usually include synchronistic tables and cross-references as we do today. Synchronisms were the subject of special and separate historiographic works.[60] In biblical terms, Judges as a narrative with a historico-religious purpose does not deal with synchronisms (except with oppressors as part of its story), while Kings is a synchronous history of Israel and Judah (while also a selective religious writing) in some degree comparable with the so-called 'synchronous histories' of Assyria and Babylonia.[61] Here, an Egyptian example will be instructive as a parallel problem. For the five Dynasties Thirteen to Seventeen (the so-called Second Intermediate Period in Egyptian history), the Turin Papyrus of Kings[62] records – or did when it was com-

---

[60] For example, the synchronous lists of Assyrian and Babylonian kings, especially Assur 14616c. See E. F. Weidner, *Die Könige von Assyrien*, 1921 (=*MVÄG* 26:2), pp. 10 ff., and S. Smith, *Early History of Assyria*, 1928, pp. 349 ff. For Assur 14616c, *cf.* Weidner, *op. cit.*, pp. 15 f., and *AfO* 3 (1926), pp. 66 ff., and A. Poebel, *JNES* 2 (1943), pp. 60, 61. *Cf.* also next note. English version, *ANET*, pp. 272–274.

[61] *Cf.* H. Winckler, *Altorientalische Forschungen*, I, 1893, pp. 297 ff.; F. Delitzsch, *Die Babylonische Chronik*, 1906, pp. 43 ff. 'Babylonian Chronicle' is given complete in R. W. Rogers, *Cuneiform Parallels to the Old Testament*[2], 1926, pp. 208–219; large extracts in English, also in *ANET*, pp. 301–307, plus D. J. Wiseman, *Chronicles of Chaldaean Kings*, 1956, and A. R. Millard, *Iraq* 26 (1964), pp. 14–35. The so-called 'Synchronous History' *par excellence* may just possibly be the preamble to a treaty (Oppenheim, *Ancient Mesopotamia*, 1964, p. 146, 284); W. G. Lambert regards this as a propaganda-text, not a treaty-preamble, *Bibliotheca Orientalis* 21 (1964), p. 182 end. No full translation is available, but snippets are given in P. van der Meer, *The Chronology of Ancient Western Asia and Egypt*[2], 1955, and H. Tadmor, *JNES* 17 (1958), p. 131 (further chronicle, *ibid.*, p. 134).

[62] Text, Sir A. H. Gardiner, *The Royal Canon of Turin*, 1959; contents excerpted in Gardiner, *Egypt of the Pharaohs*, 1961, pp. 429–443 (Dyns.

plete – some 170 kings who reigned at least 520 years altogether. Now we also know that they all belong inside the period 1786 to *c.* 1550 BC,[63] a maximum period of only about 240 years at most – a hopeless contradiction? No. We know, too, that these dynasties were all *partly contemporary*: the 520 or so years are genuine enough, but were partly concurrent, not all consecutive. This may prove equally true of some of the Judges in early Israel, so that the 553-plus-x years would then fit into the roughly 300 years, just like the 520 or so into the roughly 240 in Egypt. Now in the Ancient Orient, chroniclers and other writers often used excerpts from fuller records, and this might explain the 480 years – a total of selected figures (details now unknown) taken from the larger total. The various figures are therefore not so refractory in principle, when relevant principles are applied. To work this out in practice within the book of Judges is not easy, simply because we need more detailed information on the period than is available there or from elsewhere. But neither is it beyond possibility (as is evident from an unpublished preliminary study). The problem of the book of Judges is chronologically rather less complicated than other celebrated problems of Near Eastern chronology – such as the Second Intermediate Period in Egypt, or the date of Hammurapi of Babylon, where a similar situation obtains.

Finally, in Judges 11:26, Jephthah (*c.* 1100 BC ??) speaks of Israel occupying Transjordan for 300 years before his time, *i.e.*, back to about 1400 BC if this is treated literally on modern reckoning, which does not fit a conquest at somewhere near 1240/1220 BC. But here again, *we do not know* the basis of Jephthah's figure – it could, again, be an aggregate of partly concurrent periods (*e.g.*, for Reuben, Gad and East Manasseh?), but we have no indications on which to build. Mesopotamian

---

13–17, pp. 440–443). On Egyptian lists, *cf.* also W. Helck, *Untersuchungen zu Manetho und den altägyptischen Königslisten*, 1956.

[63] For 1786 (end of Twelfth Dynasty), see R. A. Parker, *The Calendars of Ancient Egypt*, 1950, Excursus C; for about 1550 BC for start of the Eighteenth Dynasty, see E. Hornung, *Untersuchungen zur Chronologie und Geschichte des Neuen Reiches*, 1964, pp. 15–23, 108, and my review in *Chronique d'Égypte* 40/Fasc. 80 (1965), pp. 310–322, esp. 311.

monarchs sometimes give long-range dates (like this 300, or 1 Kings 6:1, 480 years) which are invariably too long in absolute years, and probably represent some kind of aggregate; these are not yet understood despite apparently plentiful information. Empty speculation is profitless, and sound method would counsel one to await fresh light on matters of this type. No-one is compelled to produce a complete answer when there is simply not enough information to do so.

When treated positively, then, nearly all of the relevant data fits together reasonably well within the context of Ancient Near Eastern studies, considering its complex nature; more than this, no-one can demand in the current state of knowledge.[64]

II. THE MONARCHY AND LATER

Here the problems are rather matters of small detail, than questions of wholesale divergences affecting centuries at a time.

(a) The United Monarchy

As something has happened to the Hebrew text of 1 Samuel 13:1, the length of Saul's reign can only be estimated.[65] But the round 'forty years' of Acts 13:21 must be quite near the truth. The biographical data available for Saul's fourth son, Ishbosheth (2 Sa. 2:10), implies that Saul was about sixty at death; he was anointed leader and king while still a 'young man' (1

[64] As hinted already above, other Near Eastern chronological problems are just as intractable as anything in the Old Testament, but this does not inhibit Orientalists from seeking constructive solutions (real or provisional) covering all the data. For example, no one solution for the date of Hammurapi will satisfy *all* the astronomical data (*cf.* A. Parrot, *Archéologie Mésopotamienne*, II, 1953, pp. 428–429) as at present understood; the later long range Assyro-Babylonian figures do not fit any solution (*ibid.*, pp. 363–365, 430–431), as already noted; and the Assyrian kinglists cause difficulties (*ibid.*, pp. 360–363). Other examples are plentiful.

[65] A figure may have fallen out of the text during the course of transmission. Mr. A. R. Millard reminds me of the omission of the year-date in Babyl. Chronicle B.M. 21901, l. 66 (Wiseman, *Chronicles of Chaldaean Kings*, 1956, pp. 62/63, 82); and 'Babylonian Chronicle', col. I:25, the reign of Tiglath-pileser III (R. W. Rogers, *Cuneiform Parallels to the Old Testament*[2], 1926, p. 209; *cf.* Grayson, *Bibbia e Oriente* 6 (1964), p. 205).

Sa. 9:2; 10:1, 17 ff.) and so he must have reigned thirty or forty years. The reigns of David and Solomon at forty years each need not be doubted; the first is thirty-three + seven years (1 Ki. 2:11), and Solomon was a younger son of David.[66]

(b) The Divided Monarchy

For the 350 years from Rehoboam of Judah to the fall of Jerusalem in 587 or 586 BC, some ninety-five per cent of the long series of reigns and cross-datings in Kings and Chronicles have been brilliantly worked out by E. R. Thiele – and that not by arbitrary juggling but by full use of proper Ancient Near Eastern procedures, objectively documented.[67] At only two main points have difficulties persisted: the interpretation of certain data from the reigns of Ahaz and Hezekiah,[68] and certain dates linked with the capture and fall of Jerusalem in the period 609–587/6 BC.[69] New data and close study may well eliminate even these quite limited problems.

[66] See first work cited in note 68, below.

[67] E. R. Thiele, *Mysterious Numbers of the Hebrew Kings*, 1951 (2nd ed., 1965), following on *JNES* 3 (1944), pp. 137–186, and supplemented in *VT* 4 (1954), pp. 185–195, in E. C. Hobbs (ed.), *A Stubborn Faith* (*FS W. A. Irwin*), 1956, pp. 39–52, and in *AUSS* 1 (1963), pp. 121–138, *AUSS* 2 (1964), pp. 120–136. The rival scheme of Albright (*BASOR* 100 (1945), pp. 16–22; *cf. BANE*, pp. 208–213 and pp. 226–228, notes 20–50) is inferior in both its methods and results (*cf.* Thiele, *Mysterious Numbers . . .*, 1951 ed., pp. 244–267, *A Stubborn Faith . . .*, pp. 39–41, and *AUSS* 1 (1963), pp. 132 ff.). The same may be said of V. Pavlovsky and E. Vogt, *Biblica* 45 (1964), 321–347, *cf.* 348–354, and Jepsen in A. Jepsen and R. Hanhart, *Untersuchungen zur Israelitisch-Jüdischen Chronologie*, 1964.

[68] See commentary to Table II in my *Hittite Hieroglyphs, Aramaeans and Hebrew Traditions* (forthcoming). Recent discussions include those of H. Tadmor, *Scripta Hierosolymitana VIII* (*Studies in the Bible*), 1961, pp. 232–271; C. Schedl, *VT* 12 (1962), pp. 88–119; S. H. Horn, *AUSS* 2 (1964), pp. 40–52; and E. R. Thiele, *VT* 16 (1966), 83–103, 103–7.

[69] Recent discussions include: W. F. Albright, *BASOR* 143 (1956), pp. 28–33; E. R. Thiele, *ibid.*, pp. 22–27; H. Tadmor, *JNES* 15 (1956), pp. 226–230; J. P. Hyatt, *JBL* 75 (1956), pp. 277–284; D. N. Freedman, *BA* 19 (1956), pp. 50–60; E. Vogt, *VTS* IV, 1957, pp. 67–96; E. Kutsch, *ZAW* 71 (1959), pp. 270–274; E. Auerbach, *VT* 9 (1959), pp. 113–121; *VT* 10 (1960), pp. 69–70; *VT* 11 (1961), pp. 128–136; and C. Schedl, *ZAW* 74 (1962), pp. 209–213.

One must remember that ancient methods of reckoning were not the same as ours. In the Ancient Near East two main kinds of regnal year are attested. By one method, a king reckoned the interval between his accession and the next New Year's Day as his accession-year (in effect, attributing that year to his deceased predecessor) and began his first regnal year with New Year's Day. This system was current in Mesopotamia. By the second method, a king counted the interval between his accession and New Year's Day as his first regnal year (in effect, attributing that whole year to his own reign), and began his second regnal year on New Year's Day. This was the Egyptian method. The official years of a king on the first system are his real total reign; but on the second system, the official regnal years of a king will always be one higher than his real total (unless he died exactly at midnight on New Year's Eve, an unlikely event). Thus, if two kings were exactly contemporary but used different systems, their regnal years would always show a difference of one year at any given time.[70] Proper understanding and application of these methods is the main key to the detailed figures in Kings and Chronicles.

(c) Exile and Later

The main framework of chronology from 600 BC onwards is on the whole well fixed,[71] and the only biblical question of note is the dispute over the relative order of Ezra and Nehemiah. Suffice it to say here that the biblical order is factually no more objectionable than the often advocated reverse order.[72]

[70] When neighbouring states also begin their calendar years at different seasons (e.g., in spring or autumn), or when civil and calendar years do not coincide (as in New Kingdom Egypt), then further complications enter into our attempts to unravel Ancient Near Eastern chronology, biblical or otherwise.

[71] For Mesopotamia, cf. R. A. Parker and W. H. Dubberstein, *Babylonian Chronology, 626 BC–AD 75*, 1956, giving tables to turn Mesopotamian dates into Julian dates; for Egyptian dates in the Twenty-sixth Dynasty, cf. R. A. Parker, *Mitteilungen des Deutschen Archäologischen Instituts, Abteilung Kairo*, 15 (1957), pp. 208–212; and E. Hornung, *ZÄS* 92 (1965), pp. 38–39 (solar eclipse).

[72] General survey (reversing order of Ezra and Nehemiah) is given by

H. H. Rowley, 'The Chronological Order of Ezra and Nehemiah' in *The Servant of the Lord and Other Essays*, 1952, pp. 131–159. A modified 're-versal' view (owing much to Albright) with further references is presented by J. Bright, *Yehezkel Kaufmann Jubilee Volume*, 1960, pp. 70–87 [English part], and *A History of Israel*, 1960, pp. 375–386. For a critique of the Albright/Bright date (428) for Ezra (but favouring 398), *cf.* J. A. Emerton, *JTS* 17 (1966), 1–19.

In favour of the biblical order, see J. S. Wright, *The Date of Ezra's Coming to Jerusalem*[2], 1958, and *The Building of the Second Temple*, 1958; J. Morgenstern, *JSS* 7 (1962), pp. 1–11; K. A. Kitchen, *TSF Bulletin* 29 (1961), pp. 18–19, reprinted as *Supplement* to *TSF Bulletin* 39 (1964), pp. vi–vii. On this age, *cf.* K. Galling, *Studien zur Geschichte Israels im Persischen Zeitalter*, 1964 (noting P. Lapp. *JBL* 84 (1965), pp. 297–300).

4. SOME HISTORICAL PROBLEMS

I. ALLEGED ANACHRONISMS

(a) Camels in the Patriarchal Age

It is often asserted that the mention of camels and of their use is an anachronism in Genesis.[1] This charge is simply not true, as there is both philological and archaeological evidence for knowledge and use of this animal in the early second millennium BC and even earlier. While a possible reference to camels in a fodder-list from Alalakh (c. eighteenth century BC)[2] has been disputed,[3] the great Mesopotamian lexical lists that originated in the Old Babylonian period show a knowledge of the camel c. 2000/1700 BC, including its domestication.[4] Furthermore, a Sumerian text from Nippur from the same early period gives clear evidence of domestication of the camel by then, by its allusions to camel's milk.[5] Camel bones were found in house-ruins at Mari of the pre-Sargonic age (twenty-fifth to twenty-fourth centuries BC),[6] and also in various Palestinian sites from

---

[1] Cf. Albright, *JBL* 64 (1945), pp. 287–288; *ZAW* 62 (1950), p. 315; *The Archaeology of Palestine*[4], 1960, pp. 206–207, Also J. Bright, *A History of Israel*, 1960, pp. 72–73, and O. Eissfeldt, *CAH*[2], II: 26a (*Palestine in the Nineteenth Dynasty* . . .), 1965, p. 6.

[2] D. J. Wiseman and A. Goetze, *JCS* 13 (1959), pp. 29, 37.

[3] By W. G. Lambert, *BASOR* 160 (1960), p. 42. No final decision can be reached until the original cuneiform tablet has been re-collated by someone competent in the Alalakh script-forms and without interests in the presence/absence of camels in this period.

[4] See Lambert, *op. cit.*, pp. 42–43, who has to admit that the natural implication of the contexts is that of a domesticated animal.

[5] See the *Chicago Assyrian Dictionary*, 7/I-J, 1960, p. 2b under *ibilu* and reference to text Ni(ppur) 9602:94 f. I owe this reference to the kindness of Mr. A. R. Millard. Jacobsen's reading has not been taken up by S. N. Kramer, *Proc. APS* 107: 6 (1963), pp. 506–507, iii: 24–26.

[6] A. Parrot, *Syria* 32 (1955), p. 323.

2000 to 1200 BC.[7] From Byblos comes an incomplete camel-figurine of the nineteenth/eighteenth centuries BC.[8] This and a variety of other evidence cannot be lightly disregarded.[9] For the early and middle second millennium BC, only limited use is presupposed by either the biblical or external evidence until the twelfth century BC.

(b) 'Philistines' in the Patriarchal Age

The mention of Philistines at Gerar in the Patriarchal age is usually dismissed as an anachronism because they are otherwise named in no ancient document before *c.* 1190 BC (texts of Ramesses III in Egypt).[10] But this is an argument from negative evidence and cannot therefore be relied on absolutely.[11] The 'Philistines' of Genesis 26 are relatively peaceful and well-Semitized, quite different in character from the alien Aegean warriors of the twelfth century BC; and we are entitled to ask whether the term 'Philistines' in Genesis 26 is not in fact a term of the thirteenth/twelfth centuries BC here applied to some *earlier* Aegean immigrants into Palestine who, like the later Philistines (Am. 9:7; Je. 47:4), had come from Caphtor (Crete and the Aegean Isles)[12]. The Caphtorim of Deuteronomy

---

[7] See, for example, R. de Vaux, *RB* 56 (1949), p. 9 (=*Die hebräischen Patriarchen und die modernen Entdeckungen*, 1961, p. 59), and B. S. J. Isserlin, *PEQ* 82 (1950), pp. 50–53.

[8] See de Vaux, *RB* 56 (1949), p. 9 n. 5 (= *Die hebr. Patr.*, p. 59 n. 5); K. A. Kitchen, *JEA* 47 (1961), p. 159 n. 1, or *NBD*, p. 182.

[9] A fuller treatment is to appear in Kitchen, *The Joseph Narrative and its Egyptian Background* (forthcoming). The most recent collection of the archaeological data is by B. Brentjes, *Klio* 38 (1960), pp. 23–52. Hitherto, the most valuable such surveys have been those by R. Walz, *ZDMG* 101 (1951), pp. 29–51; *ZDMG* 104 (1954), pp. 45–87; *Actes du IVe Congrès Internationale des Sciences Anthropologiques et Ethnologiques*, III, Vienna, 1956, pp. 190–204.

[10] For example, by J. Bright, *A History of Israel*, 1960, p. 73; or G. E. Wright, *Biblical Archaeology*, 1957, p. 40, who speaks more prudently of 'modernization'.

[11] Inscriptionally, we know so little about the Aegean peoples as compared with those of the rest of the Ancient Near East in the second millennium BC, that it is premature to deny outright the possible existence of Philistines in the Aegean area before 1200 BC.

[12] On Caphtor, Ugaritic *kptr* (=Kaptara), *cf.* C. H. Gordon, *Minos*

2:23 may have been the Aegean settlers in question. Once grant this, and the supposed anachronism disappears entirely. Caphtor is the Kaptara of the Mari archives of the eighteenth century BC – the Patriarchal Age – and one of these documents actually mentions a king of Hazor in Palestine sending gifts to Kaptara.[13] Traffic in the reverse direction at that same period is neatly proved by the occurrence of Middle Minoan II pottery at Hazor itself,[14] at Ugarit in Phoenicia,[15] and far inland in Upper Egypt.[16] If no equivalent of 'Philistines' existed in Patriarchal Palestine, the introduction of such into the Patriarchal narratives remains an enigma. The kind of evidence utilized here has been almost entirely neglected by Old Testament scholars. Finally, *if* Professor C. H. Gordon's attempted decipherment of the Minoan 'Linear A' language as Semitic *were* to be substantiated,[17] it would agree very well with the 'Philistine' king of Gerar in Genesis 26 bearing a Semitic name or title (Abimelech); but, of course, no weight must be attached to this unless Gordon's thesis proves to be true.[18]

---

3 (1954), pp. 126–127. Note goods reaching Ugarit by boat from Kaptara (*i.e.*, Crete), in Nougayrol, *Palais Royal d'Ugarit*, III, 1955, pp. xxviii, 101, 107. On Egyptian *Keftiu* = both Kaptara and Crete, see J. Vercoutter, *Égyptiens et Préhellènes*, 1954, and more fully *L'Égypte et le monde égéen préhellénique*, 1956. Other references and general survey by J. Prignaud, *RB* 71 (1964), pp. 215–229 (gives too much ground to name-speculations of the Caphtor-Cilicia theory, and too little attention to the fact that K^{e}retim ('Cherethites') are a *later* term than Caphtor and Philistines).

[13] G. Dossin in Pohl, *Orientalia* 19 (1950), p. 509.

[14] Y. Yadin *et al.*, *Hazor II*, 1960, p. 86 with plate 115:12–13; A. Malamat, *JBL* 79 (1960), pp. 18–19.

[15] C. F. A. Schaeffer, *Ugaritica I*, 1939, pp. 54 ff.

[16] References given in H. Kantor, in R. W. Ehrich (ed.), *Relative Chronologies in Old World Archeology*, 1954, pp. 10–15; 1965 ed., pp. 20–24.

[17] See C. H. Gordon, *Antiquity* 31 (1957), pp. 124–130; *JNES* 17 (1958), pp. 245–255; *Klio* 38 (1960), pp. 63–68; *JNES* 21 (1962), pp. 207–210, *cf.* pp. 211–214.

[18] For a brief critical survey of Gordon's and other 'decipherments' of Linear A, see Maurice Pope, *Aegean Writing and Linear A*, 1964 (=*Studies in Mediterranean Archaeology*, VIII, Lund); or J. Chadwick, *Antiquity* 33 (1959), pp. 269–278. On the problem of early Philistines, see T. C. Mitchell, *NBD*, pp. 988–991, and his forthcoming monograph on *The Philistines*.

F

(c) Tirhakah and Hezekiah

Two difficulties have been raised over the mention of 'Tirhakah, king of Ethiopia' (better, Kush) in connection with the
campaign by Sennacherib of Assyria against Hezekiah of
Judah (2 Ki. 19:9; Is. 37:9), usually dated to 701 BC.

First, Tirhakah did not ascend the throne of Egypt and Ethiopia (Kush) until 690 BC.[19] Some scholars therefore assume a
second Assyrian attack on Hezekiah shortly after that date.[20]
But this is probably unnecessary, because the kingly title may
merely have been added by the biblical narrator writing about
the events of 701 at some time after 690, in order to identify
Tirhakah to his readers. It should, perhaps, be stressed that this
kind of prolepsis cannot be classed as an 'error' (as some Old
Testament scholars do), because it is a common practice of
Ancient Oriental writers to refer to people and places by
titles and names acquired later than the period being described. Precisely this usage occurs in Tirhakah's own Kawa
stela IV: 7–8, when it says of *prince* Tirhakah: '*His Majesty* was
in Nubia, as a goodly youth . . . amidst the goodly youths whom
His Majesty King Shebitku had summoned from Nubia . . .'
If Isaiah and Kings are in 'error', so is Kawa IV, an undoub-

---

[19] This date depends on the new date 664 BC (*not* 663) for the beginning
of the Twenty-sixth Dynasty in Egypt (R. A. Parker, *Mitt. d. Deutsch.
Arch. Inst. Kairo* 15 (1957), pp. 208–212; E. Hornung, *ZÄS* 92 (1965), pp.
38–39), and on a twenty-six-year reign of Tirhakah (Parker, *Kush* 8 (1960),
pp. 267–269). There is no ground for accepting a six-year co-regency of
Tirhakah with Shebitku (*cf.* G. Schmidt, *Kush* 6 (1958), pp. 121–130, esp.
123–127), excluded in particular by the express words of Tirhakah himself
(stela Kawa V:14–15): 'I was crowned at Memphis, after the Falcon (=
Shebitku, his predecessor) had flown heavenward' (regular euphemism for a
king's decease).

[20] Recent treatments of this problem, with references, include J. Bright,
A History of Israel, 1960, pp. 282–287, and in *Maqqél Shâqédh* (*FS Vischer*),
1960, pp. 20–31; H. H. Rowley, *Bulletin of the John Rylands Library* 44
(1962), pp. 395–431, and (slightly revised) in his *Men of God*, 1963, pp. 98–
132; also S. H. Horn *AUSS* 4 (1966), 1–28, a very useful survey, but his apodictic claim (p. 2) that it was 'impossible' for Tirhakah to lead an army in
701 BC is itself vitiated by his uncritical acceptance of Macadam's theories,
and failure to grasp the true significance of Leclant and Yoyotte's treatment
of the Kawa texts (*cf.* note 24, below).

tedly first-hand document! A similarly clear example of prolepsis is found on a legal stela of the seventeenth century BC in which an official is referred to at least twice as 'Count of Nekheb' before actually attaining this post.[21] We do the same today, e.g., when we speak of Abraham as coming from 'Mesopotamia', a Greek term from at least fifteen centuries later than the Patriarch![22] No-one calls this an 'error'. And the occasional similar practice of the biblical writers need not be so described either.

Secondly, and more recently, a suggestion by Macadam[23] that Tirhakah was only nine or ten years old in 701 BC has gained wide currency in Old Testament studies as proving that Tirhakah could not have gone to war in 701 BC. A much improved treatment of the Kawa texts by Leclant and Yoyotte,[24] published in 1952, alters this completely and would allow Tirhakah to be about twenty or twenty-one years old in 701 BC, which makes him quite old enough to act on behalf of his brother, King Shebitku, by leading an army to defeat in Palestine. This has so far almost entirely escaped the notice of Old Testament scholars.

The underlying chronology may be baldly summarized as follows.[25] In 716 BC, Sargon II mentions Shilkanni (=Osorkon IV, 'Akheperrē') as king of Egypt,[26] but by 712 BC he is dealing with a 'pharaoh' of Egypt who is also ruler of Kush – who therefore is no Libyan kinglet[27] but a Nubian king, and in fact Shabako, not Piankhy, since the latter did *not* rule north of the Thebaid and Abydos, and had no contact with the Assyrians

[21] Cf. lines 19 and 21 of text in P. Lacau, *Une Stèle Juridique de Karnak*, 1949, and p. 34.

[22] On the origin and early history of this term, see J. J. Finkelstein, *JNES* 21 (1962), pp. 73–92.

[23] Based on inscriptions from the temple of Kawa in Nubia; see M. F. L. Macadam, *The Temples of Kawa*, I, 1949, pp. 18–20.

[24] Published in *BIFAO* 51 (1952), pp. 17–27.

[25] For a fuller statement on the chronology of the Twenty-fifth Dynasty, see Kitchen, *The Third Intermediate Period in Egypt* (forthcoming).

[26] Cf. H. Tadmor, *JCS* 12 (1958), pp. 77, 78; on the name-form Shilkanni, cf. W. F. Albright, *BASOR* 141 (1956), p. 24.

[27] Certainly not Tefnakht or Bekenranef, who never ruled Kush or southern Upper Egypt.

on his one great raid into northern Egypt against Tefnakht. As Shabako appears to have conquered all Egypt by his second year,[28] Piankhy must have died by 713 BC at latest (717/716 BC at earliest). As Tirhakah was a son of Piankhy, biologically he could *not* be only nine in 701 BC (born four to seven years posthumously?)![29] Egyptian foreign policy was one of neutrality to Assyria under Shabako,[30] but changed in 701 when Egyptian forces came out in support of Judah, as reported by Sennacherib. The basic political situation was the same as previously – hence the change of policy reflected in the cuneiform sources is best attributed to a new man in control in Egypt, Shebitku. The latter was probably king in 702/701, and Tirhakah would then be summoned to his brother's court as a youth twenty years old.[31] Once again, the evidence repays closer, more patient study than is often accorded to it.

II. FALSE IDENTIFICATIONS

(a) David and 'Dawidum'

In the Mari texts of the eighteenth century BC, a word *dawidum* was interpreted[32] as 'general' or 'commander', and compared with the name 'David'. It must be said that such a meaning for 'David' would have been quite attractive. The explanation found ready acceptance in Old Testament studies, coupled with the further suggestion that 'David' was perhaps a name or

[28] He was in control at Memphis by then (Serapeum datum), *cf.* J. Vercoutter, *Kush* 8 (1960), pp. 65–67 (whose dates BC are too low).

[29] Macadam's calculation depended on (i) an assumed six-year coregency of Tirhakah and Shebitku, which is pretty certainly erroneous (*cf.* note 19, p. 82, above), and (ii) on referring Tirhakah's age of 20 (Kawa stela V:17) to 690/689 BC, whereas it is ten or twelve years earlier (just after Shebitku's accession).

[30] Shabako repatriated Iamani of Ashdod at Sargon's request in 712 BC (*cf.* Tadmor, *JCS* 12 (1958), p. 83 and references; text in *ANET*, p. 286); sealing of Shabako from Nineveh (Tadmor, *op. cit.*, p. 84).

[31] Kawa stela V: 17. Shabako's thirteen or fourteen years in Egypt (fourteen or fifteen in Nubia) may be placed in 716/5–702/1 BC (and 717/6–702/1, respectively); fuller details in *Third Intermediate Period*.

[32] G. Dossin, *Syria* 19 (1938), pp. 109 f., and *Mélanges Dussaud*, II, 1939, p. 981 n. 1.

title adopted by the Hebrew king and was not his original name.[33]

However, this attractive theory must now, alas, be discarded. First Kupper[34] noticed the curious fact that this supposed word for 'general' or the like was virtually restricted to one kind of context: *dawidam daku*, 'killing the commander' (of a defeated enemy). No modern insurance company would ever have issued a policy on the life of a *dawidum*! Then Tadmor (following Landsberger) pointed out that in fact *dawidum* is merely a phonetic variant of the common Babylonian word *dabdum*, 'defeat'; *dawidam* (or *dabdam*) *daku* merely means 'to defeat' (an enemy). The whole tissue of theory woven round the name 'David' is thus left without any foundation in fact, and must be abandoned.[35] The name 'David' may thus simply mean 'beloved' or be derived from a word for 'uncle' as formerly thought.[36] This example well illustrates with what care we must scrutinize even the most tempting identifications.

(b) 'Solomon's Stables'

Ever since their discovery, the two blocks of Iron Age stables found at Megiddo have been connected by modern writers with Solomon's buildings mentioned in 1 Kings 9:15–19 – hence the name 'Solomon's stables'.[37] However, the precise date of these fine stables has always been subject to certain difficulties, archaeologically. As a result of Yadin's careful study of parts of the Megiddo ruins,[38] two distinct series of remains can now be clearly distinguished. First, there is the superb North Gate, with its 'casemate' walls and two citadels, which clearly

[33] For example, M. Noth, *History of Israel*,[2] 1960, p. 179 n. 2 (following W. von Soden, *Welt des Orients* 1:3 (1948), p. 197).

[34] *Les Nomades en Mésopotamie au Temps des Rois de Mari*, 1957, pp. 58–62, esp. p. 61.

[35] H. Tadmor, *JNES* 17 (1958), pp. 129–131; cf. *Chicago Assyrian Dictionary*, vol. 3/D, 1959, pp. 14–16 on *dabdû*.

[36] See J. J. Stamm, *VTS*, VII, 1960, pp. 165–183, for a full discussion.

[37] R. S. Lamon and G. M. Shipton, *Megiddo I*, 1939, pp. 44, 59, 61; G. E. Wright, *Biblical Archaeology*, 1957, p. 132; many other works likewise.

[38] Y. Yadin, *BA* 23 (1960), pp. 62–68 (esp. p. 68); *The Art of Warfare in Biblical Lands*, 1963, p. 289 and figure.

belong to Solomon's reign; secondly, we have the stables, associated with a *later* solid and recessed city wall, which in fact may be dated to the period of Omri and Ahab. What happens to 1 Kings 9? Nothing, because in fact, as far as Hazor, Megiddo and Gezer are concerned, 1 Kings 9:15 only makes a general mention of building having been done. This is well illustrated by the genuinely Solomonic remains discovered at these three sites. Then, separately, 1 Kings 9:19 mentions Solomon's store-cities and cities for chariots and horsemen, without actually naming them. Thus 1 Kings 9 does not in fact imply the existence of stables of Solomon at Megiddo at all, although this was hitherto assumed by most writers (including the present one). It illustrates the need to be sure that we correlate what the biblical text states, not what we think it states, with other data.

5. HEBREW CONTACTS WITH NEAR EASTERN RELIGIONS

I. INTRODUCTION: SOME GENERAL PRINCIPLES

(a) The Question of Relationship

A major question in the study of Old Testament and Ancient Near Eastern religion is that of the significance of similarities, real or supposed. What degree of relationship (if any) do they imply? Three degrees of possible relationship may be defined:

1. Characteristics common to human society the world over. These are so general that they are almost valueless for our present enquiry.

2. Characteristics common to, and at home with, both the Hebrews and their contemporaries. These are the mark of a common cultural heritage.

3. Characteristics which are at home in one culture (and have a history there) may suddenly appear (without any antecedents) in another culture, perhaps being modified and/or assimilated, or even dying out again.[1] This would represent a borrowing by the latter culture from the former[2] (or *transfer*, to use a more neutral term).

(b) Basis for the Investigation of these Questions

It should be said that there is nothing inherently wrong in cultural borrowing or transfer; it can be a source of enrichment.

[1] For an excellent example of this in relation to Egypt and Mesopotamia, see H. Frankfort, *The Birth of Civilization in the Near East*, 1951, pp. 83, 100–101 (Appendix).

[2] Always supposing, of course, that the 'sudden' appearance of phenomena in the second culture is not really the chance result of *lack* of evidence (*i.e.*, negative evidence) for its having a prior history there. Allowance must always be made for this source of uncertainty according to the state of documentation available.

And it is worth remarking that the God of the Old Testament is portrayed as exercising control not only over Israel but also over Israel's environment.

On the other hand, denial of the unique elements in any culture, or misreading the elements of one culture in terms of another, only produces gross distortion of the understanding, whether it be in relation to Old Testament religion and literature or to any other Ancient Near Eastern culture (Egypt, Mesopotamia, *etc.*).

In fact, it is necessary to deal individually and on its own merits with each possible or alleged case of relationship or borrowing by making a detailed comparison of the full available data from both the Old Testament and the Ancient Orient and by noting the results.[3] In the following examples, lack of space forbids any such full treatment. Instead only the main results of a few such investigations can be given and some of the more important details noted.

II. CREATION AND FLOOD STORIES

There is no indisputable evidence that the Hebrew accounts are directly dependent upon the known Babylonian epics, despite a common belief to the contrary. Patriarchal origins in Mesopotamia point back to a common stream of tradition, known to be fully developed early in the second millennium BC.[4]

(a) Creation

The aims of Genesis 1 and 2 and of the so-called 'Babylonian Creation' (*Enuma Elish*) are quite distinct. Genesis aims to portray the sole God as sovereign creator, whereas the primary purpose of *Enuma Elish* is to exalt the chief god of the Babylonian pantheon by narrating how he and his city attained supremacy,

---

[3] A good example is the recent study of the possible relationship of Proverbs with the Egyptian Instruction of Amenemope by J. Ruffle (scheduled for early publication); careful study of both books *in their full Near Eastern context* (instead of in isolation, as is commonly done) has shown how inadequate are the grounds for relationship offered hitherto.

[4] *Cf.* above, p. 41, (*c*); other indications must be passed over, here.

in cosmological terms;[5] the acts of creation attributed to the deity at the end serve this main purpose of glorifying him and also define the role of man in relation to the gods (their servant). Moreover, in this so-called 'creation-narrative', only about one-sixth deals with creative acts – all the rest is occupied by the main theme of how Marduk of Babylon became supreme, plus the list of his fifty names.[6] The contrast between the monotheism and simplicity of the Hebrew account and the polytheism and elaboration of the Mesopotamian epic is obvious to any reader. The common assumption that the Hebrew account is simply a purged and simplified version of the Babylonian legend (applied also to the Flood stories) is fallacious on *methodological* grounds. In the Ancient Near East, the rule is that simple accounts or traditions may give rise (by accretion and embellishment) to elaborate legends,[7] but not vice versa. In the Ancient Orient, legends were not simplified or turned into pseudo-history (historicized) as has been assumed for early Genesis.

Another complete fallacy is the belief that the word *tehom*, 'deep', in Genesis 1:2, shows dependence of the Hebrew upon the Babylonian. In fact the Hebrew word is linguistically a zero form (unaugmented by formative elements) and cannot be derived from the Babylonian word *Ti'amat* which is itself a derived form, principally a proper name, and in any case shows different contextual usage. In fact, *tehom* is common Semitic, as shown by Ugaritic *thm*, 'deep' (also in plural and dual) from

[5] *Cf.* A. L. Oppenheim, *Ancient Mesopotamia*, 1964, p. 233 top; Heidel in next note.

[6] On these matters, see A. Heidel, *The Babylonian Genesis*[2], 1951 (paperback, 1963), pp. 10–11. For translations of the Epic, see Heidel, *op. cit.*, and Speiser, *ANET*[2], pp. 60–72, 514.

[7] This process can be illustrated in Egypt from the legend of Sesostris (K. Sethe, *Sesostris* in *Untersuchungen Äg. Altertums*, II: 1, 1900: *cf.* G. Posener, *Littérature et Politique dans l'Égypte de la XIIe Dynastie*, 1956, pp. 141–144), and from progressive exaggerations in later traditions about the rule of the Hyksos kings in Egypt (see T. Säve-Söderbergh, *JEA* 37 (1951), pp. 53–71, esp. 55–56, 61, 64, 69–70). In Mesopotamia, *cf.* the growth of traditions around Gilgamesh king of Uruk (W. G. Lambert in P. Garelli (ed.), *Gilgameš et sa Légende*, 1960, pp. 50–52). For *Enuma Elish*, etc., *cf.* also the remarks of A. L. Oppenheim, *Ancient Mesopotamia*, 1964, pp. 177–178.

early in the second millennium BC,[8] in contexts that have no conceivable link with the Babylonian epic. Thus there is no evidence here for Hebrew borrowing from Babylonian,[9] and even the existence of any real relationship at all between Genesis and *Enuma Elish* is open to considerable doubt.[10]

(b) The Flood

In the case of Genesis 6 to 8 and the Mesopotamian stories of the Flood, the situation is different.[11] A series of basic general similarities suggests a definite relationship between the two traditions; but there are also many detailed differences (form of Ark, duration of Flood, the birds) and the Hebrew version is again simpler and less evolved. The Hebrew and Babylonian accounts may go back to a common ancient tradition, but are not borrowed directly from each other.[12] The verdict of some specialists in cuneiform literature (*e.g.*, Heidel, Kinnier-Wilson) is even more cautious,[13] a fact that ought to be remembered in Old Testament studies.

III. THE SINAI COVENANT

At the heart of ancient Israelite religion stands the concept of

[8] *Thm/thmt/thmtm* occurs in the epics of Baal and 'Anath, Aqhat (originating in the twentieth to sixteenth centuries BC; see references quoted in note 93, p. 52, above), and in the Birth of Shahar and Shalim; refs. in G. D. Young, *Concordance of Ugaritic*, 1956, p. 68, No. 1925.

[9] The basic philological facts are presented by Heidel, *op. cit.*, pp. 98–101 (*cf.* also J. V. Kinnier Wilson in *DOTT*, p. 14), however unwilling some Old Testament scholars may be to face them. Such misconceptions are also exposed by W. G. Lambert, *JTS* 16 (1965), 287–300 (esp. 289, 291, 293–299, for creation).

[10] *E.g.*, Kinnier Wilson, *op. cit.*, p. 14.

[11] Translations in *ANET*[2], pp. 42–44, 72–99; for the Gilgamesh Epic, see also A. Heidel, *The Gilgamesh Epic and Old Testament Parallels*[2], 1949 (paperback, 1963); M. David, in Garelli, *op. cit.*, pp. 153–159. For the Atrakhasis Epic, see references given above, p. 41, notes 25–27.

[12] Full and careful discussion by Heidel, *Gilgamesh Epic . . .*, pp. 224–269.

[13] *Cf.* Heidel, *op. cit.*, pp. 267–268; Kinnier Wilson, *DOTT*, p. 21 ('fundamental difference'). Lambert, *op. cit.*, pp. 291–293, 299, also delimits the possibilities of relationship, but too easily rejects 'common tradition' going far back, on inconclusive and largely negative (hence unsatisfactory) grounds.

the covenant, and in particular the covenant made between Israel and her God at Mount Sinai.[14] Mendenhall has pointed out[15] striking parallels in form between this covenant in Exodus 20 ff. (renewed in Joshua 24) and the international covenants or treaties of the fourteenth/thirteenth centuries BC recovered mainly from the Hittite archives at Boghazköy.[16] He also suggested that there was a significant difference in form between these late-second-millennium treaties[17] and treaties of the first millennium BC, and that the form of the Sinai covenant corresponded to that of the treaties of the second millennium but not to those of the first millennium BC.[18] This, if

[14] Expounded notably by W. Eichrodt, *Theology of the Old Testament*, I, 1961 (translated from sixth German edition, 1959).

[15] In *BA* 17 (1954), pp. 26–46, 50–76 (esp. 53–70), reprinted as *Law and Covenant in Israel and the Ancient Near East*, 1955. Subsequent general studies include: K. Baltzer, *Das Bundesformular*, 1960; D. J. McCarthy, *Treaty and Covenant*, 1963; H. B. Huffmon, *CBQ* 27 (1965), pp. 101–113; F. Nötscher, *Biblische Zeitschrift (NF)* 9 (1965), pp. 181–214; J. A. Thompson, *The Ancient Near Eastern Treaties and the Old Testament*, 1964. Surveys: A. S. Kapelrud, *Studia Theologica* 18 (1964), pp. 81–90; D. J. McCarthy, *CBQ* 27 (1965), pp. 217–240. On Deuteronomy, *cf.* M. G. Kline, *Treaty of the Great King*, 1963 (including studies that appeared in *WTJ* 22 (1959/60) and 23 (1960/61)). On phraseology, *etc.*: E. Mørstad, *Wenn du der Stimme des Herrn, Deines Gottes, gehorchen wirst . . .* , 1960; J. N. M. Wijngaards, *The Formulas of the Deuteronomic Creed*, 1963, and *VT* 15 (1965), pp. 91–102.

[16] The principal treaties are published in: E. F. Weidner, *Politische Dokumente aus Kleinasien*, I/II, 1923, and J. Friedrich, *Staatsverträge des Hatti-Reiches*, I/II, 1926/30 (=*MVÄG*, 31:1 and 34:1), to which add J. Nougayrol, *Palais Royal d'Ugarit*, IV, 1956, pp. 85–101, 287–289; H. Freydank, *MIO* 7 (1960), pp. 356–381; H. Klengel, *OLZ* 59 (1964), col. 437–445, and *ZA* 56/NF 22 (1964), pp. 213–217; E. von Schuler, *Die Kaškäer*, 1965, pp. 109–140. Further references for texts and studies, *cf.* A. Goetze, *Kleinasien²*, 1957, pp. 95–96, and McCarthy, *Treaty and Covenant*, 1963, pp. xiii-xiv; xv ff.

[17] Earlier treaties down to the fifteenth century BC (i) are too early for comparison with data of Moses or later time, and (ii) do not have the fully developed form of the fourteenth/thirteenth centuries BC. Hence, however relevant to earlier covenants, they require no consideration here.

[18] *BA* 17 (1954), pp. 56 end and n. 19; 61. In favour of Mendenhall's view, M. G. Kline, *WTJ* 23 (1960/61), pp. 1–15, and *Treaty of the Great King*, 1963, pp. 42–44, 48 and *passim*; Kitchen (unpublished observations from 1955); W. F. Albright, *From the Stone Age to Christianity*, 1957, p. 16 end; W. L. Moran, *Biblica* 43 (1962), p. 103, and J. Harvey, *ibid.*, p. 185 ('âge mosaique', *cf.* p. 175 with Huffmon, *JBL* 78 (1959), p. 295); S. R.

true, would suggest that the Sinai covenant (like its strictest parallels) really did originate in the thirteenth century BC at the latest,[19] *i.e.*, in the general period of Moses. However, because there are some elements common to the covenants of both the second and first millennia BC, some scholars would claim that in fact there was no basic change in covenant-forms as between the second and first millennia BC.[20] In this case, the parallel between the Sinai covenant and the second-millennium treaties would lose something of its chronological significance but not its value for our general understanding of covenants. In view of this divergence of opinion, a brief re-examination of the forms of the Ancient Oriental and Sinai covenants is desirable.[21]

(a) Covenants of the Late Second Millennium BC

These covenants show a remarkably consistent scheme, as established by Korošec[22] and summarized by Mendenhall:[23]

1. *Preamble or title*, identifying the author of the covenant.
2. *Historical prologue* or retrospect, mentioning previous re-

Külling, *Zur Datierung der 'Genesis-P-Stücke'* (*Gen. XVII*), 1964, pp. 238–239; *cf.* H. B. Huffmon, *CBQ* 27 (1965), p. 109 and n. 41.

[19] About 1200 BC, movements of peoples with the incoming Iron Age, *etc.*, altered political and other conditions in the Ancient Orient quite considerably; *cf.* Goetze, *Kleinasien*², 1957, pp. 184–187; H. Schmökel, *HdO*, II: 3, pp. 138–140, 222, 228, 230, 236–237; and esp. Kitchen, *Hittite Hieroglyphs, Aramaeans and Hebrew Traditions*, ch. 3 (forthcoming).

[20] See (*e.g.*) E. Vogt, *Biblica* 39 (1958), pp. 269, 543; D. J. Wiseman, *Iraq* 20 (1958), p. 28; F. C. Fensham, *ZAW* 74 (1962), p. 1 and n. 6; J. A. Thompson, *The Ancient Near Eastern Treaties and the Old Testament*, 1964, pp. 14–15; D. J. McCarthy, *Treaty and Covenant*, 1963, pp. 7, 80 ff. (but impelled to note differences, 'sub-groups', p. 82, *etc.*).

[21] What follows is primarily based on my own unpublished analysis of the published texts of over thirty Ancient Near Eastern treaties (six or seven of first millennium BC, the rest of late second millennium BC). Only the barest outlines can be given here; details and other aspects must await a fuller presentation elsewhere.

[22] In his fundamental work, *Hethitische Staatsverträge*, 1931 (a new edition is expected); our main concern here is with the vassal or suzerainty treaties imposed on a vassal by an overlord or Great King.

[23] *BA* 17 (1954), pp. 58–61.

lations between the two parties involved; past bene-
factions by the suzerain are a basis for the vassal's
gratitude and future obedience.

3. *Stipulations*, basic and detailed;[24] the obligations laid upon
the vassal by the sovereign.

4. (*a*). *Deposition* of a copy of the covenant in the vassal's
sanctuary and

   (*b*). *Periodic public reading* of the covenant terms to the
people.

5. *Witnesses*, a long list of gods invoked to witness the covenant.

6. (*a*). *Curses*, invoked upon the vassal if he breaks the covenant, and

   (*b*). *Blessings*, invoked upon the vassal if he keeps the
covenant.

Nearly all the known treaties of the fourteenth/thirteenth
centuries BC follow this pattern closely. Sometimes some elements are omitted, but the order of them is almost invariable,[25]
whenever the original texts are sufficiently well preserved to be
analysed. This is, therefore, a stable form in the period concerned. Earlier than this, the pattern was apparently somewhat
different.[26] Besides these written elements, there were apparently
also:

[24] For this distinction, *cf.* K. Baltzer, *Das Bundesformular*, 1960, pp.
20, 22–24 ('Grundsatzerklärung' and 'Einzelbestimmungen').

[25] Among all the late-2nd-millennium treaties analysed, only one had
its historical prologue between two lots of stipulations (with Amurru, in
Hittite and Babylonian versions; Freydank, *MIO* 7 (1960), pp. 358 ff.
(text), 366 ff. (translation), with short basic stipulations just after the title,
plus H. Klengel, *OLZ* 59 (1964), col. 437–445). And when the treaties are
concluded with tribal groups or leaders, not monarchs as vassals, the divine
witnesses can appear in this position; so E. von Schuler, in G. Walser
(ed.), *Neuere Hethiterforschung*, 1964 (=*Historia, Einzelschrift* 7), p. 38, citing
treaties with Hukkanas and the Hayasa-people (Friedrich, *Staatsverträge*,
II, No. 6), with Ishmirikka, Gasgeans, *etc.* (sources in Laroche, *RHA* 14/
Fasc. 59 (1956), pp. 78–79, Nos. 87, 95, 96).

[26] *Cf.* H. Otten, *JCS* 5 (1951), p. 132 end; W. L. Moran, *Biblica* 43
(1962), p. 104 middle; S. R. Külling, *Zur Datierung der 'Genesis-P-Stücke'*,
p. 229.

7. A formal *oath of obedience.*
8. An accompanying *solemn ceremony.*
9. A formal *procedure* for acting *against rebellious vassals.*

(b) Covenants of the First Millennium

For the first millennium BC, our material is at present much less extensive. It consists of some six Assyrian treaties of the ninth to seventh centuries BC,[27] and the Aramaic treaty or treaties[28] of the eighth century BC,[29] of Bar-Ga'yah and Mati-el. An analysis of even this limited material shows the following picture:

1. *Preamble or title* (where the beginning of the text exists).

2. ⎫
3. ⎬ then *Stipulations* and *Curses,*[30] succeeded *or* preceded by the divine *Witnesses.*[31]
4. ⎭

[27] 1. Shamshi-Adad V, *c.* 820 BC (Weidner, *AfO* 8 (1932), pp. 27–29); 2. Assurnirari VI and Mati-el, *c.* 754 BC (Weidner, *AfO* 8 (1932), pp. 17–27; McCarthy, *Treaty and Covenant,* pp. 195–197); 3. Esarhaddon and Baal of Tyre, *c.* 677 BC (Weidner, *op. cit.,* pp. 29–34; McCarthy, *op. cit.,* p. 72 n. 15, pp. 197–198; R. Borger, *Die Inschriften Asarhaddons,* 1956, pp. 107–109); 4. Esarhaddon and the Medes, 672 BC, nine duplicates on one pattern (Wiseman, *Vassal-Treaties of Esarhaddon = Iraq* 20 (1958), pp. 1–99); 5. Assurbanipal as crown prince (Weidner, *AfO* 13 (1940), p. 215 (c); Taf. 14, VAT 11534); 6. Assurbanipal, his brother, *etc.* (*cf.* Harper, *Assyrian and Babylonian Letters,* 1105, recto 5–25; L. Waterman, *Royal Correspondence of the Assyrian Empire,* II, 1931, pp. 266–269); 7. Sin-shar-ishkun (Weidner, *op. cit.,* p. 215, n. 69, Assur 13955z); 8. Other fragments (*e.g.,* Clay-Borger fragment, Borger, *Wiener Zeitschrift für die Kunde des Morgenlandes* 55 (1959), pp. 73–74).
[28] Three copies of one treaty, or up to three related treaties (Sfîré I, II, III). *Cf.* M. Noth, *ZDPV* 77 (1961), pp. 126 ff., 147–151, 168–170, *etc.,* and McCarthy, *Treaty and Covenant,* 1963, p. 62.
[29] A. Dupont-Sommer, *Les Inscriptions Araméennes de Sfîré (Stèles I et II),* 1958, and in *Bulletin du Musée de Beyrouth* 13 (1956/58), pp. 23–41 (=III). Subsequent studies include: J. Fitzmyer, *CBQ* 20 (1958), pp. 444–476; *JAOS* 81 (1961), pp. 178–222; F. Rosenthal, *BASOR* 158 (1960), pp. 28–31; J. C. Greenfield, *Acta Orientalia* 29 (1965), pp. 1–18; also, works cited in notes 30, 32, below.
[30] Or reversed: *i.e.,* Curses then Stipulations. For treaty-curses, *cf.* F. C. Fensham, *BA* 25 (1962), pp. 48–50; *ZAW* 74 (1962), pp. 1–9; *ZAW* 75 (1963), pp. 155–175; K. R. Veenhof, *Bibliotheca Orientalis* 20

While the second- and first-millennium covenants have a common core of Title, Stipulations, Witnesses and Curses, and also share some vocabulary and forms of expression,[32] yet these are the banal, obvious things. One expects a title to any formal document; any covenant must have stipulations or conditions; witnesses are necessary guarantors for many kinds of legal documents; the curse was an automatic sanction against disobedience; and some common terminology is only to be expected. Much more significant are the *differences*:

1. In the late-second-millennium covenants so far as preserved, the divine witnesses *almost always*[33] come between the stipulations and the curses, whereas in the first-millennium covenants so far known they *never* do.

2. A historical prologue is *typical* of late-second-millennium covenants, but is *unknown* in our first-millennium examples.[34]

(1963), pp. 142–144; and esp. D. R. Hillers, *Treaty-Curses and the Old Testament Prophets*, 1964.

[31] Witnesses precede Stipulations and Curses in the Aramaic covenant and the seventh-century Assyrian treaties; they follow in at least one of the earlier Assyrian treaties.

[32] On common modes of expression, *cf.* Fensham, *loc. cit.*, and *JNES* 22 (1963), pp. 185–186, and W. L. Moran, *ibid.*, pp. 173–176, and *CBQ* 25 (1963), pp. 77–87; D. R. Hillers, *BASOR* 176 (1964), pp. 46–47; A. R. Millard, 'For He is Good', *THB* 17 (1966), pp. 115 ff.; these studies usually include OT terminology; for possible Syrian and Egyptian references (2nd millennium) to *berît*, *cf.* Albright, *BASOR* 121 (1951), pp. 21–22, and McCarthy, *Treaty and Covenant*, 1963, p. 105 and n. 26. The Aramaic treaty also has (in I, C: 16–24; II, C:1–16) additional curses upon anyone who damages the inscription, but this is not peculiar to treaties; *cf.* S. Gevirtz, *VT* 11 (1961), pp. 137–158, esp. 140–146.

[33] For a special class of exceptions, *cf.* above, p. 93, note 25.

[34] Thompson's expedients to explain away the lack of historical prologues in first-millennium treaties (*The Ancient Near Eastern Treaties and the Old Testament*, 1964, pp. 14–15) are hardly convincing. The Sfiré and esp. Esarhaddon/Medes treaties are well enough preserved to rule out loss of historical prologues in those cases (*re* the latter, if the prologue was on a separate tablet – then how curious that *no* fragments of such tablets should turn up among those of the 'other' tablet for *nine* parallel treaty-documents!). His appeal to possible oral declaration only, for historical prologues, is an empty guess, unsupported by evidence (and contrast n. 3, end). Where differences exist among groups of treaties, there is no merit in glossing over

3. In late-second-millennium covenants, the blessings are a *regular*, balancing pendant to the curses; in the first-millennium documents, the curses have *no* corresponding blessings.[35]

4. The order of elements in late-second-millennium treaties shows *great consistency*, but the first-millennium ones show *varying usage*: stipulations and curses may occur in either order and be either preceded or succeeded by the witnesses.

Thus, on the evidence now available, there *are* clear and undeniable differences in form and content between covenants of the late second and the first millennia BC.

(c) Analysis of the Sinai Covenant

The Sinai covenant is first preserved in Exodus 20 to 31; it was broken by the idolatry of the people (Ex. 32–33), and so had to be renewed immediately (Ex. 34). In the plains of Moab, this covenant was renewed with a new generation (Dt. 1–32: 47; (recapitulated in 29–30)), and again at Shechem (Jos. 24). In the analysis below, the three main (and one subsidiary) parallel sets of references are lettered A, B, (C), D, for clarity. The following elements may be discerned:

1. *Preamble:* A. Exodus 20:1. B. Deuteronomy 1:1–5. (C. Dt. 29:1?). D. Joshua 24:2.
2. *Historical prologue:* A. Exodus 20:2. B. Deuteronomy 1:6–3:29.[36] (C. Dt. 29:2-8). D. Joshua 24:2–13.

---

them. On the other hand, it is just possible that the so-called 'Synchronous History' was part of the prologue of a treaty (A. L. Oppenheim, *Ancient Mesopotamia*, 1964, pp. 146, 284); however, its inordinate time-span of events (700 years, fifteenth–eighth centuries BC) marks it off from all others, and this and its general scheme are more reminiscent of certain chronicle-texts (*e.g.*, Chronicle P); see also p. 73, note 61, above.

[35] In Sfiré II, B:4, there seems to be just one blessing – a far cry from the antithesis of Curses/Blessings in late-2nd-millennium covenants. That in Sfiré I, C: 15-16 relates to respect of the inscription, not the treaty (*cf.* Lipit-Ishtar and Hammurapi laws, epilogues), while III: 28–29 might even be a curse on bribery (entirely uncertain), *cf.* version of Rosenthal, *BASOR* 158 (1960), p. 31; Fitzmyer, *CBQ* 20 (1958), p. 464.

[36] In this passage, the 'we-form' has no relevance to its status as a historical prologue (*contra* Moran, *Biblica* 43 (1962), p. 105); one must not forget that Moses is here not only spokesman from God (as Sovereign) but

3. *Stipulations:* A. Exodus 20:3–17, 22–26 (basic); Exodus 21–23, 25–31 (detailed), plus Leviticus 1–25 ?? B. Deuteronomy 4, 5–11 (basic); 12–26 (detailed). (C. Dt. 29:9–31:8). D. Joshua 24:14–15 (plus 16–25, the people's response, *etc.*).

4. (*a*). *Deposition of Text:* A. Exodus 25:16;[37] Exodus 34:1, 28, 29; *cf.* Deuteronomy 10:1–5 (retrospect). B. Deuteronomy 31:9, 24–26. D. *Cf.* Joshua 24:26 (written in the book of the law).

    (*b*). *Public reading:* B. Deuteronomy 31:10–13.

5. *Witnesses:* The gods of paganism were excluded, so the god-lists of the Ancient Oriental covenants are not found in the biblical ones. Instead, memorial-stones could be a witness (A. Ex. 24:4; *cf.* D. Jos. 24:27), or Moses' song (B. Dt. 31:16–30; Dt. 32:1–47),[38] or the law-book itself (B. Dt. 31:26), or even the people as participants (D. Jos. 24:22).

6. *Curses and Blessings* occur not in this order but reversed in the Old Testament, following the witness.[39] A. Perhaps, *cf.* Leviticus 26:3–13 (blessings), 14–20 (curses; with more for repeated disobedience, 21–33).[40] B. Deuteronomy 28:1–14 (blessings), 15–68 (curses).[41] D. Implicit in Joshua 24:19–20.[42]

---

also leader of the subject people who had shared with them these historical experiences.

[37] The 'testimony' to be put in the Ark of the Covenant was the tablets of that Covenant, *i.e.* bearing the ten commandments (basic stipulations); for the word concerned (*'edūth*), see below, p. 108, note 84.

[38] Note the appeal to 'heaven and earth' (Dt. 32:1); on Dt. 32, see just below, item 9.

[39] In the sequence Blessings-Curses-Witness (*exact* reversal). This would appear to be a specifically OT feature, not unconnected with the difference in kind of witnesses invoked. For a similar (but not identical) special variation in late-second-millennium treaties, those made with peoples (as Israel was one), *cf.* above, p. 93, note 25.

[40] The addition of a period of discipline (verses 34–39) and of a promise of restoration (verses 40–45) seems particular to the Old Testament.

[41] For the curses being longer than the blessings section, one may suitably compare the same situation at the end of the Lipit-Ishtar laws (*ANET*,

G

Over and above this, one may see indications of items 7 and 8, the *oath* and *solemn ceremony*: A. Exodus 24:1–11. B. Deuteronomy 27[43] (fulfilled, Jos. 8:30–35). And finally, the Old Testament equivalent for the *procedure* for action *against a faithless vassal* or covenant-partner (9) is the so-called 'controversy (Hebrew *rîb*) pattern', in which (ultimately through the prophets) the God of Israel arraigns this people for breaking the covenant. The relevant form taken by the 'controversy pattern' in such cases directly reflects the covenant-form (historical retrospect, *etc.*),[44] finds its starting-point in Deuteronomy 32, and has appropriate good parallels in the second millennium BC.[45]

(d) Comparison and Consequences

Now if we take the nature and order of nearly all the elements in the Old Testament Sinai covenant and its renewals as briefly listed above, and compare these with the patterns of the late-second and the first millennium treaties already outlined, it is strikingly evident that the Sinai covenant and its renewals

---

p. 161: three blessing-clauses; fragments of eight or nine curses out of others now lost), and the Hammurapi laws (*ANET*, pp. 178–180: two blessing-clauses (rev. xxvi: 2 ff.) and forty curses ('may . . .')). The motive of additional deterrent may inspire the inclusion of more curses than blessings; and Ex.-Dt. are laws as well as covenant.

[42] *Cf.* K. Baltzer, *Das Bundesformular*, 1960, p. 35; McCarthy's remarks on this verse (*Treaty and Covenant*, 1963, pp. 146–147 and n. 11) fail entirely to allow for the conditional nature of the curses explicit in verse 20, showing that verse 19 is merely strongly expressed. No 'chronological' clue exists here, and still less in Deuteronomy.

[43] The parallel between the Ex. and Dt. passages is here noted also by McCarthy (*Treaty and Covenant*, p. 173 and n. 11), but not there recognized as constituting the oath and ceremony of treaty-form.

[44] See the valuable studies by H. B. Huffmon, *JBL* 78 (1959), pp. 285–295, esp. 294–295, and J. Harvey, *Biblica* 43 (1962), pp. 172–196; also M. Delcor, *VT* 16 (1966), 8–25 (esp. 19–25).

[45] Texts of Tukulti-Ninurta I of Assyria, late thirteenth century BC, and of Yarim-lim of Aleppo (Yamkhad) in the eighteenth century BC; see Harvey, *op. cit.*, pp. 180–184.

must be classed with the late-second-millennium covenants;[46] it is entirely different in arrangement from the first-millennium covenants and shares with them only the indispensable common core (title, stipulations, witness and curses) and some terminology. In other words, on the total evidence now available, Mendenhall's original view is correct, that in form the Sinai covenant corresponds to the late-second-millennium treaties and not to those of the first millennium.

Accordingly, the obvious and only adequate explanation of this clear fact is that the Sinai covenant really was instituted and renewed in the thirteenth century BC (presumably under Moses at Sinai and in the plains of Moab, and under Joshua at Shechem)[47] – at *precisely* the period of the other late-second-millennium covenants (fourteenth to thirteenth centuries BC) – and is directly reflected in the frameworks and text of Exodus, Leviticus (chapter 26 at least), Deuteronomy and Joshua 24.[48] This provides tangible, external ground for suggesting that considerable portions of these books (or, at least, of their contents), including almost the entire framework of Deuteronomy, originated in this same period.[49]

---

[46] G. von Rad now admits freely (*Old Testament Theology*, I, 1962, p. 132) that a comparison with the Ancient Near Eastern treaties (especially the Hittite ones) shows 'so many things in common between the two, particularly in the matter of form, that there must be some connection between these suzerainty treaties and the exposition of the details of Jahweh's covenant with Israel given in certain passages of the Old Testament' (*cf.* Kline, *WTJ* 27 (1964), p. 5 and n. 10).

[47] As far as I know, no other tradition, biblical or extra-biblical, is available to provide names for alternative leaders to Moses and Joshua; and yet *someone* has to take a leading role when a covenant is instituted or renewed. Hence the natural suggestion of Moses and Joshua, despite the phobia attaching to these figures in Old Testament studies, esp. in Germany.

[48] Otherwise, as noted by K. Koch, *Was ist Formgeschichte?*, 1964, p. 24, this clear relationship (noted even by von Rad) remains 'yet unexplained'.

[49] I am thinking here primarily of the covenant-structure and content of the passages concerned. On the laws-aspect, much also can be said but must be left aside for presentation elsewhere. Useful comparisons between the curses of Dt. and Neo-Assyrian treaties are made by R. Frankena,

If these works first took fixed literary forms only in the ninth to sixth centuries BC[50] and onward, why and how should their writers (or redactors) so easily be able to reproduce covenant-forms that had fallen out of customary use 300 to 600 years earlier (*i.e.*, after about 1200 BC), and entirely fail to reflect the first-millennium covenant-forms that were commonly used in their own day? It is very improbable that Hebrew priests under the monarchy or after the exile would go excavating in Late Bronze Age ruins specially to seek for treaty/covenant forms that in their day would be merely exotic literary antiquities; so far, there is not a scrap of tangible evidence to show that the late-second-millennium pattern survived into the first millennium anywhere but in Israelite religious tradition – and the positive existence and wide use of new forms in the first millennium speak suggestively against the idea of any extensive survival of the older forms. It is surely entirely more rational to admit the plain explanation of a Sinai covenant actually made and renewed in the thirteenth century BC. If this result, attained by a *Formgeschichte* controlled by an external standard of measurement, perchance clashes either in general[51] or in detail[52]

Oudtestamentische Studien 14 (1965), 122–154, and M. Weinfeld, *Biblica* 46 (1965), 417–427, following on R. Borger, *ZA* 54/NF 20 (1961), 191–192. However, they betray some naïvety in assuming that similarity automatically spells Hebrew dependence on late Assyrian usage. The Old Babylonian data cited by Weinfeld (pp. 422, 423) already point toward a different answer – to a long-standing tradition going well back into the second millennium at least, which could have become known in the Westlands even before Moses.

[50] *E.g.*, Deuteronomy considered to be written just before 621 BC, or at some period before or after this date (survey in Eissfeldt, *The Old Testament, an Introduction*, 1965, pp. 171–173).

[51] As Old Testament scholars are now recognizing, Wellhausen's denial of the priority of the covenant in Israel in favour of the prophets (themselves suitably emended) must be firmly discarded; *cf.* (*e.g.*) W. Zimmerli, *The Law and the Prophets*, 1965, pp. 30, 61, 68, 93, and *passim*, or R. E. Clements, *Prophecy and Covenant*, 1965 (=*SBT*, No. 43), pp. 15, 17, and esp. 22–23; also *passim*. But retrograde steps can occur. In *JNES* 22 (1963), pp. 37–48, C. F. Whitley simply evaded the clear structural correspondences between the Sinai and second-millennium covenants established by Mendenhall (independently of either terminology or assumptions about covenants and

with certain long-cherished theories of Hebrew religious evolution or of literary criticism, then (with all due respect) so much the worse for the theories in this field. Facts must take precedence,[53] and theories be adjusted to fit them or else (like

amphictyony), merely reiterating Wellhausen's position and, like the latter, gaily emending the prophets in order, as Hillers bluntly but justly observed, 'to make the facts fit a preconceived notion' (*Treaty-Curses and the Old Testament Prophets*, p. 83). E. Gerstenberger (*JBL* 84 (1965), pp. 38–51) quite failed to see the significance of the *written forms* of both Ancient Oriental and biblical covenants; reduction to three main elements (p. 45) is illusory. His evident feeling that the Sinai covenant is also law is justified, but does not exclude it from the covenant-category or -form.

[52] It is becoming increasingly evident that – regardless of the date of forms – the literary characteristics of the Ancient Near Eastern treaties make nonsense of the usual criteria of conventional literary criticism. A typical selection of such criteria from Steuernagel, König, Wright and Welch (used by many others) as applied to Dt. 28 are exposed as worthless in practice when compared with the first-hand texts of other Near Eastern covenants; see in particular D. R. Hillers, *Treaty-Curses and the Old Testament Prophets*, 1964, pp. 30–35. Furthermore, one should note that it is only the *complete* text in Gn., Ex., Jos., etc. – and *not* the supposed 'J' or 'E' (*etc.*) documents – of OT covenant-forms that corresponds to the Ancient Oriental analogues; examples, *cf.* J. A. Thompson, *THB* 13 (1963), pp. 3–5; *TSF Bulletin* 37 (1963), pp. 7–8; summarizing, *Ancient Near Eastern Treaties and the Old Testament*, 1964, pp. 33–35. The explanation is surely that our existing Hebrew text exhibits an original literary form actually used in antiquity – but 'J', 'E', *etc.*, do not; their *Sitz im Leben* is really the eighteenth/nineteenth centuries AD. For other indications of this kind, *cf.* below: Chapter 6, *Literary Criticism*, pp. 127 f. Changes of person, recurrent formulae, varied forms of command or curse, *etc.*, simply cannot be used as mechanical criteria.

[53] Thus McCarthy's difficulties (*Treaty and Covenant*, 1963, ch. 12, *etc.*) in appreciating the covenant form in Ex. (incl. Decalogue) and Jos. are at heart artificial because they are of his own making. Instead of using the extant text of Ex. and Jos., he dragged in the hypothetical J, E documentary fragments. As also noted by M. G. Kline (*WTJ* 27 (1964), p. 20, n. 30), this will not do; *cf.* previous note. In *Treaty and Covenant*, p. 154, McCarthy blithely makes the astonishing assumption that the casual combination of J, E sources and rearrangement of text in Exodus (by redactors *centuries* later than second-millennium covenants, of course) should just happen to produce a direct correspondence with a covenant-form half a millennium obsolete! A miracle indeed. On Jos. 24, note Huffmon's comment, *CBQ* 27 (1965), p. 104, n. 16. For omission of curses in second-millennium covenants (McCarthy, *op. cit.*, pp. 166–167), *cf.* omission with space available

Sethe's 'Hatshepsut theory', p. 22, with n. 18, above) be discarded. At least there can be little doubt that the early Hebrews thus used a set form which was common all over the Ancient Near East and used it in a unique way – to express the relation between a people and its sovereign God, their real Great King, something which was far beyond any merely political relationship between human rulers and other states.

The study of covenant in its setting has also been fruitful for covenants other than Sinai,[54] and has been of help in the theological field.[55]

IV. ENTHRONEMENT FESTIVALS AND DIVINE KINGSHIP

Some Old Testament scholars (notably Mowinckel) insist that such a festival, on a Babylonian model, was celebrated at New Year in ancient Israel,[56] reflecting a supposedly widespread Near Eastern usage. But there is no proper (*i.e.*, explicit)

in the Hattusil III–Benteshina treaty (E. Weidner, *Politische Dokumente aus Kleinasien*, II, 1923, pp. 134–135, n. 3). These incidental criticisms do not detract from the general value of McCarthy's useful book.

[54] *E.g.*, F. C. Fensham, *BA* 27 (1964), pp. 96–100 (Israel and the Gibeonites); *BASOR* 175 (1964), pp. 51–54 (Israel and Kenites); *JBL* 79 (1960), pp. 59–60 (Solomon and Hiram); J. Muilenberg, *VT* 9 (1959), pp. 347–365, esp. 360 ff. (Samuel); M. Tsevat, *JBL* 78 (1959), pp. 199–204 (Ezekiel and breach of oath); D. J. McCarthy, *CBQ* 26 (1964), pp. 179–189 (Gn. 21, 26, 31).

[55] At random, *cf.* K. Baltzer, *Das Bundesformular*, 1960, who follows the covenant-form into the Dead Sea Scrolls and extra-biblical early Christian writings; D. F. Payne, *THB* 7-8 (1961), pp. 10–16; M. G. Kline, *WTJ* 27 (1964), pp. 1–20, and pp. 115-139; J. A. Thompson, *Journal of Religious History* 3 (1964), pp. 1–19; F. C. Fensham, *ZAW* 77 (1965), pp. 193–202.

[56] For example, S. Mowinckel, *Psalmenstudien II*, 1922 (repr. 1960); *He that Cometh*, 1956; *The Psalms in Israel's Worship*, I–II, 1962, esp. ch. V. Excellent surveys on the use of the Psalms by Mowinckel and others can be found in A. R. Johnson, 'The Psalms', in H. H. Rowley (ed.), *The Old Testament and Modern Study*, 1951, pp. 162–209, esp. 189–206; H. Cazelles, *Dictionnaire de la Bible, Supplément*, VI, 1960, cols. 622–632; J. Coppens in R. de Langhe (ed.), *Le Psautier* (=*Orientalia et Biblica*, IV), 1962, pp. 1–71, esp. 20–42; and esp. on 'royal psalms', E. Lipinski, *ibid.*, pp. 133–272, esp. 133–137, 177–272. Coppens and Lipinski in particular give extensive bibliography.

evidence in the Old Testament for this at all.[57] No such major festival features among the feasts and rituals of the pentateuchal writings;[58] the historical books know of passovers and renewals of covenant on significant occasions, but not of Enthronement or New Year celebrations.[59] It is indeed conceivable that during the monarchy there was a New Year feast associated with the temple at Jerusalem which ended with the monarchy, copied, like that monarchy, in some measure from 'the nations round about' and not revived by post-exilic orthodoxy.[60] But this remains purely a speculation, and so is of no value at present.

Mowinckel's festival is principally based on the highly questionable use of supposed allusions in the Psalms,[61] and on a scheme inspired by supposed Babylonian models (through Canaanite intermediaries).[62] The phrase YHWH *mâlāk* in certain Psalms, despite assertions to the contrary, means simply 'YHWH reigns' (or, '. . . exercises kingship'), and not 'YHWH has become king' (implying enthronement) as partisans of the theory have held.[63] No adequate reason has been offered why

[57] Mowinckel and others tend to associate their festival with the Feast of Booths (or 'Tabernacles') in the seventh month, and assume an autumnal New Year (spring and autumn New Years are both attested). But our available evidence shows no New Year aspect for Booths; *cf.* briefly also E. J. Young, *The Book of Isaiah*, I, 1965, App. III, pp. 494–499.

[58] Even those who assert a post-exilic date for Ex., Nu., Lv. and Dt., referring their cultic data to 'H' and 'P', *etc.*, usually admit these days that earlier material is contained in these writings. We might therefore expect *some* explicit evidence here; and the supposedly late date of these books cannot be invoked to explain the absence of clear evidence of the assumed feast in them.

[59] Familiar examples are 2 Ki. 11:17 (Joash) and 23:2 ff., 21 ff. (Josiah). It is ludicrous to force specific historical occasions like 2 Sa. 6, or 1 Ki. 8, or even Lamentations, into a New Year mould.

[60] *Cf.* for example, the judicious review by H. Cazelles, *Dictionnaire de la Bible, Supplément*, VI, 1960, cols. 632–645 (apart from questionable use of OT data on calendar and autumn feasts).

[61] The chronic ambiguity inherent in such 'allusions' is well illustrated by K.-H. Bernhardt, *Das Problem der Altorientalischen Königsideologie im Alten Testament* (=*VTS*, VIII), 1961, pp. 291–300, esp. 295 ff.

[62] *Cf.* Mowinckel, *The Psalms in Israel's Worship*, I, pp. 132–136.

[63] For 'YHWH reigns' or the like, *cf.* O. Eissfeldt, *ZAW* 46 (1928), pp.

Israel should import and celebrate an entirely alien type of festival from distant Babylonia, and so far Canaan has failed to yield indisputable evidence for assumed intermediary forms.[64]

Arguments for a uniform basic pattern of myth and ritual throughout the Ancient Near East[65] have been shown up as inadequate in more than one recent study.[66] The Mesopotamian evidence is not quite what it was formerly believed to be. The extant text of the Babylonian *akitu* festival dates to the Seleucid period (*c.* 300–100 BC),[67] and one cannot guarantee how much older it is in precisely this form.[68] Furthermore, Old

81 ff. (esp. 100–102) = his *Kleine Schriften*, I, 1962, pp. 172 ff. (188–191); L. Köhler, *VT* 3 (1953), pp. 188–189; N. H. Ridderbos, *VT* 4 (1954), pp. 87 ff.; and esp. D. Michel, *VT* 6 (1956), pp. 40–68, among others. Mowinckel's latest defence of his view (*The Psalms in Israel's Worship*, II, 1962, pp. 222–224) does not begin to answer the Hebrew and comparative facts put up by Michel in particular. That God was never off the throne, so could not be enthroned is countered by H. Ringgren (*The Faith of the Psalmists*, 1963, p. xv) and others with the examples of the (metaphoric) re-enactment of deliverance from Egypt in Passover celebrations, or Christian hymns like 'Jesus Christ is risen today'. Ringgren forgets (i) this is pure metaphor, and (ii) these were once individual events that happened, and can be thus commemorated, whereas the kingship of God did not 'happen' or begin on some past date (real or supposed) in history. The analogy is therefore imaginary. Nothing new comes from A. S. Kapelrud, *VT* 13 (1963), pp. 229–231, except resort to LXX, or from E. Lipinski, *Biblica* 44 (1963), pp. 405–460, overly speculative and much irrelevant matter.

64 Contrary to Scandinavian dogma, the texts from Ugarit do *not* offer clear and unambiguous data for sacral kingship (of real kings of Ugarit, as distinct from the gods) in cult, New Year festivals or the like; *cf.* R. de Langhe, in S. H. Hooke (ed.), *Myth, Ritual and Kingship*, 1958, pp. 122–148 (*cf.* p. 140, for Kapelrud's methodologically erroneous assumption of a position itself in need of formal proof).

65 See references in note 74, p. 105, below; also T. H. Gaster, *Thespis*, 1950, 2nd ed. (and paperback) 1961.

66 *E.g.*, H. Frankfort, *Kingship and the Gods*, 1948; *The Problem of Similarity in Ancient Near Eastern Religions*, 1951; S. G. F. Brandon in S. H. Hooke (ed.), *Myth, Ritual and Kingship*, 1958, pp. 261–291; J. de Fraine, *Biblica* 37 (1956), pp. 59–73, and work in note 76 below; and K.–H. Bernhardt, *Das Problem d. Altorient. Königsideologie im AT* (*VTS*, VIII), 1961, pp. 57–66, 291–300.

67 So A. Sachs, *ANET*, p. 331; F. Thureau-Dangin, *Rituels accadiens*, 1921, pp. 127–154, Translation, Sachs, *ANET*, pp. 331–334.

68 Note the cautionary remarks of A. L. Oppenheim, *Ancient Mesopotamia*, 1964, p. 178, and his example, pp. 178 ff.

Testament scholars have used principally the reconstructions of Zimmern, Langdon and Pallis[69] as a basis for their theoretical reconstructions of an Israelite and general Near Eastern festival. But the accepted reconstruction of the Babylonian feast by Pallis *et al.* is now known to be partially incorrect in that the texts (particularly VAT 9555 and 9538)[70] supposedly relating the death and resurrection of Marduk (Bel) have no connection with a New Year feast or a death and resurrection, but seem to constitute an Assyrian propaganda-piece against Marduk, probably composed under Sennacherib.[71] Theoretical reconstructions for Israel and elsewhere that are based on the non-existent episodes are therefore quite imaginary. This inspires no confidence in the rest of the guesswork based on allusions.[72] In any case, *akitu*-celebrations were not uniform in Mesopotamia, not even in annual periodicity (or time of year), as shown, for example, by the twice-yearly festivals attested at Ur, Uruk and Nippur.[73]

Other Old Testament scholars have suggested[74] – again on supposed Mesopotamian patterns – that the Hebrew king was

[69] H. Zimmern, *Zum babylonischen Neujahrsfest*, II, 1918; S. Langdon, *The Babylonian Epic of Creation*, 1923, pp. 32 ff.; S. A. Pallis, *The Babylonian Akitu Festival*, 1926.

[70] *E.g.*, Pallis, *op. cit.*, pp. 221 ff.

[71] Shown by W. von Soden, *ZA* 51/NF 17 (1955), pp. 130–166, plus *ZA* 52/NF 18 (1957), pp. 224–234; *cf.* B. Landsberger, *Brief des Bischofs von Esagila an König Asarhaddon*, 1965, p. 15 (313), n. 9, citing a counterpart text. Note also Bernhardt, *op. cit.* (*VTS*, VIII), pp. 256 n. 2 and 257 n. 2. Marduk's defeat of Tiamat, not death and rising(?), occasioned joy at the *akitu* festival; *cf.* W. G. Lambert, *Iraq* 25 (1963), pp. 189–190.

[72] As a salutary warning against the vagaries of the method, note R. T. O'Callaghan's application (*Orientalia* 22 (1953), pp. 420–421) of Gaster's scheme for the Psalms (*Thespis*, 1950, p. 107; 1961, p. 452), on the latter's kind of reasoning, to the historical building-text of Asitiwada king of Que!

[73] Cf. A. Falkenstein, *Festschrift für Johannes Friedrich*, 1959, pp. 152, 160, 165; and add a Mari-reference for an *akitu*-feast in the month Aiaru (G. Dossin, *ARMT*, I, 1950, Letter 50:7, 13, 15, with *Chicago Assyrian Dictionary*, vol. 1: 1/A-alz, 1964, p. 267).

[74] *E.g.*, I. Engnell, *Studies in Divine Kingship in the Ancient Near East*, 1943; G. Widengren, *Sakrales Königtum im Alten Testament und im Judentum*, 1955; *cf.* S. H. Hooke (ed.), *Myth and Ritual*, 1933, *The Labyrinth*, 1935, and his cautious essay in *Myth, Ritual and Kingship*, 1958, pp. 1–21.

perhaps regarded as a divine or semi-divine being who was identified with a dying and rising god of fertility at a New Year festival. For this view, there is no adequate evidence whatsoever.[75] The Israelite king is never a divinity or a demi-god; had he ever made such claims, the Old Testament prophets would have denounced them bitterly.[76]

V. JUDAEAN AND EGYPTIAN KINGSHIP

In 1947, von Rad ingeniously compared details of the coronation of Judaean kings with that of Egyptian kings, and more especially the Egyptian *nekhbet* (understood as a titulary and decree of adoption or recognition of the king from the gods) with Hebrew *'edūth* given to the Judaean king with his crown

[75] See M. Noth, *Gesammelte Studien zum Alten Testament*, 1957 ([2]1960), pp. 188–229 (in English as: 'God, King, People in the Old Testament . . . ', in R. W. Funk and G. Ebeling (eds.), *Journal for Theology and the Church* I (1965), 20–48). The dying and rising of Marduk is illusory, *cf.* p. 105 and note 71, above. So is most of the supposed evidence for the resurrection of Tammuz, *cf.* O. R. Gurney, *JSS* 7 (1962), pp. 147–160 (one Assyrian text, p. 154). A new text (*UET*, VI: 10) for Inanna's (Assyr.: Ishtar's) Descent to the Underworld was taken by S. N. Kramer (*Proc. APS* 107:6 (1963), p. 515) to indicate that Dumuzi would have two visitors in the Underworld; but A. Falkenstein would interpret the text as saying that Dumuzi/Tammuz spent only half the year 'down under', and half the year on earth, his sister being substitute (XVI. Deutsche Orientalistentag, 1965; *cf. Frankfürter Allgemeine Zeitung*, 9 August 1965 – courtesy Frau I. Fuhr); *Orientalia* 34 (1965), 450–451. However, what may be true of Tammuz proves nothing for Marduk. *Cf.* also E. M. Yamauchi, *JBL* 84 (1965), pp. 283–290 (pp. 288–289 for Gurney, *op. cit.*, p. 154), and *JSS* 11 (1966), pp. 10–15.

[76] See G. Cooke, *ZAW* 73 (1961), pp. 202–225; J. de Fraine, *L'aspect religieux de la royauté israelite*, 1954; K.-H. Bernhardt, *Das Problem der Altorient. Königsideologie im AT* (*VTS*, VIII), 1961. The prophets did not hesitate to decry the pretensions (divine and otherwise) of foreign monarchs (*e.g.*, Is. 14:4 ff., 12 ff.; Ezk. 28:1–19), or other idolatries of Judah and Israel with which divine kings would belong if the claim had been made, the crux of Ps. 45:6 notwithstanding. In Old Testament and comparative studies (as in Egyptology), the divinity of the Egyptian pharaoh has been much emphasized; for some corrective to over-emphasis, *cf.* G. Posener, *De la Divinité du Pharaon*, 1960, and H. Goedicke, *Die Stellung des Konigs im Alten Reich*, 1960.

and also taken to represent a titulary and decree of adoption, *etc.*[77] This suggestion attracted several supporters.[78]

Unfortunately, the Egyptian parallel is not so well founded as it appears. The Egyptian *nekhbet* refers solely to the actual five-fold titles of a pharaoh,[79] and is not a decree or 'protocol' in any wider sense. A *nekhbet* (titulary) can be the subject of a decree, but is not itself a decree, merely titles. Compare the court circular or 'decree' (*wd*) of King Tuthmosis I (*c.* 1500 BC) in which he announces his *nekhbet* of five titles, and then turns to other matters.[80] There is no question of a *nekhbet* containing in itself a commission to rule or any declaration of divine sonship; the passages cited by von Rad (for example, of Hatshepsut, *Urk. IV*, p. 285:2–6)[81] mention the *nekhbet* (titulary) and sonship and/or commission wholly separately: Amūn declares his relationship to Hatshepsut, makes her ruler, *and* also writes her *nekhbet* (separate from these and not including them).

The titulary and the legitimation of a pharaoh are two distinct things; crowning was apparently the decisive moment

---

[77] G. von Rad, 'Das judaische Königsritual', *Theologische Literaturzeitung* 72 (1947), col. 211–216; now *Gesammelte Studien zum AT*, 1958, pp. 205 ff. (in English in von Rad, *The Problem of the Hexateuch and Other Essays*, 1966, pp. 222–231).

[78] *E.g.*, A. Alt, *KS*, II, p. 219; G. Cooke, *ZAW* 73 (1961), pp. 213–214; J. Gray, *Archaeology and the Old Testament World*, 1962, pp. 80, 141–143; *I and II Kings*, 1964, pp. 518–519. *Cf.* Bernhardt, *op. cit.*, p. 251 note (2); and (sceptical) Z. W. Falk, *VT* 11 (1961), pp. 88–90.

[79] A. Erman and H. Grapow, *Wörterbuch der Aegyptischen Sprache*, II, 1928, p. 308: 1–6, and R. O. Faulkner, *A Concise Dictionary of Middle Egyptian*, 1962, p. 138. The essential facts on the Egyptian royal titulary will be found in Sir A. H. Gardiner, *Egyptian Grammar*[3], 1957, pp. 71–76. Gods were sometimes given a titulary in imitation of those of the kings.

[80] *Urk. IV*, p. 80; in English, J. H. Breasted, *Ancient Records of Egypt*, II, 1906, §§54–60. In *Urk. IV*, p. 160:10–161:13, the *nekhbet* consists solely of the five names of Tuthmosis III accompanied by puns; it is similarly limited to the usual five titles in the Coronation Inscription of Haremhab (Helck, *Urk. IV*, p. 2118: 11–15, *cf.* Helck, *Urkunden d. 18. Dynastie, Deutsch* (*Hefte 17–22*), 1961, p. 406; A. H. Gardiner, *JEA* 39 (1953), p. 15; R. Hari, *Horemheb et la Reine Moutnedjemet*, 1965, p. 212:19).

[81] For a better edition of this text, see H. W. Fairman and B. Grdseloff, *JEA* 33 (1947), p. 15 and plate III: 4; von Rad's 'continuation' of this text does not in fact follow it at all, and must be derived from elsewhere.

in becoming king.[82] Thus, if the Hebrew *'edūth* is a protocol of titles combined with a declaration of adoption by YHWH, then it is wholly different from the Egyptian *nekhbet*. But the *'edūth* is rather the basic stipulations of the Sinai covenant, particularly the 'ten commandments' on the two tablets placed in the Ark.[83] With *'edūth* belongs *'edoth*, its plural equivalent, to be understood not so much as 'testimonies' as 'covenant-stipulations' or 'commandments', hence 'laws' (in Torah). Thus, the Ark is the Ark of the Covenant (*b'rīth*, general word; or *'edūth*, principally the covenant-stipulations), rather than Ark of the 'Testimony' as often translated. The parallelism of *b'rīth* and *'edūth* is well known, as von Rad remarks (*op. cit.*, p. 214, n. 4); like him, one may mention the association of crown and covenant (*b'rīth*) in Psalm 89:40 as a parallel to crown and *'edūth* in 2 Kings 11:12. Presenting the king with the covenant-stipulations as is done in the latter passage is in the same spirit as Deuteronomy 17:18 ff. Early external evidence for the word *'(e)d(ū)t* comes from Egypt, where it occurs as an early Canaanite loanword[84] in the twelfth century BC with a secondary nuance of 'conspiracy' derived from the idea of covenant or agreement on terms. The word *ḥoq*, 'statute', also occurs in parallel with the terms *b'rīth* (Ps. 105:10) and *'edūth* (Ps. 99:7). This is

[82] *Cf.* Fairman in S. H. Hooke (ed.), *Myth, Ritual and Kingship*, 1958, pp. 78–79, 81. The casket with the title-deeds of the kingdom (*op. cit.*, p. 79) is *mks* in Egyptian, in this use belonging to the Graeco-Roman period (*cf.* Erman and Grapow, *Wörterbuch d. Aeg. Sprache*, II, p. 163: 16). It has absolutely nothing to do with the *nekhbet* or *ren wer*, 'titulary', as J. Gray, *I and II Kings*, 1964, p. 519, assumes. His 'protocol' consisting of title-deeds plus titulary (*nekhbet*) is an imaginary conflation of unrelated entities and terms.

[83] Functionally, if not also etymologically, *cf.* Assyrian *adē*, 'treaty-stipulations' (Wiseman, *Iraq* 20 (1958), pp. 3, 81). *Cf.* also provisionally Albright, *From the Stone Age to Christianity*, 1957 edition, pp. 16–17. The meaning of *'edūth* was seen on context over a century ago by Samuel Lee, *A Lexicon, Hebrew, Chaldee, and English . . .* , 1840, p. 451a.

[84] *'Edūth* is therefore not a late Aramaism as is erroneously supposed by L. Rost, *Festschrift Baumgärtel*, 1959, p. 163. In the Turin Judicial Papyrus, 4: 5; translated by A. de Buck, *JEA* 23 (1937), p. 154. The word *'dt*, 'Verschwörung', is No. 300 in M. Burchardt, *Altkanaanäischen Fremdworte und Eigennamen im Ägyptischen*, II, 1911.

natural, seeing that *ḥoq* commonly indicates the statutes which in fact constitute the covenant-stipulations (*'edūth*, *'edoth*) and thus are central to the covenant (*bᵉrīth*). *Ḥoq* also has other meanings: decree, limit, prescribed allowance or task, as the evidence collected in the standard lexicons makes clear. In Psalm 2:7, the adoption of the Hebrew king by YHWH is given the status of a *ḥoq* – a divine law or decree – but in view of the poetic context and the varied meanings of *ḥoq*, this has no bearing on the meaning of *'edūth*. In Psalm 2:7, *ḥoq* is a decree or a single statute without reference to a covenant (*bᵉrīth* or *'edūth*).

The net result of all this is that 2 Kings 11:12 can be held to show that a Judaean king was crowned at his accession and was given a copy of the essence of the national Sinai covenant (so-called 'ten commandments') to which – like the people – he was subject (*cf.* Dt. 17:18 ff.), possibly on two small tablets like those in the Ark.[85] Hebrew kings sometimes took throne-names,[86] but Egypt is not the only other example of this. From Assyria, perhaps compare Tiglath-pileser III as Pulu (in later chronicles) and Shalmaneser V as Ululai;[87] and among the Hittites, certainly compare Urkhi-Tesup as Mursil III[88] and Sharri-kushukh of Carchemish as Piyassilis,[89] among others. As *'edūth* and *nekhbet* are not the same, as most kings are crowned, and as double names are fairly widespread, the evidence for Egyptian influence on Judaean coronation-ritual simply evaporates. Two other items of possible evidence may be briefly considered.

[85] We are under no obligation to imagine that the tablets of the law were anything like as heavy or unwieldy as Bernhardt (*VTS*, VIII, p. 251, §2 in note) seems to think.

[86] Examples: Azariah is called Uzziah (*cf.* 2 Ki. 15:1 and 2 Ch. 26:1–2); Eliakim was re-named Jehoiakim by Necho (2 Ki. 23:34), and Mattaniah, Zedekiah by Nebuchadrezzar (2 Ki. 24:17). Shallum was another name of Jehoahaz (*cf.* 2 Ki. 23:30, 31, 34 and Je. 22:11). On Hebrew royal throne-names, *cf.* A. M. Honeyman, *JBL* 67 (1948), pp. 13 ff.

[87] *Cf.* *ANET*, p. 272, nn. 3, 4; H. Schmökel, *HdO*, II: 3, 1957, pp. 264, 265.

[88] H. Otten, *MDOG* 87 (1955), pp. 19–23.

[89] See H. G. Güterbock, *JCS* 10 (1956), pp. 120–121.

First, von Rad suggested[90] that in Isaiah 9:6 we have four titles of a messianic king which would reflect Judaean use of a formal titulary based on the Egyptian five-fold titulary. While this verse may indeed reflect a Judaean usage, there is no evidence that this is based on an Egyptian model. Recent study of 1 Samuel 8 on the inauguration of Hebrew kingship[91] in which the significant parallels come from Syria – culturally closer to the Hebrews than was Egypt – suggests that we should seek our parallels in another direction. Some time ago, Virolleaud published[92] a broken tablet from North-Canaanite Ugarit which appears to give a formal titulary of Niqmepa of Ugarit, as follows:

line: 1. [? Names of N]iqmepa
2. [son of Niq]mad (II),
3. [king of] Ugarit:
4. Lord of Justice
5. Master of the (Royal) House
6. King who protects (frontiers)
7. King who builds
8f. (two more epithets, uncertain).

A series of epithets of this kind is stylistically much closer to Isaiah 9:6 than is the rather specialized titulary of the pharaohs.

Secondly, following on von Rad's suggestion[93] that David's promised great name in 2 Samuel 7:9 and Solomon's good name in 1 Kings 1:47 may mean not renown but a ceremonial titulary, Morenz attempted[94] to equate the 'great name' (*shem gadol*) of David with its literal Egyptian equivalent *ren wer*, 'great name'. But this seems to be a fallacy. Despite von Rad's dissenting view, the context of 2 Samuel 7:9 refers beyond all reasonable doubt to David's great *renown* – how can one possibly translate: '. . . and I was with thee wherever thou didst go,

[90] *Op. cit.*, cols. 215–216; followed by A. Alt, *KS*, II, pp. 219 f., and S. Morenz, *Theologische Literaturzeitung* 74 (1949), p. 699, and *ZÄS* 79 (1954) p. 74. Alt wished to emend the verse in order to produce five titles to correspond with the Egyptian five-fold usage.

[91] I. Mendelsohn, *BASOR* 143 (1956), pp. 17–22; *cf.* below, pp. 158 f.

[92] In *Palais Royal d'Ugarit*, II, 1957, p. 20; *cf.* C. F. A. Schaeffer, *ibid.*, pp. xvi–xvii, suggesting an original Egyptian influence here; this is possible, but not essential.

[93] *Op. cit.*, col. 215.   [94] *ZÄS* 79 (1954), pp. 73–74.

and have cut off all thine enemies, and will make for thee a noble titulary . . .' ? Surely, '. . . and will give thee great fame' is the obvious and necessary meaning in such a context. Likewise in 1 Kings 1:47, the formal wish for Solomon to have a greater throne (*i.e.*, kingdom) than David is unlikely to be paralleled by a wish for a better ceremonial titulary, but rather for an even greater renown! The Egyptian term *ren wer*, 'great name', is above all a technical term referring to the *nekhbet* or five-fold titulary,[95] and thus is used entirely differently from its literal Hebrew counterpart. Comparisons between Egyptian and Hebrew data can be very illuminating, but they must be soundly based, especially if any degree of direct relationship is postulated.

[95] 'Great name' (*ren wer*) and 'titulary' (*nekhbet*) are synonyms, directly followed by the fivefold royal titles in Haremhab's Coronation-Inscription (see above, p. 107, n. 80, end); also *Urk. IV*, p. 261 : 3 ff., 11 ff., where four of Hatshepsut's five titles are each called *ren wer*. This term, Erman and Grapow, *Wörterbuch d. Aeg. Sprache*, II, p. 427: 19–23.

6. THE QUESTION OF LITERARY CRITICISM

I. DOCUMENTARY HYPOTHESES

(a) Some Basic Criticisms

Brief reference has already been made to the physiognomy of Old Testament studies (pp. 17–20, above). Based ultimately on the dilettante speculations of the eighteenth century (*e.g.*, on the supposed significance of variant names of deity), the literary-critical theories of the composition of the Pentateuch in particular (and in some measure, of the Old Testament generally) which were elaborated in detail in the late nineteenth and early twentieth centuries are still dominant in Old Testament studies today.[1] In their classical form, these theories rest on three main grounds.

1. Supposed doublets (two versions of a story or event, usually held to be incompatible) are explained as the result of the conflation of differing original accounts into the present books.

2. The evolutionary theories of development of religion (drawn from philosophical premises, not facts) required a unilinear development of concepts from 'primitive' to 'advanced'; therefore, the Old Testament writings (especially the Pentateuch) *had* to be split up and the resulting fragments rearranged in a sequence to fit this theoretical scheme.

3. The various source-documents posited have been marked off by various criteria: *lexical* (double names for deity, for per-

---

[1] *Cf.* J. Bright, *History of Israel*, 1960, p. 62 ('still commands general acceptance'); H. H. Rowley, *The Growth of the Old Testament*, 1950 (repr. to 1964), p. 10 ('. . . necessary still to present "critical orthodoxy" to the reader'); O. Eissfeldt, *The OT, An Introduction*, 1965, p. 241 ('Modern' Pentateuchal criticism, now more than 200 years old).

sons,[2] groups,[3] places,[4] *etc.*[5]), and *stylistic* (distinction between narrative, ritual, poetry, law, *etc.*), besides the doublets referred to, and the 'theological' criterion (late dating of so-called 'advanced' concepts, *i.e.*, the unilinear theory of development mentioned above).

Usually, both the source-documents and the conflated books based on them are alike dated differently from (and later than) the dates indicated by statements and other explicit evidence in the biblical books themselves. Of course, every piece of literature has sources of inspiration or information, whether these are acknowledged (as in Kings and Chronicles) or not, but it is an entirely different matter to take a piece of literature and profess to divide up its text physically among various 'hands' or authors, so as to recover the supposed constituent parts or documents. This distinction must always be borne in mind.

It is my duty in all conscience to level some very serious basic criticisms against these superficially imposing theories on all three grounds.

First, unilinear evolution is a fallacy. It is valid only within a small field of reference for a limited segment of time, and not for whole cultures over long periods of time. One thinks of Egypt's thrice repeated rise and fall in and after the Old, Middle and New Kingdoms respectively,[6] or of the successive flowerings of Sumerian civilization, Old Babylonian culture and the Assyro-Babylonian kingdoms in Mesopotamia.[7] This

---

[2] *E.g.*, S. R. Driver, *Genesis*[12], 1926 (Westminster Commentaries), p. xiii; A. Bentzen, *Introduction to the Old Testament*, II, 1952, pp. 27–28, 47.

[3] *E.g.*, S. R. Driver, *Introduction to the Literature of the Old Testament*[9], 1913, p. 119; C. R. North in H. H. Rowley (ed.), *The Old Testament and Modern Study*, 1951, p. 80; O. Eissfeldt, *The OT, An Introduction*, 1965, p. 183.

[4] Driver, *Genesis*, p. xiii; Bentzen, *op. cit.*, II, p. 47; Eissfeldt, *loc. cit.*

[5] Various elements of ordinary vocabulary; *cf.* (*e.g.*) G. W. Anderson, *A Critical Introduction to the OT*, 1959, pp. 25–26, 46.

[6] *Cf.* standard histories of Egypt: J. A. Wilson, *The Burden of Egypt*, 1951 (paperback as *The Culture of Ancient Egypt*, 1956 and repr.); Sir A. H. Gardiner, *Egypt of the Pharaohs*, 1961 (paperback, 1964); the Egyptian chapters by E. J. Baumgartel, I. E. S. Edwards, W. S. Smith, W. C. Hayes, H. W. Fairman, J. Černý *et al.*, in *CAH*[2], I–II, 1961 ff.; É. Drioton and J. Vandier, *L'Égypte*, 1962 (*Coll. 'Clio'*).

[7] *Cf.* surveys by H. W. F. Saggs, *The Greatness that was Babylon*, 1962;

H

oscillation and mutation applies to all aspects of civilization: artistic standards, literary output and abilities, political institutions, the state of society, economics, and not least religious belief and practice. Intertwined with the multicoloured fabric of change are lines of continuity in usage that show remarkable consistency from early epochs. As extended unilinear development is, therefore, an invalid assumption, there is no reason whatever to date supposed literary fragments or sources by the imaginary level of their concepts on a scale from 'primitive' to 'advanced'. To this extent, at least, Kaufmann is absolutely justified in making the supposed Priestly source earlier than both the Babylonian Exile and Deuteronomy.[8]

Secondly, the supposed doublets or 'contradictions' which these theories were partly elaborated to explain can usually be accounted for by use of much simpler means; such extravagantly elaborate theories are then superfluous. Furthermore, some of the alleged difficulties are merely the illegitimate product of the literary theory itself. Theories which artificially *create* difficulties that were previously non-existent are obviously wrong and should therefore be discarded.

Thirdly, the stylistic criteria and assumed mode of composition-by-conflation are illusory. For, worst of all, the documentary theory in its many variations has throughout been elaborated *in a vacuum*, without any proper reference to other Ancient Oriental literatures to find out whether they had been created

---

A. L. Oppenheim, *Ancient Mesopotamia*, 1964; the Mesopotamian chapters by C. J. Gadd, J.-R. Kupper, D. J. Wiseman *et al.*, in *CAH²*, I–II, 1961 ff.; H. Schmökel, *HdO*, II: 3, *Keilschriftforschung und Alte Geschichte Vorderasiens*, 1957.

[8] And earlier than the writing prophets, or at least independent of them. See Y. Kaufmann, transl. by M. Greenberg, *The Religion of Israel*, 1961, chapter V, esp. pp. 157–166 (on pre-prophetic pentateuchal matter), 169–170 (P before D, not dependent on it) and esp. pp. 175–200, 205 and n. 16, 206–207. Hence, works that adhere to the conventional sequence and dating of J, E, D, P and exilic/post-exilic P must be considered as obsolete in their consequent presentation of Hebrew history and the history of Hebrew religion and literature. This includes works that have appeared since the English version of Kaufmann's book (1960–1) and have paid no attention to the facts marshalled by Kaufmann.

in this singular manner. In the eighteenth and earlier part of the nineteenth centuries, of course, no comparative data were available from the Ancient Near East; but from the late nineteenth century onward, Egyptian, Mesopotamian and even West-Semitic material became increasingly available, and the failure of Wellhausen and almost all of his earlier and later contemporaries to heed this material is inexcusable. It is a most serious omission, because – in the forms actually preserved to us in the extant Old Testament – Hebrew literature shows very close external stylistic similarities to the other Ancient Oriental literatures among which (and as part of which) it grew up. Now, nowhere in the Ancient Orient is there anything which is definitely known to parallel the elaborate history of fragmentary composition and conflation of Hebrew literature (or marked by just such criteria) as the documentary hypotheses would postulate. And conversely, any attempt to apply the criteria of the documentary theorists to Ancient Oriental compositions that have known histories but exhibit the same literary phenomena results in manifest absurdities.

It is sometimes suggested that it is not so much the particular criteria in themselves that are significant, as the alleged recurrence of the same stylistic criteria over a large body of literature, apparently showing a large measure of consistency and conforming in some measure to a 'historical pattern'. However, this approach betrays an inadequate grasp of the real nature of the problems involved.

First, if one is not prepared to produce and use definite and tangible criteria, then there can be no question of isolating definite, individual documents. Mere 'feelings' about passages or supposed styles are of no evidential value.

Secondly, if the chosen criteria prove to be inherently *false*, then they will be false regardless of whether one applies them to whole books or to half-verses, or to anything in between.

Thirdly, the supposed consistency of criteria over a large body of writing is contrived and deceptive (especially on vocabulary, for example)[9], and will hold for 'style' only if one in the

---

[9] *Cf.* the kind of material critically reviewed by (*e.g.*) Allis, *Five Books of Moses*, chapter II.

first place picks out everything of a particular kind, then proclaims it as all belonging to one document separate from the rest, and finally appeals to its remarkable consistency – a consistency obtained by deliberate selection in the first place, and hence attained by circular reasoning. 'P' owes its existence mainly to this kind of procedure, and was not even recognized to have existed for the one hundred years from Astruc in 1753 until Hupfeld in 1853.

Fourthly, appeal to 'some' conformity to a possible historical pattern proves nothing of itself. 'Internal agreement' of rearranged literary material is readily achieved if contrary data are emended away,[10] and agreement with the 'history' is equally easily attained if data in the historical books have also been duly 'adjusted' to fit in with views of what Israel's history ought to have been.[11] Hence, this kind of general approach has no scientific basis and is for that reason unacceptable.

(b) Basic Criticisms Applied

The first criticism (of an historically unrealistic unilinearity) has already been covered by reference to the examples of Egypt and Mesopotamia; Asia Minor, pre-Israelite Syria-Palestine and other regions would yield the same result if space permitted an exposition in detail. Likewise, the second and third basic criticisms could be illustrated at great length, but only the merest handful of material can be briefly presented here.

1. *Supposed Doublets.* It was suggested that these could more easily be solved by other means. It is often claimed[12] that Genesis 1 and 2 contain two different creation-narratives. In point of fact, however, the strictly *complementary* nature of the 'two' accounts is plain enough: Genesis 1 mentions the creation of

---

[10] Many examples exist; *cf.* at random, Rapaport on Alt, *PEQ*, 1941, pp. 165, 166.

[11] A procedure long ago unmasked by (*e.g.*) A. H. Finn, *Unity of the Pentateuch*, chapters 23–25.

[12] *E.g.*, A. T. Chapman, *An Introduction to the Pentateuch*, 1911, pp. 60–61; S. R. Driver, *Literature of the OT*[9], 1913, pp. 8–9, and *Genesis*[12], 1926, p. 35; G. W. Anderson, *A Critical Introduction to the OT*, 1959, pp. 23, 25; H. H. Rowley, *Growth of the Old Testament*, 1964, pp. 18, 21, 24; and many more.

man as the last of a series, and without any details, whereas in Genesis 2 man is the centre of interest and more specific details are given about him and his setting. There is no incompatible duplication here at all. Failure to recognize the complementary nature of the subject-distinction between a skeleton outline of *all* creation on the one hand, and the concentration in detail on man and his immediate environment on the other, borders on obscurantism.

Precisely this relationship of a general summary-outline plus a more detailed account of one (or more) major aspect(s) – with differing styles for the two accounts – is commonplace enough in Ancient Oriental texts. From Egypt we may compare the following. On the Karnak Poetical Stela Amūn addresses King Tuthmosis III, first expressing his supremacy generally (lines 1 to 12, diversified style – J?), then with more precision in a stately poem more rigid in form than Genesis 1 (lines 13 to 22 – 'P'?), and a more varied finale (23 to 25).[13] On the Gebel Barkal stela one also finds royal supremacy in general terms (lines 3 to 9), then a narrative of specific triumphs in Syria-Palestine (lines 9 to 27) and then of tribute (27 ff.).[14] Do these stelae not show 'duplicate accounts'? Many royal inscriptions from Urartu show an initial paragraph ascribing defeat of such-and-such lands to the chariot of the god Haldi, and then repeat the same victories in detail as achieved by the king.[15] We have a 'H'(aldi) source (brief, fixed style, Haldi the victor) and 'K'(ing) source (detailed; varying formulae, king as victor), if conventional literary criticism be applied. What is absurd when applied to monumental Near Eastern texts that had *no* prehistory of hands and redactors should not be imposed on Genesis 1 and 2, as is done by uncritical perpetuation of a nineteenth-century systematization of speculations by eighteenth-century dilettantes lacking, as they did, all knowledge of the forms and usages of Ancient Oriental literature.

---

[13] Partly visible in translation, A. Erman and A. M. Blackman, *Literature of the Ancient Egyptians*, 1927, pp. 254–258 (text, *Urk. IV*, pp. 611–619).

[14] Translation, G. A. and M. B. Reisner, *ZÄS* 69 (1933), pp. 24–39.

[15] Texts, *cf.* (*e.g.*) F. W. König, *Handbuch der Chaldischen Inschriften*, 1955/57, Nos. 21, 23, 80, 103, 104, *etc.* Alternative 'analyses', *cf.* pp. 125 f. below.

Only two lines of evidence have been urged in favour of a double narrative: a differing style and theological conception in Genesis 1 and 2, and a supposedly different order of creation in each narrative. The stylistic differences are meaningless, and reflect the differences in detailed subject-matter,[16] while the supposed contrast of a transcendent God in Genesis 1 with naïve anthropomorphisms in Genesis 2[17] is vastly overdrawn and, frankly, illusory.[18] The same may be said of the order of events. In Genesis 2:19, there is no explicit warrant in the text for assuming that the creation of animals here happened immediately before their naming (i.e., after man's creation); this is eisegesis, not exegesis. The proper equivalent in English for the first verb in Genesis 2:19 is the pluperfect ('. . . had formed . . .'). Thus the artificial difficulty over the order of events disappears.[19]

[16] Besides the preceding paragraph and notes, see below, p. 125, *Stylistic Criteria*, §ii. As indicated by U. Cassuto, *The Documentary Hypothesis*, 1961, p. 54, the P-source is characterized by an arid, precise style *solely* because just this kind of material was arbitrarily assigned to a hypothetical P in the first place (*i.e.*, circular reasoning); lists in J are like those of P, and the rare narrations allowed to P are as good as J or E, which simply cancels the supposed factor of style.

[17] *Cf.*, for example, S. R. Driver, *Genesis*, 1926, p. 35; Rowley, *op. cit.*, p. 21; Chapman, *op. cit.*, pp. 59–60.

[18] This 'contrast' blandly ignores the anthropomorphisms to be found in P; any reader can see in Gn. 1 that God 'called', 'saw', 'blessed', 'rested' (*cf.* E. J. Young, *Introduction to the OT*[3], 1964, p. 51). For 'naïve' P-anthropomorphisms elsewhere in Gn., *cf.* Gn. 17:1, 22, and 35:9, 13 – God appears to, speaks to, and goes up from, man; very 'local', hardly transcendent! (*Cf.* Y. Kaufmann, *Religion of Israel*, 1961, p. 207.) The supposed restriction of *bārā'*, 'create', to P rests solely on the illegitimate division of Gn. 2:4 into two parts; this verse is the proper heading to what follows, and should not be arbitrarily divided to justify illusory criteria.

[19] Driver, *Literature of the OT*, p. 8, note, objected (rather too dogmatically) that this rendering would be 'contrary to idiom', referring to his *Treatise on Use of the Tenses in Hebrew*, 1892, §76, obs., in which he endeavoured to explain other possible examples. In translating any ancient text, the first assumption is that the writer intended it to make sense; a rendering or exegesis that imports a contradiction is unsatisfactory. The meaning of any Waw-Consecutive-Imperfective must be settled on context, not by appeal to abstract principles. Although in form and origin this construction is continuative, yet (as often in languages) this was early and easily lost

It is also often asserted[20] that Genesis 37 contains parts of two irreconcilable accounts of how Joseph was sold into Egypt: (a) by his brothers to the Ishmaelites and so into Egypt (Gn. 37:25, 28b; *cf.* 45:4, 5), and (b) by the Midianites who took him from the pit (Gn. 37:28a, 36; *cf.* 40:14, 15). The truth is much simpler.

First, the terms 'Ishmaelites/Midianites' overlap,[21] and refer to the same group in whole or in part (*cf.* Jdg. 8:24).

Secondly, the pronoun 'they' in Genesis 37:28 refers back to Joseph's brothers, not to the Midianites. In Hebrew, the antecedent of a pronoun is not always the last preceding noun. If this were not so the phrase 'he has brought an evil name ...' in Deuteronomy 22:19 would refer to the innocent father; likewise the pronouns 'his' and 'he' in Deuteronomy 22:29 go

---

sight of, so that it could serve instead of a perfective form. Thus, in Lv. 1:1 ('Now, the Lord called ... ') and Nu. 1:1 ('Now, the Lord spoke ... '), there is no immediate continuity with the directly-preceding book or verse in either case. As pluperfect meaning is included in the Perfective, we cannot *a priori* deny it to contextual equivalents of the Perfective. Hebraists and others should also remember that no special pluperfect tenses exist in the Ancient Semitic languages (or in Egyptian), this nuance being covered by perfective forms and equivalents interpreted on context as here in Hebrew. For Hebrew Waw-Consecutive-Imperfectives that require a pluperfect standpoint in English, *cf.*: Ex. 4:19 (picking up 4:12, not 18); Ex. 19:2 ('having departed ... and come ... , they pitched ... ; picks up 17:1, not 19:1; these examples, courtesy Dr. W. J. Martin). Perhaps more striking, Jos. 2:22 ('now the pursuers had sought them ... ' does *not* continue immediately preceding verbs), 1 Ki. 13:12 ('Now his sons had seen' does *not* continue or follow from 'their father said'), and Is. 37:5 (the servants' coming must have *preceded* their addressing Isaiah, just as Gn. 2:19 is to be understood in line with Gn. 1); these examples were pointed out long since by W. H. Green, *Unity of the Book of Genesis*, 1895, p. 28. Driver, *Treatise* ... , p. 87, can only dispose of 1 Ki. 13:12 by appealing to the versions; reference of Is. 37:5 to his §75 *β* does not alter the fact that there is there *no* sequence; Jdg. 1:8 depends on ambiguity of pronouns in 1:7, and is irrelevant to Gn. 2:19.

[20] For example, Driver, *Genesis*, 1926, pp. 321, 332; Eissfeldt, *The OT, an Introduction*, pp. 186–187, among many others.

[21] In fact, there are not two but three terms in this narrative: in Gn. 37:36, the Hebrew word is Medanites (*cf.* Gn. 25:2, where Medan and Midian are related), but no-one posits *three* sources on this evidence; see also Kitchen, *NBD*, p. 657.

back to an erring other man; and so elsewhere in Hebrew. In Egypt, after talking of Tuthmosis II, Ineni mentions the accession of 'his (Tuthmosis II's) son', Tuthmosis III, and then the real rule of 'his sister, . . . Hatshepsut'. But 'his' here refers back to Tuthmosis II, not to his son.[22]

Thirdly, in private conversation Joseph could be blunt with his own brothers (Gn. 45:4, 5, 'you sold . . .'), but in seeking a favour from the royal butler, an alien, he could not very well reveal the humiliating fact that his own blood brothers wanted to be rid of him (Gn. 40:14, 15) – however unjustly, what kind of impression would that admission have made on the butler? Exegesis, not surgery, is the answer to such 'difficulties', together with the use of relevant Ancient Oriental comparative data.

2. *Difficulties illegitimately created by the theory*. It has often been claimed, for example, that Genesis 7 to 8 gives two different estimates for the duration of the Flood, but in fact these are purely the invention of the theory. The biblical text as it stands is wholly consistent in giving a year and ten days (eleven, if first and last are both counted) as the total duration of the Flood episode, as clearly pointed out by Aalders,[23] Heidel[24] and others long ago. Likewise, the supposed clash between Genesis 6:19, 20 (*cf.* Gn. 7:8, 9) and Genesis 7:2, 3 over 'two by two' or 'seven pairs' is imaginary. In Genesis 6:20, *shenayim*, 'pair', is probably being used as a collective for 'pairs', seeing that one cannot form a plural of a dual word in Hebrew (no **shenayimim*!); Genesis 6:19, 20 and 7:8, 9 are general statements, while Genesis 7:2, 3 (clearly twos and sevens) is specific.[25]

The various other examples of supposed 'doublets' are no

---

[22] *Urk. IV*, pp. 59–60 following 58–59; *cf.* S. Schott, *Zum Krönungstag der Königin Hatschepsût*, 1955, p. 197 and n. 9.

[23] G. C. Aalders, *A Short Introduction to the Pentateuch*, 1949, p. 46; or *cf.* E. J. Young, *Introduction to the OT*[3], 1964, pp. 54–55.

[24] A. Heidel, *The Gilgamesh Epic and Old Testament Parallels*[2], 1954, pp. 245–247.

[25] See W. J. Martin, *Stylistic Criteria and the Analysis of the Pentateuch*, 1955, pp. 15–16; *cf.* Aalders, *op. cit.*, pp. 45–46.

more convincing or soundly based than those considered here.[26]

3. *Artificiality of Stylistic Criteria.* This is readily illustrated from Ancient Near Eastern literature.

(i) *Lexical criteria.* For multiple terms for deity,[27] compare the use of three names, a fixed epithet, and common noun 'god' for the god Osiris on the Berlin stela of Ikhernofret:[28] Osiris, Wennofer, Khent-amentiu, 'Lord of Abydos' (*Neb-'Abdju*), and *nuter*, 'god' (*cf. 'Elohim* in Hebrew). But no Egyptologist bothers to invent 'Osirist', 'Wennofrist', 'Khentamentist', Neb-'Abdjuist and Nuterist sources to match the Yahwist and Elohist of Old Testament studies. Ikhernofret shows what could be taken as 'prolixity' of expression, but it is certain that this commemorative inscription was composed (as one unit), carved and set up within weeks, or possibly even days, of the events to which it chiefly relates, and has no literary 'pre-history' of several centuries of 'hands', redactors and conflation. This applies to other texts, a few cited here and many more not. Alongside Egypt, multiple divine names occur in Mesopotamia. We might cite Enlil also called Nunamnir in the prologue to the Lipit-Ishtar laws,[29] and in the prologue to Hammurapi's laws we have Inanna/Ishtar/Telitum, and Nintu/Mama.[30]

---

[26] Space-limits preclude any more extended treatment here. On the supposed double naming of Beersheba (mistranslation), for example, *cf.* W. J. Martin, *NBD*, p. 138. The alleged triplicate story afforded by Abraham's treatment of Sarah in Egypt and at Gerar (Gn. 12; 20) and Isaac's of Rebecca at Gerar (Gn. 26) is sheer invention. Abraham's regular subterfuge is defined in Gn. 20:13; attribution of this verse to a redactor must be proved and not just assumed to serve *a priori* theory. Isaac is 'like father, like son'. Or, in Egypt, shall we assume that the Euphrates campaigns of Tuthmosis I and III are mere 'doublets', because both kings erected stelae there on similar campaigns and both hunted elephants near Niy? (References in Gardiner, *Egypt of the Pharaohs*, 1961, pp. 178–179 and 194–195.)

[27] Like YHWH and Elohim; *e.g.*, Chapman, *Introduction to the Pentateuch*, pp. 29, 52–53; Bentzen, *Intr. to the OT*, II, pp. 27–29; Eissfeldt, *The OT, an Introduction*, pp. 182–183.

[28] Text, K. Sethe, *Aegyptische Lesestücke*, 1928, pp. 70–71; translation, Wilson in *ANET*, pp. 329–330 (rendering Khent-amentiu by 'Foremost of the Westerners'); study by H. Schäfer, *Untersuchungen*, IV: 2, 1904.

[29] *E.g., ANET*, p. 159.   [30] *E.g., ANET*, pp. 164–165.

Three deities bear double names in the so-called Babylonian creation-epic (*Enuma elish*).[31] The same phenomenon may be observed in Canaan,[32] Old South Arabia,[33] and among Hurrians and Hittites.[34]

There is no real warrant for attributing any greater significance to YHWH/Elohim as literary markers. It is generally agreed that YHWH and Elohim (one a proper name; the other a term for 'God') are not inherently pure synonyms, and are *not* always and everywhere used as such, either. In some passages, it is clear that each term is used because appropriate, not as a free variant.[35] In such cases, therefore, the term concerned is in character with a given context, and not the mark of a writer; such cases are not evidence of a 'J' or 'E'. Furthermore, YHWH and Elohim can be found in the 'wrong' documents, as pointed out long ago.[36] The supposed consistency between the divine

[31] Ea is also Nudimmud (tablets I, IV); Tiamat is also 'Mother Khubur' (tablets I–III); Marduk is also Bel (tablet IV). This is visible in translation, *e.g.* in Heidel, *Babylonian Genesis*, and Speiser in *ANET*.

[32] In the Ugaritic texts, the artificer-god Kothar-wa-Khasis is also Hayyin (*e.g.*, Ginsberg, *ANET*, p. 151); and Baal is also Hadad and bears multiple fixed epithets (Aliyan Baal, Dagon's Son, Rider of Clouds, *etc.*) in numerous passages. Note the reactions of C. H. Gordon, *Ugaritic Literature*, 1949, p. 6; A. S. Kapelrud, *Baal in the Ras Shamra Texts*, 1952, p. 46.

[33] Examples in G. Ryckmans, *Les Religions Arabes Préislamiques*[2], 1951, pp. 42 ('Almaqah or 'Ilumquh has epithets Thahwan, Thwr-Ba'lm), 43 ('Amm is also 'Anbay), 44–45 (solar deities); 'Athtar/6 other names and epithets, p. 41. Further examples, A. Grohmann, *Arabien*, 1963, pp. 244–245; in texts in English, *cf.* Jamme, *ANET*[2], pp. 509, No. 10 ('Athtar/'Athtar Sharqan), 511, No. 14 (Dhat-Ṣantum/Dhat-Ẓahran/Dhat-Raḥban) and No. 15 ('Anbay Shayman/Rub' Shahar, both the moon-god).

[34] For example, the Hurrian 'Song of Ullikummi' in a Hittite version; Ullikummi is referred to not only by this name but as (the) Kunkunuzzi-Stone (Goetze's 'diorite-man') and a further fixed epithet (*nuttarias siunas*; Goetze, 'that vigorous (?) god'; Güterbock, 'this swift(?) god'). Translations, A. Goetze in *ANET*, pp. 121–125, esp. 124–125; H. G. Güterbock, *The Song of Ullikummi*, 1952 (repr. from *JCS* 5 (1951) and 6 (1952)).

[35] The essential fact is admitted by Chapman, *Intr. Pentateuch*, p. 53, and S. R. Driver, *Literature of the OT*, p. 13, note.

[36] *E.g.* by Green, *Unity of Genesis*, pp. 539–541, and latterly by Segal, pp. 78–9 (work cited just below). The 'flat contradiction' between Ex. 6:2 f. and Genesis alleged by Rowley (*Growth of the OT*, pp. 20–21) misleadingly ignores various facts, and is best viewed in the light of: W. J. Martin,

names as markers and other lexical criteria is in large measure the inevitable result of first drawing lines to delimit what is considered proper to 'P' or 'J' or 'E', and then proclaiming the resultant lexical lists as 'characteristic' of this or that source; in 'P' in particular, it merely reflects the peculiar subject-matter collected under that cipher.[37]

In Egypt, many people had double names like the Israel/Jacob or Jethro/Reuel of the Old Testament,[38] e.g., Sebek-khu called Djaa whose stela in Manchester University Museum[39] exemplifies the use of three names for one Palestinian popu-lace: Mentiu-Setet ('Asiatic Beduin'), Retenu ('Syrians') and 'Amu ('Asiatics') – just like the Ishmaelites/Midianites or Canaanites/Amorites of the Old Testament. For personal and group names elsewhere, cf. in Mesopotamia the sage Ahiqar (or Ahuqar) who is Aba'-enlil-dari[40] (not to mention Tiglath-pileser III = Pul, and Shalmaneser V = Ululai). In the Hittite Empire, a series of kings had double names,[41] while 'Mitanni' and 'Hanigalbat' and 'Mitanni' and 'Hurrians' occur as double designations of the state and people of Mitanni.[42]

Stylistic Criteria and the Analysis of the Pentateuch, 1955, pp. 16–19; J. A. Motyer, The Revelation of the Divine Name, 1959, pp. 11–17; M. H. Segal, Scripta Hierosolymitana, VIII, 1961, pp. 74–76; and S. Mowinckel (1937), see North in Rowley, OT and Modern Study, p. 54.

[37] The facts noted by, e.g., O. T. Allis, The Five Books of Moses², 1949, pp. 40/46–60, are damning.

[38] On double names in Egyptian, cf. H. Ranke, Die ägyptischen Personen-namen, II, 1952, pp. 6–8.

[39] K. Sethe, Aegyptische Lesestücke, pp. 82–83; translated in T. E. Peet, Sebekku, 1914, and by Wilson, ANET, p. 230 (but rendering both 'Amu and Mentiu-Setet merely as 'Asiatics').

[40] List of kings and their sages from Uruk; cf. J. van Dijk in H. Lenzen, XVIII. Uruk Vorläufiger Bericht, 1962, pp. 45, 51/52.

[41] See H. G. Güterbock, JCS 10 (1956), pp. 120–122, for the double names of Piyassilis, Muwatallis, Mursil III, Tudkhalia IV; apparently Suppilu-liuma I; and also Mattiwaza of Mitanni as Kili-Teshup. Cf. E. Laroche, Les Noms des Hittites, 1966, pp. 358–362.

[42] See I. J. Gelb, Hurrians and Subarians, 1944, pp. 72–74, for the kingdom of Tushratta as Mitanni and Hanigalbat in Amarna Letters 20 and 29, for Tushratta as 'king of Mitanni' and 'Hurrian king' in Letter 24, and for the interchange Mitanni/Hurri-land and combination of Mitanni and the Hurrians.

For place-names like Sinai/Horeb, compare in the text of Merenptah's 'Israel Stela' two names for Egypt (Kemit, Tameri) and five names and variants for Memphis (Mennefer; Ineb-hedj, Inbu, Ineb-heqa; Hatkuptah).[43] Similarly, examples can be found elsewhere.[44]

For common nouns which are synonyms or para-synonyms like Hebrew *'amā/shiphā*, 'bondmaid'/'handmaid',[45] one may compare in Egypt the use of five different words for boats on the historical stela of King Kamose, *c.* 1560 BC;[46] or in Mesopotamia, the Assyrian King Assurbanipal's free use of the practically synonymous terms *rakbu* and *mar-shipri*, 'envoy' and 'messenger', in a prism-inscription about Gyges of Lydia.[47] Even the varying use of two forms of personal pronoun (in Hebrew, first person singular, *'ani/'anōki*)[48] can be compared in Egyptian with the mixture of Middle and Late Egyptian forms in the Contendings of Horus and Seth,[49] and within West

[43] Obvious in the original text, W. M. F. Petrie, *Six Temples at Thebes in 1896*, 1897, plates 13, 14, but hidden by the blanket terms 'Egypt' and 'Memphis' in translation either wholly (as in *ANET*, pp. 376–378) or partly (as by Spiegelberg in Petrie, *op. cit.*, pp. 26–28, and by Erman and Blackman, *Literature of the Ancient Egyptians*, 1927 (repr. 1966), pp. 274–278).

[44] *E.g.*, Nippur also called Dur-an-ki, in prologue to Hammurapi's laws (*ANET*, p. 164).

[45] Used as a criterion (with other words, similarly) by Driver, *Genesis*, p. xiii; Bentzen, *Intr. to the OT*, II, p. 47; Eissfeldt, *The OT, an Introduction*, p. 183, *etc.* However, certain differences in meaning of these two words make them entirely unsuitable for use as criteria; *cf.* A. Jepsen, *VT* 8 (1958), pp. 293–297, 425.

[46] The words *'aḥa'u*, *'imu*, *ba'u*, *mik* and *djat* respectively (the vocalizations are an artificial convenience); stela published by L. Habachi, *ASAE* 53 (1955), pp. 195–202, or M. Hammad, *Chronique d'Égypte* 30/fasc. 60 (1955), pp. 198–208.

[47] Observable (*e.g.*) in text in A. Ungnad (ed. M. San Nicolo), *Grammatik des Akkadischen*[3], 1949, pp. 138–139, or with interlinear translation in L. W. King's venerable *First Steps in Assyrian*, 1898, pp. 81–87. Also, *tamtum||aiabu* for 'sea' in text of Iahdun-Lim of Mari, eighteenth century BC, Malamat, *Studies . . . Landsberger*, 1965, p. 367.

[48] *E.g.*, Driver, *Genesis*, p. xiii, and *Literature of the OT*, pp. 134–135.

[49] A. H. Gardiner, *Library of A. Chester Beatty*, 1931, p. 11; Old Testament scholars would profit from reading Gardiner's comments on the inconsistencies of this essentially unitary tale, *ibid.*, pp. 10–13.

Semitic itself with the occurrence of *both* first person singular forms in one text on three tablets from Ugarit, just as in Hebrew.[50] 'Criteria' of this kind, separately or in conjunction,[51] are worthless. This fact must inevitably raise the most serious doubts about the validity of using such artificial methods on ancient literature.[52]

(ii) *Major Variations in Style*. These are so universal in ancient texts whose literary unity is beyond all doubt, that just one or two brief examples must suffice here. Thus, the biographical inscription of the Egyptian official Uni (*c*. 2400 BC) includes flowing narrative (like 'J', 'E' ?), summary statements ('P' ?), a victory-hymn ('H' ?), and two different refrains ('R$_1$', 'R$_2$'?) repeated at suitable but varying intervals.[53] Yet there can in fact be no question at all of disparate sources here, in what is a monumental inscription composed and engraved as a unitary whole at the volition of the man whom it commemorates. Or compare, again, the royal inscriptions of the kings of Urartu. Here, one finds fixed formulae for the going forth of the god Haldi ('P' ?), a triple formula (and variants) for that of

[50] Tablets 49, 51, 67, in the numbering of C. H. Gordon, *UM*, II, and *UT*, II.

[51] It is a waste of time to talk about the 'cumulative force' of arguments that are each invalid; $o+o+o+o=o$ on any reckoning. The supposed concordance of assorted criteria whose independence is more apparent than real has had to be rejected above (p. 122, with notes 36–37) on evidence far too bulky to include in this book.

[52] Some of the foregoing points I made earlier in *JEA* 47 (1961), pp. 162-164; *F/T*91 (1960/61), pp. 188–190; *NBD*, pp. 348–351. Others, too, are sceptical of traditional literary-critical methods (quite apart from Engnell *et al*.). So C. H. Gordon, *Ugaritic Literature*, 1949, pp. 6–7, 132; *Hebrew Union College Annual* 26 (1955), pp. 67, 95–97 (=*Homer and Bible*); *Christianity Today* 4 (1959), pp. 131–134, using Ancient Oriental evidence; M. H. Segal in *Scripta Hierosolymitana*, VIII, 1961, pp. 68–114, on internal evidence; W. W. Hallo, *IEJ* 12 (1962), pp. 13, 14, 26 end, preferring objective comparative data to unverifiable hypotheses. For a most lively (and cruelly appropriate) treatment of equally useless criteria in the Homeric field (with reference to Milton, Min and Plo), see D. Young, *Greece and Rome* (2nd series) 6 (1959), pp. 96–108.

[53] Text in K. Sethe, *Urkunden des Alten Reiches*², 1933, pp. 98–110; translations by J. H. Breasted, *Ancient Records of Egypt*, I, 1906, §§306–315, and (second part only) by Wilson in *ANET*, pp. 227–228.

the king ('K$_1$,' 'K$_2$,' 'K$_3$' ?), compact statements of success ('S' ?) or first personal narrative ('N' ?), and intermittent statistics of Urartian forces or of prisoners and booty ('P' again ?). Again, these are immediate and unitary texts without prehistories and rival proto-authors; and their style lasted through at least four reigns of nearly a century (ninth to eighth centuries BC).[54]

(iii) *'Advanced' theological concepts*. These are often denied to the Israelites until during or after the Babylonian exile (sixth century BC and after). However, this is merely a reflex of the fundamental error of unilinear development (*cf.* pp. 112–114, above), and in fact many such concepts are explicitly known from written documents to have been the common property of the whole Ancient Near East in the second millennium BC, and even in the third millennium when material is available. With this ubiquitous and inescapable background, there is no reason whatever for denying consciousness of such concepts to the Hebrews at *any* period in their history.[55] The personification of Wisdom in Proverbs 8 and 9 is a good example. This has nothing whatever to do with Greek influence in the fourth –third century BC (as is often claimed),[56] but is precisely the same

[54] From Ishpuini to Sardur II (König: III), *c.* 820–730 BC; typical texts are Nos. 6, 6a, b, 7 (Ishpuini and Menua), 21, 23–28 (Menua and son), 80–82, 89 (Argistis I), 102–104 (Sardur II/III), in F. W. König, *Handbuch der Chaldischen Inschriften*, 1955–7 = *AfO*, Beiheft 8.

[55] This is in parallel with the common but distorted view that (*e.g.*) 'the Exodus . . . took place in the morning twilight of the historical era', much being obscure (C. R. North, in Rowley (ed.), *Old Testament and Modern Study*, 1951, p. 76). To talk of events in the Near East in the thirteenth century BC as belonging to a 'morning twilight' is more than faintly ludicrous; a thirteenth-century Moses came after some *seventeen centuries* of literate civilization in Egypt and Mesopotamia since *c.* 3000 BC (preceded by millennia of pre-literate higher culture), and in the whole Ancient East from *c.* 2000 BC. While there is plenty of scope for investigation for long enough to come, too much 'obscurity' is merely the product of inherited fashions of dealing with the Old Testament source-material; a good example is early OT chronology, pp. 35–78, above.

[56] *Cf.* R. H. Pfeiffer, *Introduction to the Old Testament*, 1941, p. 659; O. Eissfeldt, *The OT, an Introduction*, 1965, p. 473; same dating, Rowley, *Growth of the OT*, p. 140, and G. W. Anderson, *A Critical Introduction to the OT*, 1959, p. 188. The dating-argument from long passages is, bluntly,

as the personification of Truth, Justice, Intelligence, Understanding, *etc.*, from the third and second millennia BC in both Egypt and Mesopotamia, and during the second millennium BC among Hittites, Hurrians and Canaanites as well.[57] Universalism – the rule of God over the known world as well as over one people – was (for example) still dated by Mowinckel in 1955 (referring to Psalm 67)[58] to 'relatively late times', despite the fact that just such universalism was current throughout the Ancient Near East from the third millennium BC onward on evidence cited back in 1940,[59] some of the best second-millennium evidence having been available for thirty years in a well-known work designed especially for Old Testament studies.[60] It is a matter for genuine regret when adherence to long-standing theories prevents scholars from seeing essential primary facts and realizing their direct implications.

(c) An Emergent Tension between Myth and Reality (cf. pp. 25–28, above)

Finally, one may briefly note the repeated clash between the results (as well as procedures) of the conventional hypotheses on the one hand, and the existing Near Eastern literary forms

---

fatuous – or are the miniature essays and 'long' passages in Egyptian works like Ptahhotep (*c.* 2300 BC) or Khety son of Duauf (*c.* 1980 BC) also to be credited to Hellenistic influence? (Impossible, because we have second millennium MSS of these.) These and other matters will be dealt with elsewhere.

[57] Sufficiently comprehensive references in Kitchen, *THB* 5/6 (1960), pp. 4–6. For personification of Magic (*Ḥikē*), Command (*Ḥu*) and Understanding (*Sia*) in Egypt, see Gardiner, *PSBA* 37 (1915), pp. 253–262; *ibid.*, 38 (1916), pp. 43–54, 83–95; *ibid.*, 39 (1917), pp. 134–139; also H. Bonnet, *Reallexikon der ägyptischen Religionsgeschichte*, 1952, pp. 586–588. In Near East, *cf.* (*e.g.*) Babylonian *Mesharu*, 'Justice', in Hittite prayers, *c.* 1400 BC (Güterbock, *JAOS* 78 (1958), pp. 241, 242), *etc.* In general, *cf.* also H. Ringgren, *Word and Wisdom*, 1947.

[58] *VT* 5 (1955), p. 29.

[59] In Albright, *From the Stone Age to Christianity*; = pp. 213–217, *etc.*, in the 1957 edition.

[60] H. Gressmann (ed.), *Altorientalische Texte zum Alten Testament*², published in 1926 (*e.g.*, Ebeling, pp. 263–265).

and other phenomena (agreeing with the *extant* Old Testament text) on the other hand.

1. *Covenant-forms.*[61] It is curious indeed that it is *not* the 'J' or 'E' versions but only the *full*, unitary text of passages such as Genesis 31; Exodus 19, 20 ff., 34; Joshua 24 that corresponds directly with the forms of actual treaty-documents in the Near East; in each of 'J' and 'E', essential features are mysteriously missing.[62] And it is the structure of Deuteronomy 1 to 32[63] *as it stands* which clearly reproduces that of first-hand covenants or treaties of the late second millennium BC – the 'structures' of the nuclei and strata commonly postulated are wholly imaginary.[64] In all these cases, we are being asked to believe in a series of separate documents ('J', 'E'; the fragments of 'D'), suspiciously unique in form, that were combined in the course of centuries so that, by some miracle unexplained, each resulting conflated covenant corresponded with real forms (particularly of the long-past late second millennium) quite unknown to the imagined redactors.

2. *Natural Phenomena.* It is also curious that the integral text of

[61] *Cf.* above, p. 101, note 52.

[62] *Cf.* references to Thompson, and to McCarthy and Kline, p. 101, notes 52, 53, above.

[63] Dt. 33, Blessing of Moses, belongs in the same category as the Blessings of Isaac (Gn. 27), the Blessings of Jacob (Gn. 48, 49), and doubtless the last blessings found elsewhere in the Near East in the second millennium (*e.g.*, Nuzi; C. H. Gordon, *BA* 3 (1940), p. 8); Dt. 34 is simply a supplement to record the end of Moses. As above, my remarks are concerned primarily with the structure, or framework; they do not automatically imply or preclude later additions to (*e.g.*) legal matter, if factual evidence should require it – but any such additions must be within the total main framework required not by theory but by the tangible comparative data.

[64] *Cf.* the able surveys of imaginative but obsolete guesswork on Dt. in Eissfeldt, *The OT, an Introduction*, 1965, pp. 171–176, 219–233; the speculations there on the relation of D and B cannot be taken very seriously; *cf.* (*e.g.*) n. 6, p. 149, below. Here and on P, *etc.*, he inexcusably fails to deal with Kaufmann, *Religion of Israel*, 1961; his remarks on Kline (p. 176) are hardly just, as the correspondence of Dt. to the second-millennium pattern is a matter of observable *fact*, not of mere declaration.

Exodus 7 to 10 fits remarkably well into what is known of the natural phenomena of the Nile Valley and North-East Africa – but not so the 'J' and 'E' versions;[65] precisely the same is true of Numbers 16.[66] Perhaps we have here another literary miracle; in each case, original and parallel narratives that do not correspond to any reality are put together and suddenly then correspond to relevant sets of rather special natural conditions. It is difficult to suppress at least a mild scepticism!

3. *Linguistic, Literary and Textual Details.* Certain difficult expressions and passages in Leviticus could be solved only with cuneiform data of the eighteenth to fifteenth centuries BC. As noted by Speiser, these were archaic and obscure by the post-exilic period and by their distribution show a callous disregard for the distinction commonly drawn between 'H'(oliness Code) and 'P', *etc.* Four swallows do not make a summer – but this is a hint of future trends.[67] In literary matters, the variation in ancient curse-collections invalidates conventional criteria applied to them;[68] the variations of grammatical person or number (as in Deuteronomy: 'ye/thou') on Near Eastern comparative evidence are no criterion.[69] In text-study, adduction of LXX variations can be a hazardous venture.[70]

[65] On the plagues of Egypt; see below, p. 157 and note 20.

[66] On the twin rebellions of Korah and Dathan and Abiram, and the probable phenomenon (*kewir* mudflats) in the Arabah; see G. Hort, *Australian Biblical Review* 7 (1959), pp. 2–26, esp. 19–26; brief summary, Kitchen, *NBD*, p. 1329.

[67] E. A. Speiser, 'Leviticus and the Critics', *Yehezkel Kaufmann Jubilee Volume*, 1960, pp. 29–45 (English section); *cf.* Chapter 8, p. 149, below.

[68] As clearly shown by Hillers, in relation to typical efforts by Steuernagel, Wright and others; *cf.* note 52, p. 101, above.

[69] *Cf.* K. Baltzer, *Das Bundesformular*, 1960, pp. 29 n. 4; 43 n. 1; 44 n. 3; 49 and n. 2, in every case with appropriate Near Eastern data, to which add W. L. Moran, *Biblica* 43 (1962), p. 103. Analyses that use these variations must be politely but firmly discarded – or else applied to first-hand Near Eastern documents with absurd consequences; in their human aspect, the OT writings cannot be exempted as a special case, merely out of *pietas* for time-worn theory.

[70] One may mention here the old idea that the LXX order of Ex. 35–40 was more original than that of the Hebrew text, and would possibly

I

II. FORM CRITICISM

Form criticism (*Gattungsforschung* or *Formgeschichte*) in relation to the Old Testament was mainly initiated and inspired in modern times by Hermann Gunkel.[71] He sought to examine and classify the forms and units of literary expression used in the Old Testament; to determine the function of each form or unit; and to show how Hebrew literature might have grown from brief, early forms (originating in oral tradition) to longer compositions and eventually whole books. This he first applied to the narratives of Genesis,[72] and later to the Psalms.[73] Others followed in his steps.[74] The original idea of investigating the various literary structures and units employed in Hebrew literature (and turning the knowledge gained to exegetical account) was excellent in principle, and added a new dimension to Old Testament studies otherwise dominated by hypotheses of the documentary kind. Some use was made of Ancient Oriental literature, but only to a limited extent.

---

support literary dissection of that part of Exodus. However, a close scrutiny of the LXX material shows that its order is derivative and that of the Hebrew, original; see D. W. Gooding, *The Account of the Tabernacle*, 1959 (= *Texts and Studies*, new series, VI). The LXX cannot, therefore, offer any support for dissection of Ex. 35–40.

[71] See the excellent outline in H. F. Hahn, *The Old Testament in Modern Research*, 1956, pp. 119–156, and exposition of the method by K. Koch, *Was ist Formgeschichte?*, *Neue Wege der Bibelexegese*, 1964.

[72] H. Gunkel, *Die Genesis*, 1901 (repr. 1964); the Introduction was also produced separately as *Die Sagen der Genesis*, 1901. The latter appeared in English as *The Legends of Genesis*, 1901, being reprinted in 1964 (paperbound) with an introduction by W. F. Albright appraising Gunkel's work, with criticisms that are just but inadequate as far as Genesis is concerned.

[73] *E.g.*, H. Gunkel, *Die Psalmen*, 1926, and esp. H. Gunkel and J. Begrich, *Einleitung in die Psalmen*, I–II, 1928–33. On this aspect of Gunkel's work (more constructive than on Genesis), see the richly documented surveys by J. Coppens, in R. de Langhe (ed.), *Le Psautier* (*OBL*, IV), 1962, pp. 1–71 (esp. 9 ff.), A. Descamps, *ibid.*, pp. 73–88, and E. Lipinski, *ibid.*, pp. 133–272 (esp. 166 ff.). Handy summary by A. R. Johnson in Rowley (ed.), *The OT and Modern Study*, 1951, pp. 162–181.

[74] *E.g.*, H. Gressmann, *Mose und seine Zeit*, 1913, and the contributors to *Die Schriften des Alten Testaments*, I–III, 2nd ed., 1920–5; A. Alt (*e.g.*, on law) and M. Noth (pentateuchal matters, Jos.); and particularly the Scandinavians, but with special reference to oral tradition (see below).

So far so good; unfortunately, various assumptions and elaborations that underlie or have become attached to the basic idea of literary categories are open to serious objections, especially in the light of the actual history and forms of Ancient Oriental literature.

First, the idea of a unilinear evolution from smaller, 'primitive', literary units to larger, more complex entities (and of growth of a work by gradual accretion) is a fallacy from the mid-third-millennium BC onwards, as far as Ancient Oriental literature is concerned. Albright began to point this out some time ago in relation to form criticism and biblical and Homeric studies.[75] The truth is that literary works (and units within them) vary considerably in length, even within a given class, at any one period. Thus, among Sumerian literature of *c.* 1800 BC, Kramer mentions[76] nine epic tales that vary in length from about 100 up to 600 lines; scores of hymns (of four different types) ranging from less than fifty to over 400 lines in length; several laments for Dumuzi (Tammuz) varying from less than fifty to over 200 lines. In the Sumerian proverb-collections of this time, individual proverbs vary in length from one line to a maximum of ten lines,[77] and so on. In Egypt, the story of Sinuhe (*c.* 1900 BC)[78] is just a little longer than the Tale of the Two Brothers[79] and the Contendings of Horus and Seth[80] (both in versions of the thirteenth century BC). These exhibit a constancy of average length over six centuries (alongside

[75] In *VTS*, III, 1955, p. 4, and especially in *American Journal of Archaeology* 54 (1950), pp. 162–164.

[76] In *BANE*, pp. 255, 257, *etc.*

[77] Compare statistics in E. I. Gordon, *Sumerian Proverbs*, 1959, pp. 26, 154; *JAOS* 77 (1957), p. 67; *JCS* 12 (1958), p. 3. On this material, *cf.* E. I. Gordon, *Bibliotheca Orientalis* 17 (1960), pp. 125–134.

[78] Translations (partial) by Wilson in *ANET*, pp. 18–22, (complete) by G. Lefebvre, *Romans et Contes Égyptiens*, 1949, pp. 1–25, among others.

[79] Full translations in Lefebvre, *op. cit.*, pp. 137–158, and (ageing) in A. Erman and A. M. Blackman, *Literature of the Ancient Egyptians*, 1927, pp. 150–161; only the first half is given in *ANET*, pp. 23–25.

[80] Full translations, Lefebvre, *op. cit.*, pp. 178–203, and A. H. Gardiner, *The Library of A. Chester Beatty*, 1931, pp. 13–26; summarizing, Wilson, *ANET*, pp. 14–17.

shorter and longer pieces, both 'late' and 'early'), and they did not grow by gradual accretion. Excessive atomization of Hebrew literature, for example, the prophets, was most effectively criticized by the Assyriologist, Sidney Smith.[81] He was able to show that the smallest units by themselves are incomplete unless understood as parts of an integral whole.

Secondly, while use of varied literary forms for different purposes is a useful distinction, it should not be overpressed in a mechanical way, and one must recognize that ancient writers were not entirely hidebound by customary form. Thus, for example, in Egypt the so-called Instruction of Sehetepibrē', by outward criteria a wisdom-work (like Amenemope or Proverbs), is virtually a loyalist hymn to the king; 'wisdom' here is narrowed to loyalty to the Crown, the language is hymnic, and forms and uses no longer correspond neatly.[82]

Thirdly, the idea that form can determine the historical worth of a tradition is fallacious.[83] In Egypt, the warlike exploits of Tuthmosis III (c. 1460 BC) are no less real whether they appear in formal statistical annals, in anthologies of his outstanding deeds, or in victory-hymns.[84]

Fourthly, a word of caution is called for on the search for *Sitz im Leben* (situation in life; or better, cultural context). Besides studying literary forms and units, Gunkel sought also to attribute each form to an appropriate situation in the life of the people.[85] Again, this has its due place if properly applied. But

---

[81] S. Smith, *Isaiah Chapters XL–LV*, 1944, pp. 1–23 (Lecture I).

[82] For this work (nineteenth century BC), see C. Kuentz in *Studies Presented to F. Ll. Griffith*, 1932, pp. 97–110; evaluation and further references, G. Posener, *Littérature et Politique dans l'Égypte de la XIIe Dynastie*, 1956, pp. 117–124.

[83] Already correctly stated by J. Bright, *Early Israel in Recent History Writing*, 1956, pp. 90–91 (in dealing with Noth). Note also Albright's remarks on the Patriarchs in his introduction to Gunkel, *The Legends of Genesis*, 1964, pp. viii–xi, modifying Gunkel.

[84] Parts of the Annals and of the Gebel Barkal and Armant 'anthology' stelae are given by Wilson in *ANET*, pp. 234–241; for the Karnak Poetical stela and Gebel Barkal stela, see already p. 117, with notes 13–14, above.

[85] Effectively exemplified by Koch, *Was ist Formgeschichte?*, 1964, pp. 3 ff., from circulars for weed-killer and then biblical examples. An outline of

too often it has been applied in direct opposition to clear biblical data (and without reference to external controls). And as too
often happens in the Old Testament field, some scholars' imagi-
nations ran riot, examples of cultic *Sitz im Leben* were seen on
every side,[86] and the eager quest for cultural contexts has un-
doubtedly produced some of the most exotic flights of fancy and
conjecture in Old Testament studies.[87] All manner of 'lists', for
example, are noted in the Old Testament; but some are characterized as genuine (*i.e.*, historical) and others as mere inventions of late date in flat contradiction of context and on the
basis of current theory, not of tangible control.[88] The renewed
emphasis on the connection of the Psalms with religion and cult
is fair enough. But in Mowinckel's case this has passed over into
a one-sided compulsion of nearly all Psalms into a cultic strait-
jacket regardless of other aspects.[89]

---

categories and conventional judgments on them, Eissfeldt, *The OT, an
Introduction*, 1965, pp. 9–127.

[86] 'There was no portion of the [OT] literature which could escape such
an interpretation' (Hahn, *The OT in Modern Research*, pp. 142–143).

[87] See, for example, certain Scandinavian experiments quoted by Hahn,
op. cit., pp. 145–146, and p. 149 (noting that Mowinckel's treatment of Ex. 34
for cultural context rested on conjecture [not facts]; 'freeing the laws . . .
from their literary context', however, is not a 'merit' (to use Hahn's word)
but simply an arbitrary destruction of covenantal context).

[88] *Cf.*, for example, Eissfeldt, *The OT, an Introduction*, pp. 25–26. The high
numbers in Nu. 1 and 26 are not a sufficient ground for dismissing these
chapters from their explicit contexts; numbers constitute a special class of
problem in both OT and Ancient Orient, and there is much archaic matter
here (*e.g.*, names of princes in Nu. 1). Rejection to a hypothetical later age
and cultural context as 'invention' (also route-lists, Nu. 33) rests wholly upon literary-critical presupposition, not on tangible facts or external control.

[89] While the hymn of Ex. 15 could well have been used in worship (or,
'cult'), as Mowinckel thinks, yet his further conviction that it is a 'festal
hymn . . . originally no doubt belonging to the cult' (*The Psalms in Israel's
Worship*, I, 1962, p. 126) goes against both the context and the external
background. This is a triumph-hymn, the Hebrew counterpart of the
Egyptian triumph-hymns of Tuthmosis III, Amenophis III, Ramesses II
and Merenptah, or even that of Tukulti-Ninurta I of Assyria; its archaic
character has been partly brought out by F. M. Cross and D. N. Freedman,
JNES 14 (1955), pp. 237–250, and N. C. Habel, *Yahweh versus Baal*, 1964,
pp. 58–62, 64–66; more could be done. Again, the term *le-Dāwîd*, 'by/for/per-

The question of cultural context is much more complicated than generally realized. The partial fluidity of function with literary forms (*cf.* preceding two paragraphs) forbids a mechanical application of the principle. Furthermore, the interaction with historical event or individual activity should not be obscured or lost sight of. Thus, it is easy to group social laws and cult-regulations into small collections on the basis of their content or form and postulate their gradual accretion in the present books, with practical elimination of Moses. One may do this equally to the Hammurapi laws (on content), and postulate there a hypothetical process of accretion of laws into groups on themes prior to conflation in Hammurapi's so-called 'code'. But this does not eliminate Hammurapi from 'authorship'[90] of his 'code'. His laws are known from a monument of his own time in his own name; therefore, any accretions of laws in his collection occurred before his work. This could also apply in the Old Testament. Furthermore, there are apparent contradictions or discrepancies in the Hammurapi 'code' that are 'no less glaring than those which serve as the basis of analysing strata in the Bible'.[91] These obviously have no bearing on the historical fact of Hammurapi having incorporated them in his collection. And so the similar phenomena in the Old Testament cannot be used to eliminate Moses at those points where the text (as opposed to any later traditions) assigns him a role

taining to David' cannot be limited in the ways suggested by Mowinckel, *op. cit.*, I, p. 77; II, pp. 98 ff., but because of space-limits, this must be taken up elsewhere.

[90] This term implying, at minimum, ultimate responsibility for ordering the collection of the laws and their recording on stelae, *etc.*, provided with suitable prologue and epilogue. Hammurapi claims a little more than this, however, even though one does not take his every phrase literally ('my words which I wrote on my stela'); *cf.* M. Greenberg, *Yehezkel Kaufmann Jubilee Volume*, 1960, pp. 9–10 and n. 10 (English section). *Cf. ANET*, p. 178 *passim*.

[91] Quoting Greenberg, *op. cit.*, p. 6. Note also his instructive contrast between Koschaker's 'literary-critical' approach to the Hammurapi laws and that of Sir J. C. Miles which seeks for the real legal distinctions that underlie the superficial difficulties (*op. cit.*, p. 7); *e.g.*, in the laws on theft (see G. R. Driver and Sir J. C. Miles, *The Babylonian Laws*, I, 1952, pp. 80–86).

in setting certain laws before the Hebrew tribes. In short, given material may in its ultimate origins have a 'cultural context' and yet subsequently be caught up in particular historical circumstances (Hammurapi, possibly Moses) and even pass from one setting to another within a culture. At all events, the usual guesswork needs to be ruthlessly pruned; much wider and more complex possibilities need to be examined, and external form-critical controls are sorely needed to be used in practice.

III. ORAL TRADITION

In this branch of study, Scandinavian scholars have been particularly prominent,[92] taking their cue from Nyberg.[93] They lay great stress on the alleged primacy of oral tradition (even beyond Gunkel), and would even claim that in the Ancient Orient writing is always secondary.[94] They suggest also that much Hebrew literature was handed down orally until quite late before being finally fixed in writing. Appeal is made to Ancient Oriental data, but in somewhat superficial (and sometimes misleading) fashion. The positions adopted by this school are open to considerable doubts and qualifications which can find only brief treatment here.

First, the term 'oral tradition' is inadequate and confusing, because it is used for two or three separate processes: oral composition of a work, and more particularly its oral *dissemination* to contemporaries, and oral *transmission* of a work down through time to posterity. Dissemination and transmission must be distinguished. In the Ancient Near East, oral dissemination doubtless was of primary importance except in official and ruling circles. But it was often done from written documents. A classic example is 2 Chronicles 17:9, in which we see King

---

[92] E.g., H. Birkeland, *Zum hebräischen Traditionswesen*, 1938; I. Engnell, *Gamla Testamentet*, I, 1945; and in English, especially E. Nielsen, *Oral Tradition*, 1954 (=*SBT*, No. 11).

[93] H. S. Nyberg, *Studien zum Hoseabuche*, 1935, pp. 1–20; cf. also J. Pedersen, *ZAW* 49 (1931), pp. 161–181.

[94] E.g., Birkeland, cited by Nielsen, *op. cit.*, p. 13; cf. Nyberg, *op. cit.*, p. 7 (on primacy; but note his resort to late Arabic, *etc.*, for examples).

Jehoshaphat sending out Levites to teach the people *orally* from a *written* law. For transmission of anything important to posterity, the Ancient Orient insistently resorted to written rather than oral transmission. This is sufficiently illustrated by the hundreds of thousands of clay tablets from Mesopotamia and the acres of hieroglyphic texts and scenes from Egypt covering all aspects of life. The pompous annals of energetic kings and the cuneiform litigation or humble hieroglyphic stelae of citizens of very modest means alike show that neither national traditions nor the repute of individuals was left to the care of campfire bards in the Ancient Near East.[95]

Secondly, it is significant how often Nielsen, for example, has to draw his parallels not from Ancient Oriental literature proper but from different and thus mainly irrelevant historical periods and cultures: for example, Old Iceland, Islam, Persia, the works of Plato, Hindu India, *etc.*[96] His use of Ancient Oriental data can be quite misleading. For oral transmission, he cites the colophon of a Babylonian hymn to Ea.[97] But this colophon does not place any value on oral transmission. Rather it gives a warning: 'This text is taken *only* from oral tradition, it has not been copied from a proper written original!' And in Egypt, it is simply not true that the scribes were all recruited from the highest class of the population,[98] at least not for the 1,000 years from the end of the Old Kingdom to the end of the New Kingdom (*i.e.*, *c.* 2100–1100 BC).[99] The assertion that writing was the affair of the specialist in Palestine[100] is grotesque; an alphabet

[95] On limits of oral tradition in Mesopotamia, *cf.* recently A. L. Oppenheim, *Ancient Mesopotamia*, 1964, pp. 22–23, 258–259.

[96] *E.g.*, Nielsen, *op. cit.*, pp. 21–24, 32, 33, 35, 37, *etc.*

[97] *Ibid.*, pp. 28–29; the colophon reads, 'written from the scholar's dictation; the old edition I have not seen'.

[98] *Ibid.*, pp. 25, 28.

[99] See H. Brunner, *Altägyptische Erziehung*, 1957, pp. 40–42 and p. 169 (Quellen XXXII and XXXIV). Nor were the scribes at Deir el Medineh in Western Thebes generally of exalted origin; for this community, see J. Černý, *CAH²*, II: 35, *Egypt from the Death of Ramesses III to the End of the Twenty-first Dynasty*, 1965, pp. 17–23, or more briefly W. Helck and E. Otto, *Kleines Wörterbuch der Aegyptologie*, 1965, pp. 243 f.

[100] Nielsen, *op. cit.*, p. 56.

of twenty-six letters or so is no strain on anyone's memory. Furthermore, Engnell's argument[101] that the written literature of Ugarit seems to be unique in Syria-Palestine, and that nothing analogous has been found in this well-explored region, overlooks various facts,[102] most especially the fact that in Syria-Palestine (particularly in the first millennium) papyrus was extensively used, but has nearly all perished. Thus, we know that the princes of Byblos in Phoenicia c. 1100 BC had kept rolls of timber-accounts for generations[103] – but no scrap of these or any other papyri has ever been found by the French excavators at Byblos in what is a very productive site. Still more might be said by way of legitimate criticism and qualification.

The truth is that all three approaches criticized on factual and methodological grounds above rest much too heavily on preconceived theories imposed upon the Old Testament, instead of proceeding from an inductive and exhaustive survey of actual Ancient Oriental evidence for literary forms, methods and usages in the biblical East. For this fundamental reason, the results of these schools are suspect to a very large extent, and ultimately must be discarded in favour of new and properly-based results securely founded on the maximum relevant comparative data[104] with a more intelligent treatment of the Hebrew text in the light of that material. Biblical criticism in the proper sense there must be. We advocate not its abolition, but its radical reconstruction, conditioned by the context of the biblical world instead of by Western philosophical schemes,

[101] Quoted by Nielsen, *op. cit.*, p. 17.

[102] *E.g.*, the occurrence of documents in Ugaritic script away from Ugarit, at Tell Sukas, Mount Tabor, Beth Shemesh, and Taanach (for Tell Sukas excavations, *cf.* refs. in D. J. Wiseman, T. C. Mitchell, R. Joyce, W. J. Martin, K. A. Kitchen, *Notes on Some Problems in the Book of Daniel*, 1965, p. 45, n. 76; for the others, *cf.* D. R. Hillers and W. F. Albright, *BASOR* 173 (1964), p. 45 n. 2, 45–53); the everyday nature of linear alphabetic epigraphs from Late Bronze Age Palestine. The mounds of Syria-Palestine are still much less well-explored in depth than Engnell seems to have realized.

[103] From the Travels of Wenamun, c. 1090 BC; mostly translated in *ANET*, pp. 25–29 (the 'journal rolls', p. 27a bottom).

[104] Note already the remarks in passing by W. W. Hallo, *IEJ* 12 (1962), pp. 13–14, 26 end.

medieval and Western literary categories, particularly of the eighteenth to twentieth centuries AD. The material presented in the foregoing sections is only a tiny fraction of all that is available or that could be done – and that in the future will have to be done.

7. PRINCIPLES OF LINGUISTIC STUDY

I. THE NEED FOR SOUND METHOD

Alongside the data provided by the Ancient Near East, one must employ sound principles established by modern linguistic study when dealing with the languages of the Bible. However, in some recent so-called 'biblical theology' much stress has been laid on the supposed differences between Hebrew and Greek thought and usage, accompanied by a theory that the grammar and vocabulary of a given language (in this case, Hebrew) can be equated with the thought-patterns of its speakers, and that these supposed patterns can be read off from the alleged special characteristics of the language. These ideas seem very attractive, but unfortunately they are very questionable. They have not been based on sound linguistic procedure (which has been neglected), but have been accompanied by misuse of etymologies and by confusion of the diachronic (historical) and synchronic (contextual) aspects of biblical semantics (study of the meanings of words). Even more unfortunately, these mistaken theories and untenable methods are not merely the property of some minor party in biblical or theological study, but largely underlie even so justly famed a project as the great Kittel-Friedrich, *Theologisches Wörterbuch zum Neuen Testament*,[1] and characterize the quite independent study by Thorleif Boman, *Hebrew Thought Compared with Greek* (1960).[2]

These erroneous procedures and the urgent need for ordinary, sound linguistic method in theology and biblical study were appropriately treated with care and in some detail by J.

[1] At least in conception and intention; this massive work is of very considerable value, particularly in so far as it does not adhere consistently to the procedures here criticized.

[2] English translation of *Das hebräische Denken im Vergleich mit dem Griechischen*[2], 1954.

139

Barr in a recent work[3] to which the interested reader may here be referred for fuller details. It is to be hoped that students of the Old Testament and theologians will profit by Barr's thoughtful criticisms, improve their methods of working and thereby place their own work on the soundest possible foundations.

II. THE ROLE OF EMENDATION

One may state a principle echoed by leading Egyptologists long ago: 'Emendation serves only for the removal of the absolutely vicious', and '. . . is always to be avoided if possible'.[4] In other words, it is to be used only when no other valid course is open to the interpreter of a text. Until recent decades, Old Testament scholars were much too partial to emendation of the consonantal text of the Hebrew Bible (the notes in the *Biblia Hebraica*, edited by Kittel, exhibit this fault to a degree, as is widely recognized), but nowadays they show a much greater and commendable caution in this regard. The evidence of the Dead Sea Scrolls and the rich harvest of linguistic gains from Ugaritic or North Canaanite have repeatedly demonstrated the essential soundness of the consonantal Hebrew text at many points where obscurity had hitherto tempted to emendation. In the Ancient Near East, moreover, there were definite ideals of accurate scribal copying of manuscripts (a point often overlooked). One example from Egypt must here suffice. A funerary papyrus of about 1400 BC bears the colophon: '[The book] is completed from its beginning to its end, having been copied, revised, compared and verified sign by sign.'[5] There is no reason to assume that the Hebrews would be less careful with their literary products, a further reason for the exercise of due caution in emending the consonantal Hebrew text.

[3] J. Barr, *The Semantics of Biblical Language*, 1961, supplemented by the same writer's *Biblical Words for Time*, 1962 (=*SBT*, No. 33) and 'Hypostatization of Linguistic Phenomena in Modern Theological Interpretation', *JSS* 7 (1962), pp. 85–94.

[4] The latter quotation from A. M. Blackman, *JEA* 16 (1930), p. 63.

[5] J. Černý, *Paper and Books in Ancient Egypt*, 1952, p. 25; H. Grapow, *Chronique d'Égypte* 14/fasc. 28 (1939), p. 225. Mesopotamia would probably yield even more evidence on this topic than does Egypt.

One particular form of emendation is especially to be avoided, namely, emendation *metri causa*. This has often been imposed on Hebrew poetry in the past to give it a mechanical regularity of syllabic or accentual or strophic structure that it in fact never originally possessed. A lesson in this field has been administered by studies like that of Ugaritic prosody by G. D. Young[6] who showed that mechanical regularity is quite alien to Ugaritic poets, the literary and linguistic forms of whose works are very close indeed to Hebrew. In Egypt, too, absolute regularity of structure was not always specially sought, as can be seen, for example, by examining the structure of works like the 'Kahun' hymns to Sesostris III,[7] or the poems in the *Lebensmüde*.[8]

III. LEXICAL CRITERIA AND THE DATING OF OLD TESTAMENT LITERATURE

(a) *Three Essential Principles*

Sometimes a word may occur only a few times in the Old Testament or only in restricted contexts (ritual, poetry, *etc.*), and then never again in existing available sources until post-biblical writings of the Roman period, for example, the Mishna. This phenomenon is invariably interpreted by Old Testament scholars in one way only, although in fact it can be explained in any of *three* different ways:

1. The common occurrence of a word only at a very late period may imply that a few apparently 'early' occurrences should also be considered as 'late' and (if original in the text) carrying down to a similarly late date the production of the writings in which they occur. This is invariably the line of

---

[6] *JNES* 9 (1950), pp. 124–133; C. H. Gordon, *UM*, I, p. 108 and n.1 (*UT*, p. 131 and n.2). *Cf.* also M. Held, *JBL* 84 (1965), pp. 272–282, on wrong emendation of verb-repetition.

[7] Translated in A. Erman and A. M. Blackman, *Literature of the Ancient Egyptians*, 1927, pp. 134–137; *cf.* also H. Grapow, *MIO* 1 (1953), pp. 189–209, and G. Posener, *Littérature et Politique dans l'Égypte de la XIIe Dynastie*, 1956, pp. 128–130.

[8] Translations by Wilson, *ANET*, pp. 405–407, and R. O. Faulkner, *JEA* 42 (1956), pp. 21–40; but see also R. J. Williams, *JEA* 48 (1962), pp. 49–56, on this text.

reasoning followed in Old Testament studies – hence some of the arguments for, for example, an exilic or later 'P'-source in the Pentateuch, late Psalms or post-exilic dates for wisdom-literature. The other two possibilities seem almost never to be envisaged in works on the Old Testament.

2. The 'early' occurrences of such words (say, in the Pentateuch and then not until the Mishna) *may* in fact be valuable evidence of how *early* the word really was used, and its absence otherwise before late times would then be the accidental result of negative evidence.

3. A genuinely 'late' word which appears in a supposedly 'early' composition *may* be a later substitution for another term which has become obsolete, or offensive, or has changed its meaning. Such a substitute can only date itself, and not the composition in which it now appears.

Now, principles 2 and 3 are *not* simply a piece of theoretical special pleading. They are well-attested as real facts of experience from the objectively-dated literary remains of the Ancient Near East. One example for each of these principles is but a token of many more.

In accord with principle 2, it is a well-known phenomenon in Egyptology for words to occur sporadically in, say, the Pyramid Texts of about 2400 BC – and then to disappear largely or even entirely from our view until they suddenly reappear (sometimes in more frequent use) in the Ptolemaic and later temple-inscriptions of the Graeco-Roman period.[9] Now, if the one-sided emphasis on principle 1 that occurs in Old Testament studies were to be applied identically in Egyptology, the Pyramids of the Sixth Dynasty (*c.* 2400 BC) would have to be dated (because of 'late words' in their texts) some twenty-one centuries later to the Greek period (*c.* 300–30 BC)! To compress

---

[9] Examples from A. Erman and H. Grapow, *Wörterbuch der Aegyptischen Sprache*: II, p. 274:10, *nnt*, a kind of reed; II, p. 489: 3, *ḥp mꜥ*, 'to free from'; IV, p. 72:4–6, *swḥ*, 'to wrap, cover'; V, p. 37:7–8, *ḳmꜥ*, 'to mourn' and a derivative; or words like *ḥnwt*, 'vessel', so far known only twice in an Eighteenth-Dynasty tomb, between the Old Kingdom and the Graeco-Roman period (III, p. 106: 18–22). Full references in the *Belegstellen* volumes to the *Wörterbuch*.

2,100 years of intervening Egyptian history into two hundred years by this means is, of course, absurd. Yet by their indiscriminate use of the 'late word' argument, Old Testament scholars can hardly avoid committing absurd distortions of this kind within the history of Hebrew literature and religion.

In illustration of principle 3, one may cite the occurrence of *yam*, 'sea', 'waterflood', and the Late-Egyptian negative *bw* in the Ashmolean Ostracon text[10] of the story of Sinuhe which would, on the principle-1 reasoning of Old Testament scholarship, suggest a date of composition about 1500 BC or later, for this work and not in the twentieth century BC as required by statements made in its text. However, the existence of manuscripts[11] of about 1800 BC (with their readings also retained in other later MSS) reveals that *yam* and *bw* were actually substitutions in the Ashmolean text for the old word *nwy* and the Middle-Egyptian negative *n*, respectively; principle 1 would not be applicable, of course. In the Old Testament, it may be nothing more than the lack of *really* early and old MSS from periods long before the Dead Sea Scrolls that prevents us from finding that the same thing may sometimes be true there.

(b) The Value of Collateral Evidence

Furthermore, Old Testament scholars too often ignore collateral evidence for the early existence and use of words that they have considered to be 'late', evidence contained, for example, in Ugaritic, West-Semitic loanwords in Akkadian (Assyro-Babylonian) or in Egyptian, and they persist in this even after that evidence has been pointed out (*cf.* § (*c*), below).

Thus, it has already been noted above[12] that Hebrew *'edūth*, 'covenant (stipulations)', is not a late Aramaism but an early Canaanism, being already known as a loanword with a secondary meaning in Egyptian in the first half of the twelfth century BC. Also found as a loanword in Egyptian at this

---

[10] J. W. B. Barns, *The Ashmolean Ostracon of Sinuhe*, 1952, pp. 12 (rt. 45) and 22 (vs. 25).

[11] See Posener, *loc. cit.* (p. 24, note 20, above).

[12] See p. 108, note 84.

period is *ktm*, 'gold', (as *ktmt*) with a prehistory reaching back to Sumerian.[13] It should not of itself, therefore, be considered as 'late'.[14] The words *krz*, 'make proclamation', and *krwz*, 'herald', in biblical Aramaic have been assigned a Greek origin[15] and more recently an Old Persian origin.[16] But a study of Hurrian *kirenzi* (from a **kirezzi*), 'proclamation', in a Nuzi document of about 1500 BC[17] indicates that forms from *krz* had begun to enter Semitic at least a millennium earlier than any of us had hitherto suspected. The word *ḥmr* for 'wine' in biblical Hebrew and Aramaic may well be poetic but cannot now be described as late,[18] being attested in Ugaritic (thirteenth century BC at latest) and Mari Akkadian (*c.* eighteenth century BC).[19] Similarly, *špr* in biblical Aramaic (and once in Hebrew, Psalm 16:6) for 'be fair', 'acceptable', 'pleasant' may possibly be rare but is certainly not 'late'.[20] Known in Aramaic of the eighth and fifth centuries BC (Sfiré stelae; Ahiqar papyrus), it is not restricted to Aramaic but is common West Semitic as is shown by its occurrence in personal names of that kind (*cf.* Shiprah, Ex. 1:15) in the eighteenth century BC in both Egyptian and cuneiform sources.[21] The vast linguistic treasury of the Ancient Near East is constantly enriching our background for biblical lexicography and counsels the greatest caution over what may really be termed 'late'.

[13] See T. O. Lambdin, *JAOS* 73 (1953), pp. 151–152, following on M. Burchardt, *Die Altkanaanäischen Fremdworte und Eigennamen im Aegyptischen*, II, 1911, p. 53, No. 1036, and W. F. Albright, *The Vocalization of the Egyptian Syllabic Orthography*, 1934, p. 61 (XVII: C: 11).

[14] As, for example, in F. Brown, S. R. Driver, C. A. Briggs, *Hebrew and English Lexicon of the Old Testament*, 1907, p. 508b.

[15] *E.g.*, *ibid.*, p. 1097b (and others).

[16] *E.g.*, H. H. Schaeder, *Iranische Beiträge I*, 1930, p. 254 [56].

[17] A. Shaffer, *Orientalia NS* 34 (1965), pp. 32–34.

[18] As (*e.g.*) in Brown, Driver, Briggs, *op. cit.*, p. 1093a.

[19] *UM*, III, No. 713 (*UT*, No. 972; differently, Dahood, *Biblica* 45 (1964), 408–9); M. L. Burke, *ARMT*, XI, 1963, p. 133, §11.

[20] *E.g.*, Brown, Driver, Briggs, *op. cit.*, p. 1117.

[21] References in D. J. Wiseman *et al.*, *Notes on Some Problems in the Book of Daniel*, 1965, pp. 33–34, note 18, to which add the cuneiform references in H. B. Huffmon, *Amorite Personal Names in the Mari Texts*, 1965, p. 252.

(c) The Question of Aramaisms

The common dictum that Aramaisms are necessarily late is all too often erroneous.[22] In the first place, a great number of so-called Aramaisms (i.e., Aramaic loanwords in Hebrew) are really just early West Semitic terms found not least in poetry and are not specifically Aramaic at all (even if commoner in that language). By way of a purely random example, Eissfeldt in 1964–5 still labelled[23] qibbel, 'receive' (Pr. 19:20), and naḥat, 'go down' (Pr. 17:10) – with other words – as 'Aramaisms' and therefore late, implying an exilic or later date for the relevant parts of Proverbs. Yet over twenty years earlier, Albright had pointed out[24] that the very same term qibbel occurs (in the form tiqa(b)bilu) – and actually in a proverb – in an Amarna letter from the Canaanite king of Shechem to the pharaoh in the fourteenth century BC! It is, therefore, an early Canaanism[25] and not a late Aramaism. The same is true of naḥat, first noted in the Ugaritic epics some thirty years ago.[26] Eissfeldt has never heeded these facts; and so far as these two words are concerned his statements on their date and nature are wrong and the dependent deductions for the date of those parts of Proverbs are unjustified. There is no reason to believe that the other two words he cites exemplify anything more than negative evidence and the inevitable use of principle 1.[27] Nor is this case unique in Old Testament studies at large.

[22] Demonstrated long ago by R. D. Wilson, A Scientific Investigation of the Old Testament, 1926 (repr. 1959), pp. 112–126.

[23] In The OT, an Introduction, 1965, p. 474.

[24] BASOR 89 (1943), p. 31 n. 16.

[25] Or more strictly, an old West Semitic word shared by Canaanite, Hebrew and Aramaic, later perhaps more common in Aramaic but still used archaistically in Hebrew.

[26] Ugaritic nḥt, C. H. Gordon, UM, III, p. 295, No. 1231 (=UT, No. 1635); first identified by C. Virolleaud, Syria 14 (1933), p. 145, and its relevance noted by E. J. Young, Introduction to the Old Testament¹, 1949, p. 303 (³1964, p. 313). A different treatment of nḥt by J. Aistleitner, Wörterbuch der Ugaritischen Sprache, 1963, p. 204, No. 1771, depends on an unnecessary Arabic etymology and is less suitable in contexts; cf. (e.g.) M. Dahood, Proverbs and Northwest Semitic Philology, 1963, pp. 45–46.

[27] Thus, rʿʿ appears in Old Aramaic as rqq in Sfiré stela III: 6 in the eighth century BC; cf. A. Dupont-Sommer, Bulletin du Musée de Beyrouth

K

Secondly, it should be remembered that Aramaean penetration of Syria and Mesopotamia was well under way in the twelfth to tenth centuries BC,[28] and Israel was in constant contact with Aramaeans from at least the time of David, when Syrian Aram was politically subject to Israel. Hence some Aramaisms could be expected at any time from about 1000 BC onwards. It has been suggested that early Aramaic or 'proto-Aramaic' forms (like final -$\bar{a}$)[29] can be found that go back to the days of the Patriarchs,[30] although this question requires great caution.[31] Even measuring from about 1000 BC, there is no warrant nowadays for treating genuine Aramaisms (when they can be proved to exist) as automatically 'late'.

---

13 (1956), p. 32 (meaning here 'to capture'). For '/q, cf. Kitchen in Wiseman et al., *Notes on Some Problems in the Book of Daniel*, 1965, p. 56, (iii).

[28] From the district of Palmyra eastward along the Middle Euphrates in the time of Tiglath-pileser I, for example (c. 1100 BC); cf. *ANET*, p. 275a, §b; E. Forrer in E. Ebeling and B. Meissner (eds.), *Reallexikon der Assyriologie*, I, 1928, pp. 131–139 (*Aramu*).

[29] In Cappadocian and Old Babylonian texts, W. Semitic personal names from Mari, *etc. Cf.* with references, C. F. Jean in A. Parrot (ed.), *Studia Mariana*, 1950, p. 71 n. 33, and p. 74; M. Noth, *Geschichte und Altes Testament (FS Alt)*, 1953, pp. 135–136, 152; and M. Tsevat in A. Berger *et al.* (eds.), *Joshua Bloch Memorial Volume*, 1960, pp. 89–91. On the basis of the Mari material, any connection with the Aramaic emphatic state is doubted by H. B. Huffmon, *Amorite Personal Names in the Mari Texts*, 1965, pp. 104 ff., 115–116. However, one would not expect to find the fully developed later usage in the early second millennium even if some classes of -$\bar{a}$ were ancestral to the later Aramaic article.

[30] *Cf.* W. F. Albright, *AfO* 6 (1930/31), p. 218 n. 4; Kitchen, *NBD*, p. 56.

[31] *Cf.* the 'proto-Aramaisms' suggested by M. Noth, *Die Ursprünge des alten Israel im Lichte neuer Quellen*, 1961, esp. pp. 34–40, and the critique (and virtual elimination) of these by D. O. Edzard, *ZA* 56/NF. 22 (1964), pp. 142–149. On 'early Aramaeans', *cf.* my *Hittite Hieroglyphs, Aramaeans and Hebrew Traditions*, ch. 2 (forthcoming).

8. FURTHER ASPECTS OF BIBLICAL AND ORIENTAL STUDIES

Much could be added to the preceding sections, and more work is being done in still other fields, with striking and valuable results. Law and topography are two such fields.

I. ANCIENT LAW IN THE BIBLICAL WORLD

Law has benefited from the discovery of several ancient collections of laws since the recovery of Hammurapi's stela in 1901–2.[1] Renewed interest in biblical law was stimulated by Alt's study in 1934, in which he emphasized the distinction in formulation as between 'casuistic' or case law ('If a man . . .') and 'apodictic' law ('Thou shalt/shalt not . . . '),[2] classing the former as Canaanite and the latter as more particularly Israelite. Unfortunately, the distinction has been over-emphasized, and apodictic formulations are not unique to Israel, as is clearly shown by the mixture of 'casuistic' and 'apodictic' forms in the treaty-covenants and laws of the Ancient Near East.[3]

[1] For the Ur-Nammu laws, cf. S. N. Kramer and A. Falkenstein, *Orientalia* 23 (1954), pp. 40–48; for those of Lipit-Ishtar, from Eshnunna, of Hammurapi, the Middle Assyrian, Hittite and Neo-Babylonian laws, see the translations with bibliographies in *ANET*, pp. 159–198; also R. Haase, *Einführung in das Studium Keilschriftlicher Rechtsquellen*, 1965, and *Die Keilschriftlichen Rechtssammlungen in Deutscher Übersetzung*, 1963.

[2] A. Alt, *Die Ursprünge des Israelitischen Rechts*, 1934, in *Berichte über die Verhandlungen der Sächsischen Akademie d. Wissenschaft*, Ph.-Hist. Kl., 86:1; repr. in *KS*, I, pp. 278–332.

[3] Note the criticisms by I. Rapaport, *PEQ*, October 1941, pp. 158–167, T. J. Meek, *Hebrew Origins*[2], 1950 (repr. 1960), p. 72, and S. Gevirtz, *VT* 11 (1961), pp. 137–158, esp. 156–157; a more elaborate critique is offered by E. Gerstenberger, *Wesen und Herkunft des 'Apodiktischen Rechts'*, 1965. For apodictic style (incl. 2nd person) in covenant-stipulations, cf. D. J. Mc-

A much more fruitful approach to Ancient Oriental and biblical law has been opened up by Greenberg.[4] As noted above (p. 134), he pointed out that 'discrepancies' occur within Hammurapi's laws that are just as severe as anything in the Pentateuch that has tempted Old Testament scholars into literary-critical schemes of unilinear development between 'codes'. The presence of such 'difficulties', deliberately included within a single law-collection such as Hammurapi's, is a signal warning that merely to arrange the offending laws in a unilinear scheme is not a proper solution at all – particularly as it 'leads to a disregard of [valid legal] distinctions' (Greenberg, pp.7–8). And comparison of biblical and extra-biblical laws has too often ignored the cultural backgrounds of both. Hence, one must work out the proper legal distinctions that exist within a given series of usages current with a people (be they Babylonians or Hebrews), and one must observe and apply the differences in the values that are basic to each culture (whether Hebrew, Babylonian or other). These two principles are brilliantly worked out and illustrated by Greenberg, using examples from the realm of criminal law. On the second principle, the underlying contrast in values between the Babylonian and Hebrew outlook emerges clearly: the latter sets a supreme value on human life in a religious context, while the former sets most store on the sanctity of property.[5] For illustration of the other principle, the reader must refer to Greenberg's study;

Carthy, *Treaty and Covenant*, 1963, pp. 36–37 and list, p. 49; 3rd person apodictic laws occur in the laws of Eshnunna, Hammurapi and the Middle Assyrian laws. Both 2nd and 3rd persons are used in West Semitic curse-formulae (Gevirtz, *loc. cit.*). G. von Rad, *Studies in Deuteronomy*, 1953, (=*SBT*, No. 9), pp. 17–36, over-emphasizes formal stylistic distinctions much as does Alt, and fails entirely to regulate his form-criticism by external controls (p. 24, combination of apodictic and conditional statutes in Near Eastern laws is ignored; p. 29, 'negative style' was never peculiar to any age).

[4] M. Greenberg, 'Some Postulates of Biblical Criminal Law' in *Yehezkel Kaufmann Jubilee Volume*, 1960, pp. 5–28 (English section).

[5] *Cf.* Greenberg, *op. cit.*, p. 18, on biblical severity and non-biblical leniency over homicide, and biblical leniency and non-biblical severity over property-offences.

at several points the supposed 'early–late' distinctions of the uni-linear kind simply fall away as meaningless.[6]

Not only the subject-matter and the form of biblical laws but also the linguistic usage can be so old that it is only fully ex-plicable in terms of external data (especially cuneiform) from the first half of the second millennium BC. As already men-tioned above (p. 129), this has been shown by Speiser[7] for some difficult expressions in Leviticus. This can apply both to in-dividual words and verses (*e.g.*, Lv. 19:20, 21; 27:12) and to connected passages (*e.g.*, Lv. 5:15 ff.; 25:35–54).[8] Further-more, it is probably misleading to use the word 'code' both of the Near Eastern law-collections[9] and of the biblical laws,[10] and so this term (with overtones of 'Code Napoléon') should be dropped in favour of more neutral terms such as 'law-collec-tions', 'laws', or (legal) usage.

II. THE TOPOGRAPHY OF BIBLE LANDS

Topography has always been a concern of biblical and Near Eastern studies since the pioneer days of Edward Robinson,[11]

[6] This has a direct and unfavourable bearing on the conventional kind of speculations indulged in by (*e.g.*) Eissfeldt, *The OT, an Introduction*, 1965, pp. 220 ff. (esp. on the relationship of D(eut.) and B(ook of the Covenant) in Ex.). On the real relationships between the laws of Ex., Nu., Lv., and Dt., the unpretentious little volume by G. T. Manley, *The Book of the Law*, 1957, esp. chapters vi–ix, is far more realistic than the kind of romancing exemplified by Eissfeldt (who cites Manley's book, but ignores his evidence), and is much closer methodologically to Miles's treatment of the Hammurapi laws in Sir J. C. Miles and G. R. Driver, *The Babylonian Laws*, I, 1952, as well as to the important issues raised by Greenberg.

[7] E. A. Speiser, *Yehezkel Kaufmann Jubilee Volume*, 1960, pp. 29–45 (Eng-lish section).

[8] The passages quoted are those dealt with by Speiser, *loc. cit.*

[9] On the possible function and nature of the 'codes' of Lipit-Ishtar, Hammurapi, *etc.*, and their indirect relation to royal edicts at the begin-ning of a king's reign, *cf.* J. J. Finkelstein, *JCS* 15 (1961), pp. 100–104, and D. J. Wiseman, *JSS* 7 (1962), pp. 161–172, with earlier references.

[10] Thus, in Ex., Dt., Jos., and possibly Lv., the commandments and 'laws' also come within the framework of covenant-form and its stipulations (*cf.* pp. 90–102, above).

[11] E. Robinson, *Biblical Researches in Palestine (etc.)*, I–III, 1841, and

and not least in studies by Alt and Noth between the two world wars.[12] More recently, a great deal of valuable work has been done by scholars in Israel; for example, surveys and excavations in Philistia,[13] the Negeb and Arabah,[14] Carmel and environs,[15] and studies in the historical topography of Eastern Palestine and Aramaean inroads.[16]

Later Biblical Researches in Palestine, 1856. Standard is still F. M. Abel, *Géographie de la Palestine*, I–II, 1933–8; J. Simons, *Geographical and Topographical Texts of the Old Testament*, 1959, is virtually undocumented and of very limited utility. D. Baly, *The Geography of the Bible*, 1957, and *Geographical Companion to the Bible*, 1963, are quite useful. On atlases, *etc.*, *cf.* p. 167, notes 53, 54, below.

[12] Numerous studies in *ZDPV*, *Palästina-Jahrbuch*, *etc.*; some of Alt's are in *KS*, I–III.

[13] *E.g.*, J. Naveh, *IEJ* 8 (1958), pp. 87–100, 165–170, and B. Mazar, *IEJ* 10 (1960), pp. 65–77; *cf.* also H. E. Kassis, *JBL* 84 (1965), pp. 259–271.

[14] Y. Aharoni, *IEJ* 8 (1958), pp. 26–38, and *IEJ* 13 (1963), pp. 30–42.

[15] Y. Aharoni, *IEJ* 9 (1959), pp. 110–122.

[16] B. Mazar, *JBL* 80 (1961), pp. 16–28; H. Tadmor, *IEJ* 12 (1962), pp. 114–122.

PART TWO

ILLUMINATION AND ILLUSTRATION

9. NEAR EASTERN LIGHT ON
THE BIBLICAL TEXT

We now turn to see briefly how the Ancient Orient can further our understanding of the Old Testament by helping to clear up individual textual difficulties and by lending greater vividness to what is said in the biblical writings. For the purpose of the present work, I shall employ the following definitions:

1. 'Illumination' is here used of clarifying the meaning of what was previously obscure, or the full force of something imperfectly understood.

2. 'Illustration' is here taken as the use of parallels or other background information to underline, and to make more vivid, statements and lessons which are already clearly intelligible in the biblical text as it stands. Naturally, however, this distinction between the two terms is not absolutely rigid; much of what 'illumines' provides illustration, while many 'illustrations' help also to 'illuminate'.

3. To this we may add the term 'confirmation', which may be defined as the use of extra-biblical data to illustrate or demonstrate the reliability and accuracy of the biblical writings or of their individual parts. Here also there is overlap, because the agreement between biblical data and material that illumines or illustrates it also serves in some measure as confirmation. We shall deal mainly with illumination.

I. ANCIENT LEGAL CUSTOM AND THE PATRIARCHS

(a) *Laws of Inheritance*

The family customs of the Patriarchs in Genesis 15 to 31 are unfamiliar to modern readers, but their significance has been remarkably illumined by parallels from cuneiform tablets found at Ur[1] and especially Nuzi,[2] in Mesopotamia. According to the usage in these documents a childless couple might adopt as heir one of their servants, just as in Genesis 15 Abraham adopted his servant Eliezer as heir.[3] Or else the wife might produce an heir 'by proxy' (so to speak) by giving her hand-maid to her husband. Thus was Ishmael born to Abraham by Hagar as a result of Sarah's initiative (Gn. 16). But if a couple did subsequently have a son of their own, then he automatically became chief heir in place of any servant or hand-maid's son (so Isaac; cf. Gn. 15:4; 17:18–21). These documents also indicate that the handmaid and her son should not norm-ally be sent away after the birth of a true heir;[4] thus Abraham needed divine direction on the matter before he could heed Sarah's irregular request to send away Hagar and Ishmael (Gn. 21:9–14). Esau was not the only person to sell his birth-right to satisfy immediate material needs (Gn. 25:29–34); Tupkitilla of Nuzi sold his for three sheep![5] An oral blessing conferred by an aged or dying father (Gn. 27; 48) was valid at law.[6]

(b) Laws of Land Tenure

Through the death of Sarah (Gn. 23) Abraham had to acquire a family burial-place. He sought to buy the cave of Machpelah from Ephron the Hittite, but eventually bought not only the cave but also the plot of land in which it lay. The main facts are clear, but their implications were first made evident when Lehmann pointed out the relevance of the Hittite Laws (§§46,

---

[1] D. J. Wiseman, *JTVI* 88 (1956), p. 124.

[2] C. H. Gordon, *BA* 3 (1940), pp. 1–12, reprinted in E. F. Campbell and D. N. Freedman (eds.), *Biblical Archaeologist Reader*, II, 1964. Much briefer accounts, cf. G. E. Wright, *Biblical Archaeology*, 1957, pp. 43–44, or D. J. Wiseman, *Illustrations from Biblical Archaeology*, 1958, pp. 25–27.

[3] A good parallel is Nuzi tablet H. 60 (E. A. Speiser in *AASOR* 10 (1930) p. 30); Ehel-teshup adopts Zigi as principal heir, unless he has a son of his own.

[4] *Cf.* Nuzi tablet H. 67 (Speiser, *op. cit.*, p. 32, *cf.* p. 22).

[5] Gordon, *BA* 3 (1940), p. 5.

[6] *Ibid.*, p. 8. The thorough realism of the patriarchal narratives could be illustrated at length. Pre-Nuzi data, *cf.* *THB* 17 (1966), p. 71, n. 26.

47).[7] These state that when a landholder disposes of only a part of his property to another person, the original (and principal) landholder must continue to pay all dues on the land. But if a landholder disposes of an entire property, then it is the new owner who must pay the dues. Thus, Abraham wanted only the cave, without complications; but Ephron knew that Abraham must buy quickly (to bury Sarah), and so he insisted that Abraham should acquire the *whole* plot of land (and so have to pay the dues as well). Abraham evidently shouldered this responsibility without complaint, for the sake of family needs – which still holds a lesson for us moderns. Recently, the narrative of Genesis 23 has been compared[8] with the 'dialogue-document' type of contracts that are known from the late eighth century BC and principally in the Neo-Babylonian period, and the conclusions drawn that Genesis 23 is a late tradition and cannot be used as evidence for practices of the patriarchal period.[9] However, it should be noted that Genesis 23 is *not itself* a dialogue contract-document, but is simply the *report* of an agreement; it is hard to conceive of an agreement being drawn up between two parties without some discussion between them! Hence, comparisons with the late dialogue-contracts are basically irrelevant, since Genesis 23 is not an actual contract-document, and these contracts are not simply narrative descriptions of the making of agreements. Furthermore, the publication of dialogue-type contracts from, for example, the early second millennium BC could at any time shatter the 'negative evidence' argument from the date of this type of contract even if it were still held to be relevant. Finally, the fact that the question of land-dues is not explicitly mentioned in Genesis 23 does not automatically exclude the Hittite Laws or related data as background[10] any more than the fact

[7] M. R. Lehmann, *BASOR* 129 (1953), pp. 15–18. Translations of the Laws, *cf.* A. Goetze, *ANET*, p. 191, and J. Friedrich, *Die Hethitischen Gesetze*, 1959, pp. 30–33, for the relevant paragraphs.

[8] H. Petschow, *JCS* 19 (1965), 103–120, a valuable study of this class of document; G. M. Tucker, *JBL* 85 (1966), 77–84.

[9] *Cf.* Petschow, *op. cit.*, p. 120, and esp. Tucker, *op. cit.*, p. 84.

[10] As is asserted by Tucker, *op. cit.*, p. 79 (negative evidence again); that such dues are not uniquely Hittite is well known. That the reference to trees

that Genesis 23 lacks a whole series of features normally found in actual contracts would exclude its being the narrative record of an agreement.[11]

II. THE PERIOD OF MOSES

(a) Bricks and Straw

As a punishment for the request of Moses that Israel should be released from work to hold a feast to their God, the pharaoh commanded that henceforth the Hebrews must find their own straw and yet still produce the same quota of bricks daily (Ex. 5:1–19). Why was the straw so necessary? The ancients had noticed that sun-dried mud bricks were stronger and kept their shape better if chopped straw or chaff was mixed with the clay. This is still done in the Near East today.[12] Investigation has shown that the straw yields organic acids that make the clay more plastic, and its presence also stops shrinkage.[13] The same concerns that moved the Egyptians in Exodus 5 – quotas and straw – reappear in Egyptian documents of this period (thirteenth century BC), some long known. One official reports that his workmen 'are making their quota of bricks daily',[14] while another bitterly complains: 'there are neither men to make bricks, nor straw in the neighbourhood.'[15]

(b) Religious Feasts and Idleness

In Exodus 5, the pharaoh charges the Israelites with laziness, and he refuses Moses' appeal to let them go and celebrate a

---

is not peculiarly Hittite is well shown by both Petschow, op. cit., p. 119, n. 129, and Tucker, op. cit., pp. 83–84.

[11] As is seen by Tucker, p. 84. His points on 'giving', etc., rather obscure the fact of common use of 'give' and 'take' for 'sell' and 'buy'. (Cf. Andersen, JBL 85 (1966), 48–49.)

[12] C. F. Nims, BA 13 (1950), pp. 24–28.

[13] A. E. Lucas, Ancient Egyptian Materials and Industries[3], 1948, pp. 62–63 ([4]1962, ed. J. R. Harris, pp. 48–50); A. A. MacRae, in Modern Science and Christian Faith, 1948, pp. 215–219.

[14] Papyrus Anastasi III, verso 3: 2; translated, R. A. Caminos, Late-Egyptian Miscellanies, 1954, p. 106.

[15] Papyrus Anastasi IV, 12:6, in Caminos, op. cit., p. 188.

feast to their God because he claims that it is just an excuse for them to stop work and be idle. In Egypt, journals of work preserved on ostraca of this period from Deir el Medineh and the Valley of the Kings at Thebes show vividly how many days were claimed as 'days off', not least for religious purposes. One ostracon (dated to Year 40 of Ramesses II) gives a full register of the working days and absences of fifty men;[16] another (Year 6 of Sethos II)[17] shows gangs of workmen idle for eight or fourteen days at a time, and several documents mention men who go 'to offer to their god',[18] while another records four days of festivity enjoyed by the workmen of the royal necropolis at a local festival.[19]

(c) The Plagues of Egypt

Although the death of the firstborn, the tenth of the plagues that afflicted Egypt on the eve of the Exodus, is avowedly in the realm of miracle, the preceding nine demonstrate God's use of the created order for His own ends. A careful study by Greta Hort[20] strongly suggests that the first nine plagues form a se-quence of unusually severe natural phenomena which began with an unusually *high* inundation of the Nile (not low, as often thought). The result of her investigation is to show that the narrative of Exodus 7 to 10 makes excellent sense as it stands and shows evidence of first-hand observation,[21] thus enabling us to understand the course of events with greater clarity. Thus, the excessive inundation may have brought with it microcosms known as *flagellates* which would redden the river and also cause conditions that would kill the fish. Decompos-

[16] Ostracon British Museum 5634, published in J. Černý and Sir A. H. Gardiner, *Hieratic Ostraca I*, 1957, pp. 22–23, plates 83–84; noted by A. Erman, *Life in Ancient Egypt*, 1894, p. 124.

[17] Ostracon Cairo 25515, published in J. Černý, *Ostraca Hiératiques*, Catalogue du Musée du Caire, 1930–5, pp. 7, 11*–12*, plates 8–9; sum-marized by G. Daressy, *RT* 34 (1912), pp. 47–49.

[18] S. Schott, *Altägyptische Festdaten*, 1950, p. 102 (No. 130).

[19] Schott, *op. cit.*, p. 99 (No. 113).

[20] G. Hort, *ZAW* 69 (1957), pp. 84–103, and *ZAW* 70 (1958), pp. 48–59.

[21] As noted above (p. 129), the hypothetical documents of conventional literary criticism fail to do so.

ing fish floating inshore would drive the frogs ashore, having also infected them with *Bacillus anthracis*. The third plague would be mosquitoes, and the fourth a fly, *Stomoxys calcitrans*, both encouraged to breed freely in the conditions produced by a high inundation. The cattle-disease of the fifth plague would be anthrax contracted from the dead frogs, and the 'blains' on man and beast (sixth plague), a skin anthrax from the *Stomoxys* fly of the fourth plague. Hail and thunderstorms in February would destroy flax and barley, but leave the wheat and spelt for the locusts whose swarming would be favoured by the same Abyssinian rains which had ultimately caused the high inundation. The 'thick darkness' would be the masses of fine dust, *Roterde* (from mud deposited by the inundation), caught up by the *khamsin* wind in March.

III. EXAMPLES FROM LATER HEBREW HISTORY

(a) *The Instituting of Kingship in Israel*

In 1 Samuel 8, when Israel requested an earthly king 'like all the nations round about', Samuel the prophet warned them of what this would mean for them, *i.e.*, conscription of labour, requisitioning of property, and so on. Old Testament scholars have sought to interpret this passage as a *denunciation* of kingship in itself, as the embittered opinion of an historical epoch much later than Samuel. But a comparison of 1 Samuel 8 with documents from Alalakh and Ugarit[22] indicates, rather, that Samuel was simply warning Israel about the *regular* civil powers (not abuses) that an earthly king would assume in order to govern them, showing them the *cost* of a monarchy. The Hebrews would have to put up with conscription for military and other state service and forced labour, with state requisitioning of private land and property, and with state taxation (*e.g.*, the royal tithe). These practices are all attested of Syrian kings in Alalakh and Ugarit centuries before Samuel, and so were of long standing in the region. Some of the techni-

[22] By I. Mendelsohn, *BASOR* 143 (1956), pp. 17–22.

cal terms in the tablets are identical with terms known in Hebrew.[23]

(b) The Sukkiim of 2 Chronicles

In narrating how Shishak (Shoshenq I) of Egypt invaded Palestine in the fifth year of Rehoboam of Judah (c. 925 BC), the Chronicler includes the enigmatic Sukkiim among Shishak's forces along with the Libyans and Ethiopians (2 Ch. 12:3). These, in fact, are known from Egyptian texts (thirteenth century BC and later) as Tjuku, Tjukten, and were scouts or light-armed auxiliaries, perhaps of Libyan origin. This identification was first made by Spiegelberg in 1904,[24] but was largely forgotten until revived by Gardiner, Albright and Caminos[25] more recently. A broken stela of Shishak as re-edited by Grdseloff[26] suggests that the Egyptians used a border-incident as the official pretext for their invasion of Palestine.

(c) Geshem the Arabian

Among the three opponents of Nehemiah when he repaired the walls of Jerusalem, the least-known hitherto was Geshem or Gashmu the Arabian (Ne. 2:19; 6:1, 2, 6). Yet among the rumours said to be circulating about Nehemiah's activities in Nehemiah 6:6, the word of Gashmu is mentioned separately as if it were specially important. A recent discovery has revealed Geshem's real identity, and thus also his importance. Among silver bowls found in the ruins of a pagan shrine in the Egyptian north-east delta was one dedicated by Qaynu 'son of Geshem, king of Qedar'.[27] Qedar is in north-west Arabia, where a

---

[23] E.g., the terms for tithe (cuneiform ma'šaru, mēšertu, cf. Hebrew ma'ašer) and for corvée (Ugaritic msm, and mazza in Amarna Letters, cf. Hebrew mas), Mendelsohn, op. cit., p. 20 and n. 16, p. 21.

[24] W. Spiegelberg, Aegyptologische Randglossen zum Alten Testament, 1904, pp. 30–31.

[25] A. H. Gardiner, The Wilbour Papyrus, II: Commentary, 1948, p. 81 n. 1; W. F. Albright in Rowley (ed.), Old Testament and Modern Study, 1951, p. 18; R. A. Caminos, Late-Egyptian Miscellanies, 1954, pp. 176–177, 180.

[26] B. Grdseloff, Revue de l'Histoire Juive en Égypte, No. 1 (1947), pp. 95–97; first published by G. Legrain, ASAE 5 (1904), p. 38.

[27] I. Rabinowitz, JNES 15 (1956), pp. 2, 5–9, and plates 6, 7.

graffito naming Jasm (=Gashmu) is also known,[28] and so Geshem was in fact the paramount Arab chief in control of the land-routes from Western Asia into Egypt. The Persian kings had always maintained good relations with the Arab rulers of this region ever since Cambyses had enlisted their aid for his invasion of Egypt in 525 BC[29] – so Geshem's word could well have endangered Nehemiah at the Persian court. Hence its separate mention.

IV. LIGHT ON OLD TESTAMENT HEBREW FROM LINGUISTIC STUDIES

(a) Ugaritic and Old Testament Hebrew

This ancient West Semitic language and literature has been recovered from clay tablets in a unique alphabetic cuneiform script of the fourteenth to thirteenth centuries BC, and is named after its place of discovery, the ancient Canaanite seaport of Ugarit (now Ras Shamra) in northern Phoenicia.[30] It presents many affinities with the language and literary forms of the Old Testament. Study of Ugaritic has enabled scholars to rediscover grammatical forms and syntactical usages in biblical Hebrew which had gone unrecognized and so given rise to textual difficulties. Likewise, 'lost' words have been restored,

---

[28] *Cf.* Rabinowitz, *op. cit., p.* 7; Albright in *Geschichte und Altes Testament (FS Alt)*, 1953, pp. 4, 6.

[29] Rabinowitz, *op. cit.,* p. 9.

[30] Excavations and texts, *cf.* reports by Schaeffer, Virolleaud and others in *Syria* since 1929 and in *Annales Archéologiques de Syrie* since 1951, plus *CRAIBL* and *AfO.* Definitive reports in *Mission de Ras Shamra* series (*Ugaritica I–V*, by Schaeffer *et al.*; *Palais Royal d'Ugarit*, II–VI, by Nougayrol and Virolleaud; *Légende phénicienne de Danel, Légende de Kéret, La Déesse Anat,* by Virolleaud; and now *Corpus des Tablettes en cunéiformes alphabétiques* . . . , *1929 à 1939,* by Herdner). Schaeffer, *Ugaritica I,* and Herdner, *Corpus,* contain very extensive bibliographies, esp. for the texts. For English translations of texts, see C. H. Gordon, *Ugaritic Literature,* 1949; H. L. Ginsberg, *ANET,* 1950/55; G. R. Driver, *Canaanite Myths and Legends,* 1956, besides treatments of individual texts. For an extensive grammar, see C. H. Gordon, *UM,* 1955, revised as *Ugaritic Textbook,* 1965.

further examples of rarer words rediscovered, and lost additional meanings of still other words recovered.[31]

(b) Ugaritic Contributions to Grammar and Syntax

1. *Enclitic mêm*. The isolation of a particle consisting of *m* plus a vowel (-*i* or -*a*) in Ugaritic as a stylistic device has led to its rediscovery in biblical Hebrew. It is usually termed 'enclitic *mêm*'.[32]

In many cases, recognition of enclitic *mêm* does not alter the meaning of a passage but simply removes a grammatical anomaly. What looks like a plural 'absolute' form (where the corresponding 'construct' form of a noun should occur) now turns out to be the 'construct' form plus an enclitic *mêm*. Thus, *hannăḥalîm-'Arnōn*, 'the wadies of the Arnon', in Numbers 21:14, can now be read better as *hannaḥălē-mi 'Arnōn* (same meaning).[33]

In other cases, recognition of an enclitic *mêm* can clarify not only the grammatical form but also the meaning of the text. Thus, in Psalm 89:50 (Heb. 89:51), in parallel with:

[31] Useful books on Ugaritic and Old Testament studies include: R. de Langhe, *Les Textes de Ras Shamra – Ugarit et leurs Rapports avec le Milieu Biblique de l'Ancien Testament*, I–II, 1945; J. Gray, *The Legacy of Canaan* (=*VTS*, V), 1957 (2nd ed., 1965); briefer but useful as introductions are E. Jacob, *Ras Shamra et l'Ancien Testament*, 1960, and C. F. Pfeiffer, *Ras Shamra and the Bible*, 1962. A. S. Kapelrud, *The Ras Shamra Discoveries and the Old Testament*, 1965, pays too little heed to the linguistic help from Ugaritic, and too much heed to certain Scandinavian theories on kingship and cults. On Ugaritic and the Hebrew text, valuable are: W. F. Albright, *CBQ* 7 (1945), pp. 5–31; M. J. Dahood, *Biblica* 40 (1959), pp. 160–170; *idem*, *Gregorianum* 43 (1962), pp. 55–79; on the Psalms, *cf.* his Anchor Bible volumes on *Psalms 1–50*, 1966, and *Psalms 51–150* (forthcoming), also *Theological Studies* 14 (1953), 452–457. H. L. Ginsberg, *JBL* 62 (1943), pp. 109–115; older, wider-ranging surveys of value include W. Baumgartner, *Theologische Zeitschrift* 3 (1947), pp. 81–100, G. D. Young, *JKF* 2 (1952/53), pp. 225–245, and R. de Langhe in *L'Ancien Testament et l'Orient* (=*OBL*,I), 1957, pp. 65–87.

[32] First isolated by Ginsberg in Ugaritic (*Tarbiz* 4 (1932), p. 388) and in Hebrew (*Kitve Ugarit*, 1936, pp. 20, 29, 63, 74, *etc.*), and fully studied by H. D. Hummel, *JBL* 76 (1957), pp. 85–107.

[33] After Hummel, *op. cit.*, p. 97 No. 1; for the definite article before a construct noun in Phoenician and Hebrew, *cf.* M. Dahood, *Orientalia* 34 (1965), pp. 170–172 (our passage, p. 172).

L

'Remember, O Lord, the reproach of (*i.e.*, on) thy servants', for he unhappy, '(How) I bear . . . all the mighty, peoples', one may substitute: '(How) I bear in my bosom all the content tions (*rîbē-mi* for *rabbîm*) of (the) peoples.'[34]

2. *Pleonastic waw.* Sometimes in the Hebrew text of the Old Testament, the letter *w* – for the little word *wᵉ*, 'and' or 'even/ yea' – appears in unexpected places before words where its presence seems superfluous. In the past, this has often led scholars to excise the offending letter, or else to re-interpret the sentence with or without more drastic emendation. However, two recent studies[35] (starting from the discovery of a similar example in Ugaritic) have shown that this apparently superfluous or 'pleonastic' *w* is a stylistic device used for emphasizing a word or for variety in style. Thus, in Job 4:6, one should probably read not as some suggest: 'Is not thy piety thy confidence, thy hope and thy perfect conduct?', but with some translators:

'Is not thy piety thy confidence,
Thy hope, indeed, thy perfect conduct?'[36]

3. *Some Prepositions.* The prepositions *lᵉ*, 'to', 'for', and *bᵉ*, 'in', 'by', 'with', can also mean 'from' as shown by examples in Ugaritic. Previously, scholars often sought to emend the Hebrew text when the hitherto accepted meanings of *lᵉ* or *bᵉ* failed to make sense, but recognition of the meaning 'from' renders such emendations superfluous.[37] This applies to passages such as Psalm 84:11 (Heb. 84:12), 'He will not withhold good from (*lᵉ*) those who walk perfectly';[38] and Job 5:21, 'From (*bᵉ*) the scourge of the tongue shalt thou be hidden.'[39] Not a few

---

[34] Hummel, *op. cit.*, p. 98 No. 7 (from Dahood). One could also read the last word as *'ammî-mi*, 'my people', with final enclitic *mêm*.

[35] By M. Pope, *JAOS* 73 (1953), pp. 95–98, and P. Wernberg-Møller, *JSS* 3 (1958), pp. 321–326.

[36] After Pope, *op. cit.*, p. 97b.

[37] See C. H. Gordon, *UM*, I, or *UT*, §10: 1; §10: 5; §10: 11; and N. M. Sarna, *JBL* 78 (1959), pp. 310–316, for examples.

[38] After Gordon, *op. cit.*, §10: 1.

[39] After Sarna, *op. cit.*, pp. 314–315.

other locutions are shared by Ugaritic and Hebrew, aiding in the interpretation of the latter.[40]

(c) Ugaritic Contributions to Vocabulary[41]

1. In Proverbs 26:23, there occurs the *crux interpretatum*, 'silver dross' (*kesep-sigim*), in the context, 'Silver dross overlaid upon an earthen pot are fervent lips and a wicked heart.' This can now be read as *kᵉ-sapsag-mi*,[42] 'Like glaze', and the whole sentence be rendered:

> 'Like glaze coated upon an earthen pot,
>   Are fervent lips with a wicked heart.'

The word *sapsag* for 'glaze' first turned up in Ugaritic (*spsg*) and has received independent confirmation from Hittite documents (in the form, *zapzagai-*, and variants).[43]

2. In Jeremiah 49:4, the word *'emeq* may now be taken not as the word for 'valley' but as a homonymous word for 'strength'. Thus one may render, not:

> 'Why dost thou boast of thy valley?
>   Thy valley flows away,
>   O faithless daughter
> Who trusted in her treasures . . .',

but rather:

---

[40] For example, finite uses of the 'infinitive absolute', J. Huesman, *Biblica* 37 (1956), pp. 271–295, 410–434; emphatic *lamedh*, Gordon, *UM*, §9:12 (=*UT*, §9:16), *cf*. J. Mejia, *Estudios Biblicos* 22 (1963), 179–190, and Dahood, *Biblica* 37 (1956), pp. 338–340; double-duty suffixes, *ibid*., and G. R. Driver, *JRAS*, 1948, pp. 164–176; vocative *l*, Dahood, *VT* 16 (1966), pp. 299–311.

[41] *Cf*. (*e.g.*) M. Dahood, 'Hebrew-Ugaritic Lexicography', I ff., in *Biblica* 44 (1963), pp. 289–303, *ibid*. 45 (1964), pp. 393–412, *ibid*. 46 (1965), 311–332; *ibid*. 47 (1966), *etc*., and other studies; A. A. Wieder, *JBL* 84 (1965), pp. 160–164.

[42] Treating -*m* as an enclitic *mêm* (Kitchen).

[43] Discovered by Ginsberg, confirmed by Albright (*BASOR* 98 (1945), p. 21 n. 55, pp. 24–25; *VTS*, III, 1955, pp. 12–13; also J. Gray, *VTS*, V, 1957, pp. 207–208). *Zapzagai-* in Hittite, J. Friedrich, *Hethitisches Wörterbuch*, 1952, p. 260a, and *ibid*., *2. Ergänzungsheft*, 1961, p. 28a.

'Why dost thou boast of thy strength?
   Thy strength has ebbed away,
   O faithless daughter
Who trusted in her treasures . . .'[44]

3. Newly detected examples of rarer words include several examples of II *'azab* 'to place', 'arrange', in Job, formerly interpreted as I *'azab* 'to forsake', 'leave'. Good examples have been found in Job 9:27; 10:1; 18:4; and less certainly 20:19.[45] A possible example of interest is in Job 39:14 on the habits of the ostrich. Dahood suggests the text be rendered, not:

'She abandons her eggs to the earth,
And lets them be warmed on the ground',

but rather:

'She places her eggs in the ground,
And she warms (=hatches) them on the sand.'

This rendering may not only restore the meaning of the text but also the character of the ostrich! And it would agree with what is known of the habits of this bird.[46]

4. A lost meaning is sometimes recovered for a well-known word. *Bāmā* is the common Hebrew word for a high place. In Ugaritic, it also means 'back', and this rendering would also fit very well in Deuteronomy 33:29, in the ancient Blessing of Moses:

'Thine enemies shall submit to thee,
   And thou shalt tread upon their backs'
      (rather than: 'on their high places').[47]

---

[44] After Dahood, *Biblica* 40 (1959), pp. 166–7; examples also in Jb. 39:21 and Je. 4:74.

[45] M. Dahood, *JBL* 78 (1959), pp. 303–9, esp. 304–7.

[46] Dahood, *op. cit.*, pp. 307–308; in Jb. 39:16, he further suggests taking *pāḥad* as 'flock' rather than 'fear' (in J. L. McKenzie (ed.), *The Bible in Current Catholic Thought (FS Gruenthaner)*, 1962, p. 74).

[47] *Cf.* J. Gray, *The Legacy of Canaan*[1] (=*VTS*, V), p. 189; E. Jacob, *Ras Shamra et l'Ancien Testament*, 1960, p. 63; C. F. Pfeiffer, *Ras Shamra and the Bible*, 1962, p. 60.

The idea expressed is then similar to that in Joshua 10:24 or in Psalm 110:1, and finds plastic expression in Egyptian reliefs and statuary.[48]

(d) Illumination from other Languages

Other Semitic languages besides Ugaritic (*e.g.*, Akkadian) could be called on; but here we take two examples from a more distant source, namely Egypt.

1. Potiphar: was he an 'officer' or 'eunuch' of Pharaoh? The word used of Potiphar in Genesis (37:36; 39:1; 40:2, 7) is *sārîs* which elsewhere in the Old Testament usually means 'eunuch'. Now this meaning creates difficulties in Genesis; not only was Potiphar a married man (Gn. 39:1), but eunuchs were not customary in ancient Egypt.[49]

The answer to this question is a simple one. Hebrew *sārîs* is probably a loanword from the Akkadian (Assyro-Babylonian) *ša-rēš-šarri* or *ša-rēši* which itself shows a change of meaning during the time that it was in use. Thus, in the second millennium BC, *ša-rēši* usually meant simply 'courtier', 'official', but by the first millennium BC it had come to mean specifically 'eunuch'. This is a valuable hint, for the same diachronic restriction of meaning can be seen to affect Hebrew *sārîs*. In the Joseph-story in Genesis, the early, general meaning of 'official', 'courtier', suits the context perfectly, and is also, therefore, a genuinely early usage preserved from the early second millennium BC. But all the other examples of *sārîs* in the Old Testament belong to books originating in the *first* millennium BC (Isaiah, Kings, Jeremiah, Daniel, Esther) and so they naturally show the later, narrower meaning of *sārîs*. The parallel development in meaning of these two related terms is not unique. In both Egypt and Mesopotamia, other and wholly unrelated

---

[48] The captives shown in P. Montet, *L'Égypte et la Bible*, 1959, plate VII, would originally be placed under the feet of a royal statue; captives are likewise shown on a royal footstool and a hassock (to come under the king's feet) from Tutankhamun's tomb (*cf.* P. Fox, *Tutankhamun's Treasure*, 1951, plates 60, 61), and a scene shows the young Amenophis II with feet on foes (W. M. F. Petrie, *A History of Egypt*, II, (v.d.), fig. 96).

[49] See J. Vergote, *Joseph en Égypte*, 1959, pp. 40–42.

words for 'official', 'courtier' also show the same change of meaning. The old Egyptian word *sr*, 'official', became *siūr*, 'eunuch', in Coptic, while in Mesopotamia in the early second millennium BC the term *girsequm*, 'eunuch', had earlier meant 'courtier'.[50]

2. In 2 Samuel 12:14, the Hebrew text describes David's sin (in his having taken Bathsheba) as having 'slighted the enemies of the Lord', usually altered in our modern versions to something like, 'Thou hast given occasion for the enemies of the Lord to blaspheme.' But the literal rendering is no fault in the text, it is simply a euphemism to avoid saying 'having slighted the Lord . . .', by transferring the insult verbally to God's enemies. Remarkably enough, *exactly* the same euphemism has been noticed[51] in an Egyptian decree of the seventeenth century BC (it having itself no direct link with the Old Testament), in which punishment is passed upon an Egyptian conspirator 'as is done to the likes of him who rebelled against (*sebi ḥir*) the enemies of his god'. There is no question of emending the Egyptian text (an original document), and no need either to emend the Hebrew construction.[52]

V. THE OLD TESTAMENT ILLUSTRATED

Illustration of the Old Testament comes from two main sources: the natural environment (and relevant sciences) and Ancient Oriental studies proper.

Today, there are excellent publications available which help us to visualize the natural setting of Old Testament history and daily life, whether it be, say, the mountains and cedars of Lebanon, or the 'wildernesses' that may vary in nature from

---

[50] Full references for this paragraph, *cf.* Kitchen, *JEA* 47 (1961), p. 160. In addition, for *siūr* see W. Spiegelberg, *Koptisches Handwörterbuch*, 1921, p. 122, and for *sr* A. Erman and H. Grapow, *Wörterbuch der Aegyptischen Sprache*, IV, pp. 188–189.

[51] R. Yaron, *VT* 9 (1959), pp. 89–91.

[52] For another striking linguistic parallel in Egyptian and Hebrew, see S. Morenz, *Theologische Literaturzeitung* 74 (1949), cols. 697–699.

pasture to sand and rock desert, or the flora and fauna of the biblical world.[53]

In the archaeological realm, two forms of pictorial illustration can make more vivid the circumstances of Old Testament people and events, and thus enliven our understanding of them.[54]

First, the monuments of Egypt and Assyria in particular preserve – sometimes in vivid colour – painted or sculptured scenes of daily life, or of historical events or of religious practice. Details of dress, furniture and much else are all portrayed for us to see. In Egypt, white linen dress and clean-shaven face are customary in the tomb- and temple-scenes and are presupposed in Genesis 41:14, 42; while in Western Asia, the Semitic and other peoples appreciated fine beards and often multi-coloured garments – again, abundantly illustrated upon Egyptian and Assyrian monuments, and underlying various biblical references.[55] For beards, one may compare Psalm 133:1, 2, and the insult in 2 Samuel 10:4, 5; for coloured dress, compare the allusion to fine dyed stuffs in Judges 5:30.

Secondly, the actual objects and buildings revealed by excavation perform a like service. Thus, from the combined

[53] Compare, for example, the excellent photographs in works such as L. H. Grollenberg, *Atlas of the Bible*, 1957 (and *Shorter Atlas of the Bible*, 1959) and in Aharoni, *etc.* (next note). Archaeology and topography are variously combined in: G. E. Wright and F. V. Filson, *Westminster Historical Atlas to the Bible*[5], 1957 (selected maps in *idem*, *Westminster Smaller Bible Atlas*, 1947 and reprs.), E. G. Kraeling, *Rand McNally Bible Atlas*, 1956, and H. G. May, R. W. Hamilton, G. N. S. Hunt, *Oxford Bible Atlas*, 1962. There is still room for a proper atlas with large-scale maps, proper relief and routes, and detailed topographical study, rather than potted biblical archaeologies with rather diagrammatic maps in the current fashion.

[54] *Cf.* (*e.g.*) the classified corpus of photographs in J. B. Pritchard, *ANEP*, 1954 (and *idem*, *The Ancient Near East*, 1958), or in colour Y. Aharoni, B. Mazar *et al.*, *Illustrated World of the Bible Library*, 5 vols., 1958–61 (and M. Avi-Yonah and E. G. Kraeling, *Our Living Bible*, 1962). An excellent brief introduction is D. J. Wiseman, *Illustrations from Biblical Archaeology*, 1958 ([3]1966).

[55] For example, *ANEP*, figs. 3, 26, 43, 47 (=Pritchard, *Ancient Near East*, figs. 2–5) or Wiseman, *op. cit.*, figs. 25, 27, 29, *etc.* Examples in colour, C. F. Nims, *Thebes of the Pharaohs*, 1965, figs. 60 and *passim*; fig. 81.

study of Old Testament words for pottery and of pottery found in Palestinian excavations, one may gain a sharper understanding of many Old Testament allusions to various such vessels.[56] The layer of ashes a metre thick which lay over the ruined walls of the Israelite citadel at Hazor, with some of the stonework torn down right to the foundations – revealed by Yadin's excavations[57] – is a graphic illustration of the ferocity of the Assyrian attack on northern Israel by Tiglath-pileser III in the time of Pekah, recounted briefly in 2 Kings 15:29.

VI. THE ISSUE OF CONFIRMATION

Many of the correspondences between biblical and Ancient Near Eastern data that have been mentioned in the foregoing chapters not only illuminate or illustrate the Old Testament but also serve to indicate the reliability of many of its allusions to the world in which it was written; these are *indirect* confirmation.

Examples of *direct* confirmation – actual extra-biblical mentions of persons and events of the Old Testament – are not lacking but are necessarily much fewer. This is because (i) Old Testament history is quantitatively only quite a small part of Ancient Oriental history as a whole; (ii) the tasks of exploration and decipherment are but well begun;[58] (iii) in any case much information has perished irrevocably at the hands of time and man;[59] and (iv) some events are of such a kind as to leave no physical traces behind.

However, some examples of direct confirmation do occur; one need only mention one or two examples. Thus, Ahab, Menahem, Pekah and Hoshea, kings of Israel, are all mentioned in due order in the Assyrian annals along with the fall

[56] See J. L. Kelso, *The Ceramic Vocabulary of the Old Testament*, 1948, and A. R. Millard, *NBD*, pp. 1012–1016.
[57] *E.g.*, Y. Yadin, *BA* 20 (1957), pp. 39–40.
[58] See above, p. 32, note 43.
[59] See above, p. 32, with notes 42, 44–45.

of Samaria in 722 BC,[60] and also Judaean kings such as Ahaz, Hezekiah and Manasseh.[61] The Babylonian chronicle-tablets in the British Museum confirm the capture of Jerusalem and the change of Judaean kings effected by Nebuchadrezzar II in March 597 BC,[62] while the actual presence of the Judaean king Jehoiachin in Babylon as an exile is independently attested by the ration-tablets that were excavated by Koldewey at Babylon and published by Weidner.[63] One may also view the sudden destruction of several Late Bronze Age cities in Canaan in the thirteenth century BC as being at any rate partial confirmation of the Israelite invasion and the start of the settlement recorded in Joshua and Judges.[64] Where problems have been raised in Old Testament studies, the information available from Ancient Near Eastern sources can, as indicated earlier above, cut down the scope of these problems considerably and sometimes solve them outright or partially.

While we must always exercise great care in deciding what constitutes confirmation of this or that detail or episode in the Old Testament and in excluding illusory examples, I cannot agree with those who would condemn the quest for such confirmation as 'improper'.[65] It is every bit as legitimate to seek for

[60] For this date see E. R. Thiele, *Mysterious Numbers of the Hebrew Kings*, 1951, pp. 122–128, and H. Tadmor, *JCS* 12 (1958), pp. 33–40. For Hebrew royal chronology, *cf*. works cited above, p. 76, notes 67–69.

[61] *Cf*. standard histories (*e.g*., Bright); Assyrian references are mainly collected in *ANET* and *DOTT*.

[62] Published in D. J. Wiseman, *Chronicles of Chaldaean Kings*, 1956.

[63] E. F. Weidner, *Mélanges Syriens offerts à R. Dussaud*, II, 1939, pp. 923–935; see also W. F. Albright, *BA* 5 (1942), pp. 49–55, and A. L. Oppenheim in *ANET*, p. 308, or W. J. Martin, *DOTT*, pp. 84–86.

[64] It should be noted that the technical problems of detail in correlating stratigraphic/occupational evidence (often incomplete) with the site-histories known from biblical and other records are not any more significant than those found in relating site-occupations at (*e.g*.) Megiddo, Samaria, Hazor, or Lachish with the site-histories in biblical and other records during the Hebrew kingdoms. *Cf*. (*e.g*.) discussions by Y. Aharoni and R. Amiran, *IEJ* 8 (1958), pp. 171–184; G. E. Wright, *BASOR* 155 (1959), pp. 13–29; O. Tufnell, *PEQ* 91 (1959), pp. 90–105; Wright, *BANE*, 1961, pp. 98–100; latterly, K. M. Kenyon, *BIA/UL* 4 (1964), pp. 143–156.

[65] As done (*e.g*.) by M. Noth, *History of Israel²*, 1960, p. 47; with his de-

real confirmation of an ancient document[66] as it is to look for errors, and no less legitimate to seek soundly-based confirmation for biblical than for other ancient literary records.

---

precation of 'over-hasty' use of parallels one must fully agree – but not with his erroneous inference (p. 48) that written records alone constitute evidence. If it were true, then non-literate archaeological material and written records should never be correlated! *Cf.* next note.

[66] Thus, in Mesopotamia, the palatial building excavated at Brak by M. E. L. Mallowan (*Iraq* 9 (1947), pp. 26 ff., 63 ff.) gives direct confirmation of the tradition of Naram-Sin's campaigning far N.W. of Babylonia (*cf.* C. J. Gadd, *CAH*², I: 19, *Dynasty of Agade* . . . , 1963, p. 29). In Anatolia, Goetze (*JCS* 11 (1957), pp. 53–57 with 59–61) has no hesitation in using archaeological data from Boghazköy to confirm the evidence of the Hittite offering-lists and Telipinus Decree. In Egypt, S. Allam, *Beiträge zum Hathorkult* (*bis zum Ende des Mittleren Reiches*), 1963, pp. 42–49, appropriately confirmed late Dendera temple tradition on the works of Pepi I, Amenemmes I, *etc.*, there from monumental indications. There is no sufficient factual reason to treat the Old Testament differently from these.

10. CONCLUSION

It is hoped that the foregoing survey will provide a small glimpse – and it is but a small one – of the contribution that Ancient Oriental studies are making and can yet make to our understanding of the Old Testament and its world today. If these studies can continue to flourish in this uncertain world, they hold the exciting promise of still further aids to understanding, new perspectives, unforeseeable discoveries.

In the future, correlation of the Old Testament and the Ancient Orient ought ultimately to be conducted on a much more fundamental and systematic basis than ever before. While a great deal of really valuable work has been done, and is constantly continuing, it is often very piecemeal and there is room for something more purposeful. Some day, there ought to be set out a kind of 'comparative grid' or graph of Ancient Oriental data to cover every aspect of contact between the Old Testament and the Ancient Orient. Thus, on a given topic, the material available ought to be fully collected and sifted both across the 'grid' and down the 'grid'. In other words, the material on a given topic must be separately collected and classified for each main culture or area in the Ancient Orient, and within each such spatial division this material must then be further classified on a chronological basis, period by period, whenever possible. A full picture of a given topic in all its variations (on available evidence) can then be gained for the whole Ancient Orient and its main epochs. Next one must plot against this background the data of the Old Testament *as it stands*, and see how it connects with an objectively-established environment.

All too obviously, this vast task cannot be done at once; but it can be pursued bit by bit consciously, and sectional results used as they are gained. Needless to say, this is work for

Orientalists rather than theologians, but the material and results would have to be made available to the latter in suitable
form. Prior theories about the Old Testament would have to be
rigorously tested against the accumulated facts. The days of
'primitive Israel', treated as though she had developed in
isolation, are over and gone, obsolete beyond recall; if the
Patriarchs had lived in 7000 or 6000 BC, and the Exodus taken
place in 5000, 'primitive Hebrews' would have been conceivable – but not so very late in the culture and history of the
Ancient Near East as the second and first millennia BC.[1]

On the other hand, it may perhaps be thought by some that
run-of-the-mill Old Testament studies have come in for considerable incidental criticism. The criticisms that have been
offered here are not, of course, directed at any such scholars
personally. Some are very highly gifted men, and the writer
has learnt much (and pleasurably) from their works.[2] The
criticisms made apply to facts and methods, and arise simply
from the basic fact that the Ancient Orient provides means
of external control upon our study of the Old Testament. The
theories current in Old Testament studies, however brilliantly
conceived and elaborated, were mainly established in a vacuum
with little or no reference to the Ancient Near East, and initially
too often in accordance with *a priori* philosophical and literary
principles. It is solely because the data from the Ancient Near
East coincide so much better with the existing observable
structure of Old Testament history, literature and religion
than with the theoretical reconstructions, that we are compelled
– as happens in Ancient Oriental studies – to question or even
to abandon such theories regardless of their popularity.
Facts not votes determine the truth. We do not here merely
advocate a return to 'pre-critical' views and traditions (*e.g.*, of
authorship) merely for their own sake or for the sake of theological orthodoxy. Let it be clearly noted that *no appeal whatsoever*
has been made to any theological starting-point in the body of
this work, not to mention the miasma of late post-biblical

---

[1] *Cf.* above, p. 37, note 10, on antiquity of pre-literate high cultures.
[2] Not least from various works of Eissfeldt and Noth, several times
cited in reference to views found untenable or unrealistic in this work.

Jewish or patristic (or later) Christian traditions. If some of the results reached here approximate to a traditional view or seem to agree with theological orthodoxy, then this is simply because the tradition in question or that orthodoxy are that much closer to the real facts than is commonly realized. While one must indeed never prefer mere orthodoxy to truth, it is also perverse to deny that orthodox views can be true.

As far as the historic Christian faith is concerned, it should have nothing to fear from any soundly-based and fair-minded intellectual investigation (anything less than this is, *ipso facto*, invalid). Its truth must stand or fall with that of Him who said, 'I am the way, the truth, and the life' (Jn. 14:6; *cf.* 7:17).

INDEX OF BIBLICAL REFERENCES

175

INDEX OF SUBJECTS